To Marie Frances Deer

Contents

Acknowledgments

This book, like most, exists thanks to the right combination of two incompatible conditions, sociability and solitude.

It is unimaginable to me to write in complete scholarly seclusion; I get my best ideas talking (and occasionally listening) to people. Thus I am happy to acknowledge all those friends and colleagues who have indulged me by listening, who have offered advice and critique, and who, without perhaps realizing it, have helped me stretch my imagination. They are why I am in academia: Robert Alter, Sacvan Bercovitch, Fritz Breithaupt, Adam Bresnick, Peter Burgard, Dorrit Cohn, Jonathan Elmer, James Engell, Donald Fanger, Stephen Greenblatt, Karl Guthke, Neil Hertz, Jochen Hörisch, Barbara Johnson, David Levin, Barry Mazur, Gretchen Mazur, William Rasch, Eric Rentschler, Judith Ryan, Eric Santner, Hinrich Seeba, Marc Shell, Juri Striedter, Maria Tatar, Sigrid Weigel, and Marc Weiner.

Particular thanks go to Frederick Beiser, Carol Jacobs, Jeffrey Librett, and Helmut J. Schneider for the meticulous and eye-opening readings they provided of the whole manuscript. I am grateful to Liliane Weissberg and David Wellbery for the interest they took in the book and the editorial advice they proffered. Houchang Chehabi encouraged me, and Ellen Hertz egged me on, just when I needed it. Fatima Naqvi-Peters, Peter Michalik, and Joel Westerdale assisted me with my research and saved me from committing many blunders.

But the book would not have been written had I not also been left alone. I would like to thank Harvard University for a semester's leave, the National Endowment for the Humanities for a fellowship, and Indiana University for a summer stipend; their generosity made solitude affordable. Judith Ryan provided the ideal working space by giving me the use of her study in Pusey Library, thoughtfully placed two floors underground and hence bereft of the temptations a room with a view would have held.

Throughout my work on this book, my family helped me negotiate the demands of solitude and society. My sons, Max and Felix Chaoulideer, made the world an infinitely richer place for me. My wife, Marie Deer, provided emotional and intellectual sustenance. Her intelligence and acuity have pressed upon every page of this book, which I dedicate to her with love and gratitude.

Note

For the sake of legibility, I use English translations throughout; Schlegel's original appears in the notes. There I have preserved all idiosyncrasies, typographical oddities, and abbreviations that the critical edition records (as well as, in square brackets, the decoding the editors suggest). Following the Press's style, I have not marked capitalizations at the beginning of quotations. When possible and practicable, I provide a reference for both non-English sources and published English translations (separated by a slash), even in cases when I provide my own translation, to make it easier for readers to check the cited source. When I use other translations, I often silently amend them. In the notes, I provide volume, page, and, where appropriate, fragment numbers. Thus "KA 2:182, No. 116" refers to fragment 116 on page 182 of volume 2 of the *Kritische Ausgabe* of Schlegel's works. A list of abbreviations follows. The notes list only short titles; full references can be found in the bibliography.

Abbreviations

AA   *Kants gesammelte Schriften.* Edited by Königlich
Preußische Akademie der Wissenschaften. Berlin:
Walter de Gruyter, 1902– .

AM   *Aesthetic and Miscellaneous Works of Friedrich von
Schlegel.* Translated by E. J. Millington. London:
G. Bell & Sons, 1915.

DP   Friedrich Schlegel. *Dialogue on Poetry and Literary
Aphorisms.* Translated by Ernst Behler and Roman
Struc. University Park: Pennsylvania State University
Press, 1968.

DW   Jacob and Wilhelm Grimm. *Deutsches Wörterbuch.*
1854–1960. Reprint, Munich: Deutscher Taschenbuch
Verlag, 1984.

KA   *Kritische Friedrich-Schlegel-Ausgabe.* Edited by Ernst
Behler et al. Munich, Paderborn, Vienna: Ferdinand
Schöningh, 1958– .

KU   Immanuel Kant. *Kritik der Urteilskraft.* In AA 5/
Critique of Judgment, trans. Werner S. Pluhar. Indianapolis: Hackett, 1987. Since the translation provides
the pagination of the original, only one page reference
is given.

LF   Friedrich Schlegel. *Lucinde and the Fragments.* Translated by Peter Firchow. Minneapolis: University of
Minnesota Press, 1971.

PF   Friedrich Schlegel. *Philosophical Fragments.* Translated
by Peter Firchow. Minneapolis: University of Minnesota
Press, 1991.

Abbreviations

TP   *Theory as Practice: A Critical Anthology of Early German Romantic Writings.* Edited and translated by Jochen Schulte-Sasse et al. Minneapolis: University of Minnesota Press, 1997.

Introduction

> *Interrupted, it goes on.* —*Maurice Blanchot*

This is a book about an unexpected encounter between the natural sciences and the theory of poetry at the end of the eighteenth century. It looks at how concepts and images borrowed from the tumultuous field of chemistry enable the most important theorist of romanticism, Friedrich Schlegel (1772–1829), to imagine the production and reception of verbal artifacts in entirely new ways—ways inaccessible to the philosophical language at his disposal, and ways crucial to what we take to be the idiom of modernity.

At the heart of these innovations in poetics and aesthetics lies a new theory of language that Schlegel both describes and, as it were, tests in his writings. We can find it in suggestive ideas, notes, images, and metaphors scattered throughout his work (chiefly his early output), but they never gather into a coherently articulated treatise. (That there are systematic reasons for this failure at being systematic will concern me later.) Instead, Schlegel offers us essays—which is to say: textual experiments—that are imagined to have, and sometimes do have, the volatility and combustibility of chemical agents. More than a decade before Goethe finds himself attracted to chemical ideas in his *Wahlverwandtschaften* (Elective Affinities), published in 1808, Schlegel relies on chemistry to effect what Derrida has called a "displacement without reversal"[1] of aesthetics. The results are far more chaotic and far less artful than in Goethe's work, yet because of their vast range, metaphors of chemistry end up having rich implications for reconceptualizing poetics.

As we shall see, chemistry provides the crucial conceptual model—the enabling allegory—for a powerful transformation of poetological theory beyond Schlegel's own work.[2] Because our own engagement with texts still occurs within a frame largely devised in early romanticism, the chemical allegory has consequences far beyond the limits of Schlegel's writings. Thus throughout this study, I have attempted to make my historical claims—the specific ways texts are processed around 1800—with an eye toward current theoretical debates. It has seemed to me that the particular form our perplexity takes when we read literature or when we relate literary claims to cultural and political acts can be understood and described with considerable precision through the model of chemical combinatorics that Schlegel develops.

I should be clearer: Schlegel does not in fact "develop" any "model" of the workings of chemistry in poetic or linguistic production. There is nothing in his writings with the requisite level of organization and coherence to merit being called "model" or "theory" in the conventional sense. Instead, he speaks endlessly of "saturation" and "condensation," of "synthesis and analysis," of "oxidation" and of "azote" (i.e., nitrogen), and above all of "eternally dividing and mixing forces." What distinguishes him from some of his contemporaries is not his knowledge of this emerging science, but in fact his lack of systematic understanding. It is a field with which everyone seems to have more than a mere passing familiarity: Kant knows it well, Schelling lectures on it at length, Novalis studies it intensively, Goethe occupies himself with it throughout his life (and not only in his novels), Coleridge has a remarkably firm grasp of it. In comparison, Schlegel's occupation with chemistry is more dilettantish, which is why it has only rarely been taken seriously by scholars.

Yet my sense is that precisely because he feels no obligation to produce a "correct" account of chemistry, his metaphors are subject to far fewer controls than those in writers who do, yielding an aesthetic model that is, paradoxically, far closer to the state of eighteenth-century chemistry than one might at first think possible. For if there is something chaotic or unaccountable in the model that emerges, that is as it should be: as we shall see, chaos and contingency reside in the very center of chemistry around 1800. The idiosyncrasy of Schlegel's metaphors, as well as their import for the history and theory of literature, becomes evident only when we recognize that they are neither random nor isolated but rather part of an extended narrative—an allegory—motivated by the complex scientific context from which they are borrowed. Taking a close look at the muddled state of late-eighteenth-century chemistry (which I do in chapter 3) allows us to see how Schlegel's metaphors cohere into an aesthetic conception with broad consequences for our understanding of romanticism, of the relationship of science and literature, and, most important, of what we mean by "understanding" literature *tout court* (discussed in chapter 1).

The fuller story of the interaction between chemical and poetic language will occupy me in the chapters to come, but it may be worth providing a glimpse of some of the main themes. Chemistry is often taken by Schlegel to stand in the middle between terms treated as irreconcilable opposites. Thus the dichotomy of life and death is loosened when he maps the taxonomic "trinity [of] animality, vegetability, minerality" onto "organic, chemical, mechanical."[3] The opposition of understanding and genius (as articulated, for example, in Kant's *Kritik der Urteilskraft* [Critique of Judgment]) is complicated by the injection of a third, chemical term: "Understanding is mechanical, wit is chemical, genius is organic spirit."[4] The conceptual triplet can even be flipped from the horizontal axis of classification to the vertical axis of temporal organization to increase the possibilities of imagining the future with a third term: thus Schlegel contrasts two kinds of ideals, one undesirable (the "mathematical phantoms of a merely mechanical mind"), the other unattainable ("only a perfect mind could conceive of ideals organically"), with a third, chemical possibility: "Whoever has a sense for the infinite and knows what he wants to do with it, sees in it the product of eternally dividing and mixing forces, conceives of his ideals at least as being chemical."[5] I will come back to some of these passages in future chapters, but one thing is evident already at this point: to say that chemistry stands in the middle by no means implies that it therefore stands in the center. It occupies a rather odd, almost untenable, perhaps even impossible place, certainly not well charted enough to be a position; if anything, it permits or consists of a movement between two positions. As we shall see, this movement between positions entails, of necessity, interruption; indeed, it will be difficult to distinguish neatly between movement and interruption.

It is just this possibility of movement as interruption that recommends chemistry as a model for the production of verbal artifacts. It helps us to understand why the proponent of "progressive universal poetry,"[6] of the synthesis of all branches of science and art, expresses these ideas in the stubbornly nonsynthetic form of fragments. For if we understand the notion of synthesis chemically, then poetry would not be the activity of enlivening all facets of a productive life with the same (organic) meaning (for which it has all too often been taken), but it would describe the process of experimentation in which some forms emerge and others decay, in which some outcomes are predictable and others are not. The concept of chemistry, I will argue, permits Schlegel to develop and practice a form of writing that is experimental down to the letter. Letters, morphemes, words, phrases— in short: fragments—are subjected to the "eternally dividing and mixing forces" over which the experimenter has only limited sway. When every move toward greater synthesis is at the same time interrupted by analysis and every analysis by an attending synthesis, then we begin to see how the fragment can be seen as the allegory of the irreducibility of interruption in movement. And not just the allegory: the fragments are themselves the place—the laboratory—in which these experiments in dividing and mixing are performed. Such an idea of experimental writing not only represents a departure from commonly held notions about romanticism, but it can be made fruitful for the analysis of post-romantic literature, notably in the work of Stéphane Mallarmé and Paul Valéry.

Rather than a notion of art dignified, but also circumscribed, by a double bond—an analogy to nature and a causal connection to a genius imagined as divine—Schlegel's chemically inspired theory promotes a notion of art that is reticulated with ideas of auto-formation, open-endedness, and uncontrollable contingency. Where eighteenth-century aesthetics imagines an enclosed work of art as the *product* created by an intentional producer, here the work consists of an open-ended *process* of combinatorial formation and deformation, a process, furthermore, over which the artist by no means retains full control.[7] One way of imagining this process is along the lines of Roland Barthes's writerly "production without product,"[8] which neglects the stable text (as it is stored, for example, in a critical edition) in favor of the fluid text consisting of a perpetual rearrangement, effected by the active reader. Indeed Barthes's idea of the "ideal text" is worth quoting at length, since it seems to me to provide an astute description of Schlegel's project of fragmentary writing:

> In this ideal text, the networks are many and interact, without any one of them being able to surpass the rest; this text is a galaxy of signifiers, not a structure of signifieds; it has no beginning; it is reversible; we gain access to it by several entrances, none of which can be authoritatively declared to be the main one; the codes it mobilizes extend *as far as the eye can reach,* they are undecidable (meaning here is never subject to a principle of determination, unless by throwing dice); the systems of meaning can take over this absolutely plural text, but their number is never closed, based as it is on the infinity of language. (12 / 5–6)

While Barthes's is ultimately a theory of reading (the mobility in this passage is generated entirely by the reader), Schlegel's poetic theory demands innovations in both the production of verbal artworks and in their reception. It allows for a process of reading that tolerates, indeed encourages, the emergence of transient configurations of thought among the fragments and essays that cannot be folded into a redemptive narrative, toward which the fragments have so often been understood to strive. While even the most "advanced," philosophically sophisticated readings of early romanticism tend to integrate it into a narrative of progression—be it organic, dialectic, or asymptotic—I argue in chapter 2 that the most consequential poetic model developed by the Jena romantics denies just this move toward redemption (while yearning for it nonetheless). But for Schlegel, the alternative is not therefore a "paratactic contiguity"[9] of starkly unconnected material elements or temporal events. The fragments are not reducible to fragmentation alone. Rather, chemistry shuttles between narrative and its absence (and hence the absence of communicable meaning), neither smoothly moving along the flow of narrative sense nor blocked entirely by the senseless interruptions of fragmentation and parataxis; interrupted, it goes on. It looks for affinities and attractions between the disjointed elements without lending them final coherence; it is always prepared to start afresh, to look for other possibilities, to read again.

In its most general form, the theory of language undergirding Schlegel's project locates the peculiar force of utterances, whether poetic or not, in the strange interaction of two distinct realms of generating symbols. One of these reduces the wealth of linguistic possibilities to a small number of elements and combinatorial operations; on this account, language is nothing more than the permutation and variation of a few elements. Rather than flowing from an ineffable spirit of genius, even the most sublime expressions of poetry are produced by an austere algorithm governing two dozen letters. Yet what emerges from this symbol-making machine can be charged with meaning—with the possibility of conveying sense and nonsense—only when it has come into contact with another realm, namely the conscious or unconscious intentions by means of which speakers and writers reach into the world. At the precise place where a speaker's or writer's wishes, fears, or curiosities interact with the external language machine, as they must if they are to be communicated, they give rise to utterances that are neither the predictable outcome of a linguistic mechanism nor the organic outgrowth of ingenious creation, but another, not quite predictable entity. We can call it "chemical," using the term in a historically precise sense: for while chemistry in the late eighteenth century means to develop a combinatorial model in which elements combine and recombine in purely mechanical fashion, it cannot explain away the fact some substances appear to be drawn to each other with far greater ardor than others. To describe this oddity, which places severe limitation on the combinatorial field, chemists rely on the notion of attraction (or elective affinity). Combination and attraction mark the two poles between which chemists attempt to forge a theory of the changes in matter: on the one hand, a force that marches on with the implacable predictability of an algorithm; on the other, an anthropomorphically imagined counterforce that introduces unevenness and contingency.

Schlegel is drawn to this highly unstable model (which chemists start abandoning in 1810 when Dalton proposes the atomic theory) because it describes what happens when we use, and in turn are abused by, language. Every utterance we venture partakes of a combinatorial system anteceding us, external to us, and accessible to others, as well as a set of motives or intention that are ours alone (though not necessarily fully accessible to our conscious selves). An intention cannot but be communicated as an utterance resulting from the application of a set of combinatorial rules to a finite set of elements, yet at the same time every intention, whether wittingly or not, skews those rules in favor of some utterances rather than others. Every utterance has, then, something human as well as something nonhuman about it, for while it would not be there without us, it must make use of—it must submit to—an apparatus beyond the reach of any single human. In the language of romanticism: it is at once organic and mechanical, yet exceeds both. One of my goals in this book is to offer an account of this point of contact between the human and the nonhuman, which is as common as communication itself, yet as perplexing as anything we are likely to encounter (for it is the perplexity of encountering itself).

Ascribing such a model of poetic writing and reading to Schlegel entails shifting our emphasis away from the organic worldview that scholars as different as René Wellek and Friedrich Kittler have attributed to Schlegel and identified as the hallmark of romantic thinking.[10] Certain features of his writing—features that yield important insights into the theory of poetic production and reception—become available for analysis only when we admit a narrative in Schlegel's work, running alongside the many explicit endorsements of the organic, that is marked by discontinuity, contingency, and occasional incoherence. As we shall see, the meaning of words cannot finally be explained through recourse to a seed of meaning buried deep within them that would, through organic augmentation, steadily grow into a meaningful word. Things are messier and more interesting than that.

Yet it would not be right to turn the received idea of a powerful critical tradition on its head, insisting that Schlegel's work is really a disguised application of mechanistic concepts of selection and permutation to poetics. Part of what his writings demonstrate is that language cannot be expected to comply fully with the force of our wishes, that "secret societies"[11] among words—and parts of words—exert a certain counterforce, which we experience as incomprehensibility. At the same time, words—and parts of words—are not therefore governed by a logic wholly external to speakers and writers. Some readings of romanticism counter the notion of the romantic enthrallment with the organic by relying on poetological and rhetorical terms borrowed from mathematics or optics.[12] Although this counter-model is meant to stress the essential modernity of romanticism and its commitment to rational forms of thought, arguments with which I am wholly sympathetic, such a conceptual shift from organicism to a mathematically inspired mechanism misses not only the many contradictions and ambivalences in Schlegel's writings; it also misses what I take to be his daring and theoretically consequential experiment of combining the two, an experiment that admittedly yields only unstable processes and formations (which Schlegel calls fragments), but that also offers rich ways of imagining the process of writing and reading poetry.

Indeed, the choice of chemistry over mathematics may constitute the point at which Schlegel's project is most sharply distinguished from that of his friend and collaborator Novalis, whose interest in mathematics as the template for language is articulated in his well-known "Monologue": "If one could only make people understand that it is with language the way it is with mathematical formulas—

They make a world of their own—They play only with themselves, . . . and for that very reason they are so expressive."[13] An entry in one of his mathematical notebooks is even clearer: "The system of numbers is a *model* [*Muster*] of a real linguistic sign system—our letters should become numbers, our language arithmetic."[14] Chemistry and mathematics share the idea of self-enclosure and self-reference, yet the chemical model allows for a much richer account of the possibilities of incomprehension inherent in the material of (written) language, namely letters, morphemes, words, etc. For unlike the symbols in a mathematically conceived language (such as the Leibnizian *ars combinatoria*), in Schlegel's model of language neither the meaning of the elements of language nor their function within a systematic arrangement remains inert. Linguistic units are imagined not as mere tokens shuffled by definable operations, nor as autonomous signifiers saturated with meaning from which ever more complex meanings grow, but rather as something located between the two, partaking of both form and matter, operation and element, and changing both. While one vector—combination—expands the number of possible outcomes (to infinity), the other vector—attraction—limits them by the idiosyncratic behavior of the elements, as though a secret urge propelled them toward some combinations and away from others.

To put the appearance of chemistry in Schlegel's writings into a larger context of intellectual history, we could say that it opens a space between mechanism and organicism. If mechanical philosophy regards everything, including the once sacrosanct human body, as "an assemblage of springs that mutually wind each other up" (as La Mettrie claims in his aptly titled *L'Homme machine* of 1747),[15] and if, on the other hand, organicist *Naturphilosophie* conceives of the cosmos essentially as one purposeful organism (as articulated by Schelling and, in weaker form, by Coleridge, Wordsworth, Novalis, Goethe, and Schlegel himself), then chemistry makes possible a picture of the world in which living and lifeless elements engage in dynamic interactions, in which the very distinction between the living and lifeless becomes ever more difficult to maintain.

This is not to say that this picture represents the philosophical or heuristic model grounding the work of chemists in the eighteenth century. As the century progresses, more and more of them become firm adherents of the mechanical position, which had already a century earlier been forcefully applied to chemistry by Robert Boyle. Nonetheless, the idea of chemistry as a middle voice (still current today in the classification of the basic sciences that places chemistry between physics and biology) is, in effect, the truth of chemistry in the eighteenth century. It is a result of monumental upheaval in the science: the late eighteenth century is the scene of the most important shift in the theory of chemistry, a shift which in the history of science is routinely described as the "Chemical Revolution." The replacement of the phlogiston theory of burning, developed by Georg Ernst Stahl early in the century, with Lavoisier's theory of oxidation in the 1780s required such a thorough rethinking of the very model of chemical interaction that it has become an exemplar of the notion of a paradigm shift as applied to the sciences, most notably in Thomas Kuhn's work.[16] As Kuhn points out, a paradigm shift is a profoundly disorienting event, because it results *from* a disciplinary confusion pervasive enough to require a new theory and it results *in* a period of confusion during which the practitioners of the field adjust to the new theory. In the case of eighteenth-century chemistry, things are more complicated still, because even the most fervent proponents of the new theory—Lavoisier himself included—have a keen sense of its inadequacy. Because the theory lacks mathematical formalization, chemists find themselves in a kind of theoretical wilderness in which they continue to work with imprecise notions such as affinity. This points to another shift taking place at the same time—exacerbating the disorientation of the paradigm shift—namely the shift from a practice steeped in occult, alchemical, medical, and pharmaceutical traditions to a rational, empirical science.[17] Chemistry at this time attempts to rid itself of alchemical traces and to replace them with a mathematical (which is to say, ultimately mechanical) explanatory model, and fails at both attempts. It is, in short, a field perched between the phlogiston and oxygen theories, between magical and rational explanations, between an artisanal practice and a theoretical science.

The two features defining late-eighteenth-century chemistry—on the one hand, the increasing formalization and quantification typical of an emerging science, and on the other, the obstinate leftovers of a matter not wholly mastered (inherited in part from alchemy)—make it into the powerful allegory of a new poetic project that it becomes in Schlegel's work: to invent an account of poetic production and reception that moves between the normative and the aesthetic, the technical and the inspirational, the mechanical and the organic, without, however, offering a "higher synthesis" of these. Linguistic elements, like chemical elements at the turn of the nineteenth century, maintain affinities and yield outcomes that remain unexplained to the experimenter; they refuse to submit to the formalizing will of the scientist or the writer. But what frustrates the program of providing a complete and coherent description of their behavior at the same time enables the emergence of a mysterious surplus—sometimes sublimely poetic, sometimes monstrous and nonsensical—that would evaporate entirely in a system exhaustively reduced to a mechanical set of operations. Since formalism breaks down at the precise point at which operation and operandum cannot be kept distinct and begin to contaminate one another, the *failure* at formalization recommends eighteenth-century chemistry as a model for Schlegel's attempts at removing linguistic, and thus poetic, production from the aegis of organicism, without at the same time submitting it to a well-ordered mechanism. Chemistry before the advent of the atomic theory in the early nineteenth century is this mechanism that cannot quite exorcise the ghost of alchemical magic, a formalism to which material remainders persistently cling. It allegorizes the textuality of texts, the literariness of literature.

What are the consequences for poetic production in conceiving of verbal artworks as chemical experiments? On the most elementary level, it entails thinking of the verbal artwork as *written*. Experiments require control and isolation (i.e., reduction of complexity), and neither of these is possible without writing (as will be shown in detail in chapters 4 and 5). But imagining poetry as expressed in letters, rather than as emanating from a soulful voice, in turn means that the medium of its appearance, its materiality, becomes an object of reflection, an object that to a certain extent remains external to the artist. These two linked possibilities—imagining writing in its materiality and thus as an externality—provide us with an instance of media studies long before there was such a discipline, and thus have great resonance for a modern understanding of literary production. "The writing of our day," Foucault has claimed in his celebrated essay "What Is an Author?" "has freed itself from the necessity of 'expression'; it only refers to itself, yet it is not restricted to the confines of interiority. On the contrary, we recognize it in its exterior deployment. This reversal transforms writing into an interplay of signs, regulated less by the content of the signifieds than by the very nature of the signifier."[18] Put into the language of aesthetics: the autonomous work of art, a notion commonly understood to have emerged in Jena romanticism, entails an autonomy of art not from social pressures but to an important degree *from the artist.* The externality of language sponsors a poetological model in which a process bereft of intention or sense is as important in giving rise to the poem as the poet's emotions, hopes, and fears. We may call it "autonomous," but *automatic* may be a more accurate term.

Nor is this externality entirely autonomously. There is no use of language without a user; language occurs exactly at the point where the external apparatus of its operational rules crosses a speaker's or writer's intentions, be they conscious or not. Neither Foucault, who makes his point carefully to avoid a digital choice between inside and outside ("*less* by the content . . . than by the . . . signifier"), nor Schlegel overlooks this fact. In the latter's writing, the manner in which the formal, external operations of language are drawn into the subjective sphere of a person's desire becomes apparent in the material composition, and decomposition, of language itself. This involves an obsessive interest in typography, syntax, semantics, morphology, even the constitution of letters, as though the secret ingredients giving rise to the verbal artwork could be found in them. "The letter is the true magic wand," Schlegel notes more than once (and demonstrates it with the pun *Buchstab / Zauberstab,* letter / magic wand, which makes use of the very magic that is being invoked here).[19] As we will see, Schlegel's early writings can be understood to pursue the question of what magic, what unlikely combination of internal wishes and external laws, joins and scatters letters in such a way as to hold our attention.

It is not merely a play on words to say that such concern for the materiality of letters is the mark of a fully self-conscious *littera-tura.* "The term 'literature,'" Harry Levin notes in his preface to Albert Lord's *The Singer of Tales*, "presupposing the use of letters, assumes that 'oral literature' is obviously a contradiction in terms."[20] I do not of course mean that in Schlegel's work we observe the transition from oral to written poetry; in Europe, that shift had been under way for more than two millennia before young Friedrich Schlegel arrived on the scene. But, as Eric Havelock has observed, "cultural habits survive their technical obsolescence."[21] Such surviving habits include not only oral conventions of composition (such as anaphora, parallelism, rhyme, rhythmic repetition) that persist long after their mnemonic function has been usurped by writing, but also—and even more insistently—ways in which a culture imagines and describes the production of verbal artworks. Changes in the technology of storage, transmission, and retrieval of words effect changes in manifest beliefs about words only slowly and unevenly. Writers and readers until romanticism (indeed, in many cases to our day) continue to conceive of writing as a container for spoken words, convenient in permitting the easy transportation of voices across space and time. It is on this level of self-understanding and self-description that Schlegel's writings register a change: they cease exclusively to imagine written poetry as essentially oral. By no means does Schlegel entirely surrender an attachment to the voice[22] (how could he, given that it is immeasurably older and richer than any writing system?), but he develops a rather fine-grained conception of the possibilities for extending the uses of writing beyond its ability to store and ship voices.

One way in which the profound change in self-description manifests itself is in the gradual and fitful replacement of *poetry* by *litera-*

ture in the late eighteenth century, a change we can also observe in Schlegel's own writing (though not in any systematic way). Poetry, in its old sense, comprises not only the verbal arts—rhythmic and non-rhythmic, written and spoken—but metonymically stands for all the arts. Indeed, through its fortuitous etymological link with the Greek *poiein*, to make, it is often regarded as the universal and quintessentially human activity of making or creating, of extending to the world our technical and imaginative capacities. Literature, by contrast, is understood in its medial, historical, and social specificity already in the late eighteenth century: it is a particular form of writing in a particular language and occurs under particular circumstances. Like other spheres of production, it employs principles and customs *internal* to its formal and material makeup.[23] It is this internal materiality that particularly interests Schlegel: the explicit and self-conscious focus of literature on its own material medium, on writing and on letters. Friedrich Kittler has argued that literature in the modern sense arises around 1880, after the invention of new recording technologies for sight and sound forces writing to specialize on specifically textual media, imposing on literature "the ascesis that knows only black letters on white paper."[24] But as I shall try to demonstrate in chapter 5, Schlegel's writings exhibit, in a more ambiguous and tentative way than Kittler might approve of, many of the features of modern literary writing, even in the absence of competition from film and phonography.

By introducing the theory (and, to a lesser extent, the practice) of an experimental combinatorics into his writing, Schlegel achieves two things that Kittler takes to be peculiar to writings after 1880: he allows the number and range of possible linguistic expressions to increase dramatically, and, by the same token, opens the way for the production of entirely meaningless configurations. Programmatic nonsense—complete incomprehensibility—is not, as Kittler would have it, reserved for literature after Mallarmé, but is already available in Schlegel's fragments and notebooks.[25] It is admittedly never present in a pure form, but is rather always contaminated by a certain dose of sense. Yet I argue that, rather than any sort of "ascesis," this mutual implication of sense and nonsense, of a poetic production directed by a sovereign mind and a writing emerging from a machine-like process, describes what actually interests us about literature, what provokes us into becoming readers who are, in Schlegel's words, "alive and exerting a counter-force."[26] Writing and reading fall into this strange and uncertain zone in which letters, words, and sentences are mere tokens of a formal system and, at the same time, deeply meaningful signs.

The loosening of the bond between the signified and the signifier (or, in the terms of the present discussion, the move from "poetry" to "literature") has often been imagined to be a kind of victory for a liberation struggle. Thus in the passage quoted earlier, Foucault says, without apparent irony, that contemporary writing "has *freed itself* from the *necessity* of 'expression,'" as though writing had been a revolutionary subject yearning to rid itself of a particularly onerous yoke. When critics, in analyzing the complicated relationship of language and reference, resort to the term "play" to designate the lack of a firm fit between linguistic terms and their referents, it is temptingly easy to place that term into opposition to concepts such as "work" or "constraint," and thus easy to read a linguistic practice as a political allegory. Such claims have also been advanced about Schlegel's writings by critics who have attempted to point to politically progressive strands of thought in the work of an author who in his later life becomes an ardent Catholic and an official in Metternich's administration (though not a terribly effective one). While laudable in intention, these arguments miss both the most innovative aspects of the linguistic and poetic theory and the most radical, and radically troubling, features of a social theory embedded in Schlegel's writings. Chapter 6 makes an attempt at showing why the identification of the "play of the signifier" with political liberation overlooks complicating elements in both.

Part of what is missed by a too hasty identification (or even analogization) of literary and political practices is the very "freeing" of writing from certain "necessities" to which Foucault alludes, including the necessity of serving as moral or political allegories. In

Schlegel's poetic practice and poetological theory (and it is unclear which of the two is the chicken, which the egg) incomprehensibility is not merely tolerated, but sought after as an effect of linguistic communication, an effect that seems aptly allegorized by the ceaseless process of synthesis and analysis in chemistry (more about this in chapter 1). The very same conditions that further a programmatic incomprehensibility, a feature of writing that has become a defining mark of post-romantic, particularly modernist, literature, would also seem to complicate the reading of literature as a political allegory. That (high) literature should be enigmatic has attained the status of dogma since Mallarmé, repeated by critics and scholars, including Foucault;[27] but just this devotion to its own material, regardless of "sense," refers literature back to literature, rather than to politics or morality.

The increase in zones of hermeneutic incoherence serves to effect precisely the shift from the idea of poetry as universal expression of human wants to the local and specific activity of literature. In sociological terms, it promotes the differentiation of literature as a social system.[28] In the chapters that follow, I will not be making specifically sociological claims, but the readings I offer here, both local and general, do not contradict the historical narrative offered by sophisticated sociological studies. Thus one of the ways in which the sphere of art asserts and maintains its systemic autonomy is precisely by producing statements that in any other context would be deemed incomprehensible. Indeed, incomprehensibility becomes an index for the autonomy of art: the more autonomous it is, the more it can tolerate and even promote incomprehensible statements. In Schlegel we can document not only a greater willingness than before for being incomprehensible, and thus a tendency toward a greater differentiation of the verbal arts toward "literature," but also a self-awareness about this process.[29] When he writes that poetry ought to be "at once poetry and poetry of poetry" and when, in using the technical language he borrows from the Kantians, he comes up with the notion of "transcendental poetry,"[30] these second-order terms point to the fact that, in Schlegel's work, poetry becomes, as it were, aware of the process of differentiation from other modes of cultural production that it has been undergoing for several centuries. It begins to observe the fact that it does not produce in the manner of or according to the rules of philosophy, politics, or religion, but rather in its own manner and according to its own rules.[31] In Schlegel's works, poetry introduces *into itself* distinctions that define its production (such as the distinction between itself and philosophy); it becomes recursive. As poetry, it performs its own differentiation from other cultural spheres; as poetry of poetry, it reflects on—it allegorizes—this performance.

1 | *Of Incomprehensibility*

Between Syntax and Semantics

One of Friedrich Schlegel's best-known works is the brief essay "Über die Unverständlichkeit" (On Incomprehensibility), published in 1800 in the journal *Athenäum,* which he and his brother August Wilhelm Schlegel edited. The essay is often regarded as the culmination of the program motivating the entire journal, because the essay contains a distillation of everything the *Athenäum* aspires to; with it—the final piece of the final issue—Schlegel seems to close the book on an astonishing literary and critical experiment. Though in existence for a total of barely three years, the journal attracted a lot of attention, albeit mostly negative, among its contemporary readers. Goethe and Schiller were both quite irritated by it (though Goethe, possessed perhaps of greater self-assurance, seems to have relished the irritation).[1] Later readers have taken the journal to be the most important source for the ideas associated with early romanticism; had the *Frühromantik* been a literary movement like surrealism or futurism, the *Athenäum* would have been its manifesto.[2] Since romanticism is in many ways still our critical moment ("our birthplace," as Philippe Lacoue-Labarthe and Jean-Luc Nancy put it with a touch of pathos)[3]—since (as we shall see) we have not quite managed to extricate ourselves from its particular entanglement with philosophy, literature, and language—the *Athenäum* can excite in us a peculiar sense of intellectual affinity. Its themes, its techniques, its worries, its ambitions, while put in language that can seem dated, are comprehensible to us without a great deal of historical and conceptual translation.

What facilitates this comprehension across two centuries is that the very notion of comprehension is no longer taken for granted by the texts in and around the *Athenäum.* Parallel to the particular content that they convey, the texts also communicate the idea that to a certain degree they will remain incommunicable. It is this basic premise, more basic than any specific theme or motif, that establishes the bond of affinity between contemporary readers and early romanticism. If literary scholars have largely subscribed to the view that some aspect or other of a work will always elude their hermeneutic skill and have thus resigned themselves to the endless process of producing interpretations, they do so not primarily in response to the work of Sigmund Freud or of Jacques Derrida, but because of two decisive steps taken by the Jena romantics. To the latter, the possibility of failed communication is not merely a consequence of incompetent participants or of a faulty code but endemic to the act of communication itself. "The purest and most splendid incomprehensibility," Schlegel writes in that final essay of the *Athenäum,* can be obtained "precisely from science and from art, . . . from philosophy and philology."[4] The romantic project accepts the possibility of incomprehensibility, and what is more—this is the second decisive step—it embraces it. Far from being seen as an unfortunate but unavoidable feature of communication, failure is actually taken to be desirable in certain communicative situations. We can see how the idea that incomprehensibility can be "pure" and "splendid" might resonate with particular force among readers of Mallarmé, of Kafka, or of Pynchon. In this view, just because a communication fails, it has not therefore been a failure. On the contrary, a moment of failure, of incomprehension, of perplexity is precisely what guarantees the overall *success* of communication, especially of poetic or aesthetic communication. The idea that we ought to seek, rather than shun, the enigmatic regions in literary texts is precisely what we share with—what we have inherited from—the *Athenäum.* And nowhere are these ideas laid out more programmatically than in "On Incomprehensibility."

And yet reading the essay is a more confounding experience than one might have been led to believe by what I have claimed so far. There are certainly stretches of the essay which include wholly comprehensible discussions of "the question of whether [the reciprocal communication of ideas] is even possible";[5] precisely by making incomprehensibility into its explicit theme, Schlegel seems to have attempted to insulate the essay from contamination by its topic. ("In order that this whole enterprise not turn in too palpable a circle, I had firmly resolved to be comprehensible at least this once," he writes.)[6] It is supposed to be an essay *on* incomprehensibility, not *of* it.

But when he declares that the essay is an "occasion to conduct experiments on this possibility or impossibility"[7] of successful communication, it begins to dawn on the reader that a self-reference is at work that can finally not permit topic and exposition to remain entirely distinct. Simply put, one cannot conduct experiments to determine the possibility or impossibility of something without running the risk of getting one's hands stained with that something. This should have been clear all along, for an essay is ultimately nothing but an experiment; the polysemy, already apparent in English, becomes plainly obvious in the German word *Versuch,* meaning both essay and experiment. An essay on incomprehensibility can therefore never simply be *on* it, but must always also court the possibility of becoming *of* it.

This is just what happens in—or better yet: happens to—"On Incomprehensibility": despite the fact that its topic and its critical idiom are familiar, despite the author's stated intentions of lucidity, the essay's brilliant flashes of insight are often obscured by vapors and smoke. Take, for example, the passage early in the essay in which Schlegel begins to consider his topic (here it is useful to have the German text present):

Der gesunde Menschenverstand . . . dürfte leicht auf die Vermutung geraten können, der Grund des Unverständlichen liege im Unverstand. Nun ist es ganz eigen an mir, daß ich den Unverstand durchaus nicht leiden kann, auch den Unverstand der Unverständigen, noch weniger aber den Unverstand der Verständigen. Daher hatte ich schon vor langer Zeit den Entschluß gefaßt, mich mit dem Leser in ein Gespräch über diese Materie zu versetzen. (KA 2:363)

Common sense . . . might easily be led to believe that the grounds for the incomprehensible lies in incomprehension. Now it is one of my peculiarities that I detest incomprehension, including the incomprehension of the uncomprehending, even more the incomprehension of the comprehending. Thus I had decided long ago to engage the reader in a conversation on this matter. (TP 119)

It is unclear what this passage might mean; what is clear is that it contains an unusually high concentration of the prefix *ver-*, ten instances to be precise. Indeed, the whole essay is riddled with *ver*-s. Over its ten-page length, I counted a hundred and two instances; in the first two pages alone *ver-* occurs thirty-five times. (To make these numbers more meaningful, we can use Schlegel's other important essays in the *Athenäum* as a control group: in the first two pages, *ver-* occurs four times in "Über die Philosophie" [On Philosophy], eight times in "Über Goethes Meister" [On Goethe's *Wilhelm Meister*], and nine times in "Gespräch über die Poesie" [Conversation on Poetry].) Besides the *ver*-s in the cognates clustering around *Unverständlichkeit* that Schlegel seems to enjoy repeating (*Verstand, Menschenverstand, Unverstand, Verständlichkeit, Verständigen, mißverstanden,* etc.), we also find *ver-* in combination with many other words: *verlieren, Verkehr, Verhältnisse, Verhältnisbegriffe, vervielfältigen, verwickeln, versetzen, Vermutung,* and *Versuche* occur on the first page of the essay.

We know that the question of whether comprehension is possible leads Schlegel to consider words and how they "often understand themselves better than do those who use them."[8] It now emerges that, while considering the comprehensibility of words on its manifest level, the essay experiments with *parts* of words on the level of its coding in language—the level of its self-implication in the medium that it means to study. The essay is on *Unverständlichkeit*, certainly, but it is also on a *part* of *Unverständlichkeit*.

Unlike some other prefixes (e.g., *aus-, über-, vor-*), *ver-* itself is not a word. By itself it means nothing.[9] Yet when added to a word (or word stem), it can change the course of its meaning considerably. For example:

stehen (to stand)	→	*verstehen* (to understand)
laufen (to run)	→	*sich verlaufen* (to lose one's way)
führen (to guide)	→	*verführen* (to seduce)
sprechen (to speak)	→	*(sich) versprechen* (to misspeak; to promise)
suchen (to search)	→	*versuchen* (to try)
		Versuch (attempt, essay, experiment)
		Versuchung (temptation)

Grimm's *Deutsches Wörterbuch* traces *ver-* back to Greek and Sanskrit forms that mean *passed* or *away*, and concludes that this meaning "has been preserved as the main Germanic meaning" (DW 25:54). Thus the dictionary's impressive list of the eleven main transformations of meaning effected by *ver-* (while not covering nearly all cases) suggests that *ver-* not only changes the meaning of the word or stem, but often causes a particular form of deviation from the path of meaning, especially in the reflexive form of verbs: it denotes disorientation (*sich verfahren*, "to go astray driving"), missed or mistaken goals (*sich verrechnen*, "to miscalculate"), excessive actions (*verschlafen*, "to oversleep"), and frequently a combination of these. Reading the history and usage of *ver-* in Grimm, one gets the sense that words had better steer clear of the prefix, for once it attaches itself to them, they are subjected to what the lexicographers call, not without mild alarm, "a moving away, a carrying away from the path taken thus far" (ibid.). Though neither of the brothers Grimm had a hand in preparing the definition of *ver-* (both had died by the time the volume with the letter *v* was prepared), one cannot help but see a gothic narrative in the way the dictionary presents the effects the prefix has on upstanding German words: on their way to the comfort of grandmother's house, they encounter a sinister figure and, "moving away . . . from the path taken," they end up in a dark, frightening place.[10] This sense of foreboding is made explicit by Max Leopold, the main author of the article on the prefix *ver-* in Grimm, in his stupendously erudite book on the topic. After methodically organizing the *ver-* material into groups according to their meaning, he concludes: "The largest groups are those with a nasty connotation. They predominate so much that *ver-* has primarily acquired this character and preserves it in the living language. New combinations made with *ver-* today almost exclusively have this meaning. The compositions of the type *verbinden* [to bind] are also richly represented and vital."[11]

Ver- is of course by no means alone in effecting transformations in stem words. Prefixes, suffixes, and other morphemes usually display a similar behavior: in attaching themselves to simple words, they create new words, new meanings, but also new uncertainties about meaning. And they do so even when the morpheme is not the slippery *ver-* but a seemingly unambiguous operator such as the operator of negation *un-* (as in *Un-verständlichkeit*). *Un-* can do odd things: unlike the mathematical "not," which in its domain applies uniformly and with predictable results, *un-* not only fails to bond with just any noun or adjective, but even when successfully attached, the outcome is not always what we might have expected. *Unmenge* means *greater* quantity, not its opposite, and *Untiefe*, "un-depth," not only refers to shallow waters but to great depths as well.[12] In a cryptic notebook entry, Schlegel registers this mix of qualities with great precision: "A lot of words (verba) can still be made with [the prefixes] *zer-/auf-*," he notes and adds parenthetically, "*be-* is also good for indeterminacy, maybe *ge-* too."[13] More combinations produce more words *and* more indeterminacy. It is the peculiar feature of this linguistic conception that it does not, and cannot, uncouple the two increases, for the same syntactic operation that permits an exponential rise in the number of possible words (e.g., the coupling function of *ver-*) introduces, as we have seen, unforeseen variations in the semantic field. In a sense, it makes semantics as a field of study possible, even necessary, insofar as semantics itself is a symptom of a malfunction in meaning. Otherwise, there would be no need to ask what or how something meant.

Syntax, in its most general sense of putting into order (*syntassein*),[14] thus opens a space of play, but also of doubt, into the referential function of words; it creates meaning as a problem, hence meaning as a category. The space for (the question of) meaning is opened not by the syntactic combination itself, nor by any of the particular instances of linguistic compounds, but by the process that leads to them; it occurs, as I hope to show, in the movement from *stehen* to *verstehen,* from *stand* to *understand.* And vice versa. For what Schlegel calls indeterminacy arises not merely in the direction of synthetic word formation (i.e., of an expansion of words such as *Un-ver-ständ-lich-keit* by a process of successive combinations) but, looping back, is introduced into what earlier I provisionally called simple words. This looping back of semantic confusion is certainly due to a historical amnesia that is a feature of language: that, for example, at any given moment "compound" and "simple" words impress users with similar degrees of semantic evidence (*understand* is not understood to stand, as it were, under *stand*), or that in some cases the pre-compound form of a word has been forgotten, making the compound into the simple word (*vergessen,* to forget, being an apt example of this). But there is also a structural reason for the appearance of semantic uncertainty, namely that the combinatorial principle, once introduced, works in two directions: synthesis and analysis. Making new combinations, as we shall see, requires breaking old ones until there is nothing left to break. Every possible division carries a possible incomprehensibility further and further into words. It is just such a model of language that we find in Schlegel.

Like other prefixes and suffixes, *ver-* is not merely acted upon by combinatorial rules; Schlegel's experiments show that it in turn acts upon *them,* pulls and warps their operations. The game of combinations produces such varying results that we are inclined to dismiss the notion that a meaning intrinsic to this prefix could have caused the swerves and manipulations. Yet *ver-* remains contaminated by a residue of "intrinsic meaning" (e.g., the primordial Sanskrit "away" detected by Grimm or the nastiness of connotation by Leopold), and this residue in turn contaminates, and hence constrains, the manner and range of combinations in which the prefix occurs. While the meanings of words to which the prefix ver- attaches itself scatter over a large range, there is nonetheless a clustering in the kinds of meanings we are likely to find. In other words: the effects of *ver-* (like that of other prefixes) is unpredictable, which is to say that it is neither determined nor random. If, as I suggested earlier, the syntax of *ver-* opens a space for semantics to occur, then the semantics of *ver-* at the same time intervenes in the working of its syntax. In Schlegel's conception, elements such as *ver-* are perched in a place that is "*neither purely syntactic nor purely semantic,*"[15] but somewhere between the two.

It is in part the very unpredictability inherent in the game of linguistic combinations that attracts Schlegel's and our attention (be it conscious or unconscious) to *ver-* ; we can certainly imagine other words or morphemes that would have served us just as well in this discussion. Does "On Incomprehensibility," already in its title, not call our attention to the fact that *all* morphemes in *Un-ver-ständ-lich-keit* play the game of combination and deviation that I have been describing? *Un-, ver-, -lich,* and *-keit* belong to the group of prefixes and suffixes that, apparently without autonomous meaning, not only add meaning in combinations but do so capriciously (though to differing degrees: *ver-* is far more unreliable than *-lich*). *Über* and *die,* the first two words of the title, are for their meanings no less dependent on the surrounding words than the prefixes and suffixes. Which leaves *ständ.* Standing there with all its semantic heft, two prefixes and two suffixes flanking it, it seems ideally suited as the pillar bolstering the whole structure. The dictionary, though, dashes such hope: according to Grimm, *ständ* derives via a series of transformations from *verstehen;* but the connection of the latter to *stehen* has given rise, Grimm notes, to "more or less ingenious attempts at interpretation" (25:1665), all of which remain speculative. There is simply no unequivocal way of grounding the mental notion of understanding in the bodily sensation of standing. Thus *ständ,* in the final analysis not grounded in *stehen* or *Stand,* depends for its meaning on the mischievous morphemes surrounding it just as they depend on it (and on each other). The structure is as marvelous as the arch under which Heinrich von Kleist passes on a stroll through the town of Würzburg. "Why, thought I, does the arch not collapse, since it has *no* support?" Kleist wonders in a letter to his bride-to-be (in fact, as it turns out his bride-*not*-to-be). "It stands, I responded, *because all stones want to collapse at the same time.*"[16] Novalis offers the same idea with a better sense of humor. "The whole," he writes, "rests approximately like those playing people who, without a chair, sit in a circle, one on the knees of the other."[17]

As critics have pointed out, "On Incomprehensibility" looks for the causes of the incomprehensibility inherent in communication in what Schlegel calls "the irony of irony,"[18] a form of irony that twists the meaning of messages—and hence their comprehensibility—in utter disregard for the designs of speakers and writers. (It occurs, for example, "when one cannot escape irony, as seems to be the case with this essay on incomprehensibility").[19] But once we note the combinatorial experiments that Schlegel conducts with *ver-*, we can see that a far more compressed account of incomprehensibility—of its inevitability as well as its desirability—can be found in the mysterious process through which the word *Unverständlichkeit* itself comes about. Somehow—and we do not quite know how—five linguistic units, each by itself without determinate meaning (though not therefore without all semantic pull), join to make a meaningful word. If we want to understand the word by analyzing its parts, our efforts will fail; it simply will not yield to comprehension on that level. But there is a further wrinkle, a folding back over itself: for *Unverständlichkeit* denotes precisely the puzzlement we experience when we attempt to fathom the process that gives rise to the word. It is a name for the unexpected ways in which linguistic parts collide and react. The irony of irony, the self-reflexivity that knows itself without being able to master itself ("as seems to be the case with this essay"), is already present, in highly condensed form, in the word *Unverständlichkeit* (and for that matter in *incomprehensibility*) itself. The word is its own illustration, description, and performance.

We can take another step to condense things even further. For does *ver-* itself, strictly speaking, not encode the very self-reflexivity in *Unverständlichkeit? Ver-* causes the swerve in meaning that it names. Like other prefixes, it leads words astray by virtue of its combinatorial quality, yet it is unlike the others in that the quality of its operation—its effective meaning—often consists, as Grimm informs us, precisely in this movement of leading astray. In short, it names and performs the incomprehensibility arising in the space between syntax and semantics.

I hope the reader will forgive me for narrowing the interpretation of Schlegel's rich and justly famous essay to one syllable. It is not my aim to provoke in him or her a sense of textual claustrophobia, but I could think of no better way of opening the view to the larger themes that interest me—Schlegel's innovations in linguistics, poetics, and aesthetics, and their interconnections—than by first tightening the aperture. In fact, to make my point convincingly, I will have to focus it even further in chapters to come, halting my analysis not at syllables but at the even more meaningless letters of which syllables and words and books are composed.

It will not come as a complete surprise if I claim that *ver-,* like the other linguistic and graphic elements that will concern me later, enacts the logic of chemistry in language. As I suggested in the Introduction, the application of the game of combinations to language opens a wealth of possibilities, including the possibility of treachery. *Ver-* names both of these, something that Max Leopold, the man who devoted a good deal of his professional life to that prefix, unwittingly points out in the passage I quoted earlier. The "nasty" connotations, he concludes, have become by far the predominant meaning in words bonding with *ver-,* but there is, we recall, also another prominent category: "The compositions of the type *verbinden* are also richly represented and vital." All we need to do is to establish a connection—a *Verbindung*—between the two: to argue that the very process of binding and bonding, of *verbinden,* opens the possibility for those nasty connotations to attach themselves to perfectly unnasty words. In short, linguistic elements, while making use of the power

of combinations to produce potentially infinite utterances, do so un-
reliably and unevenly. Schlegel's phrase about words understanding
each other better than do those who use them need not necessarily
conjure up a linguistic mysticism, but could be understood as pointing to precisely this unaccountable impurity. It prevents language
from being exhaustively described by strictly formal methods. (The
vocabulary, for instance, cannot simply be plugged into the grammar,
as students of a new language learn to their chagrin.) Just as eighteenth-century chemists are puzzled by what it is that makes the
combination of sulfur, hydrogen, and oxygen yield very different
substances, depending on circumstances, so Schlegel has no theory
about why it is that some combinations of phonemes, morphemes, or
words are permissible while others are not, let alone the question of
what makes particular combinations arouse our interest.

It is this unformalizable (or as yet unformalized) aspect of the material constitution of language that allows language (or as Lacan will
insist: the letter) to serve as a magnet for those achievements of our
consciousness for which we have no ready account. Thus puzzling
phenomena such as obsessional neurosis or fetishism become accessible to Freud through the purely material—and purely contingent—
way in which *Rate* (installment) can be plugged in for *Ratte* (rat), or
glance for *Glanz* (shine).[20] What is more: the very impurities in the
logic of linguistic substitution that call for a psychoanalytic interpretation seep into the language of psychoanalysis itself. Is it merely an
accident that many of the most crucial Freudian concepts use, and
are abused by, the prefix *ver-* ? *Verdrängung, Verleugnung, Verneinung,
Verdichtung, Verkehrung, Verschiebung* (repression, disavowal, negation, condensation, reversal, displacement) all describe a process of
substitution (an innocent dream for a trauma, *Rate* for *Ratte,* no for
yes) subject to a disfiguring shift that describes and performs the operations of the unconscious. To take the simplest and most extreme
case, the *ver-* in *Verneinung* marks the degree to which *no* may be
(mis-)understood to stand for *yes*.

This is how we can make sense out of Lacan's claim that "metaphor is the very mechanism by which the symptom, in the analytic

sense, is determined";[21] for all psychic *ver-* processes work according to the metaphoric logic of "one word [or syllable or letter] for another," a logic that is so imbued with material contingency that it permits even the substitution of *no* for *yes*. If the unconscious is structured like a language, that is because language works like eighteenth-century chemistry (and not, for example, like mathematics). Its material substrate refuses complete formalization. In this sense, chemistry is an allegory of the unconscious in language.

Hegel on Schlegel

An interpretive approach to a problem demonstrates its range, as well as its limits, by how well it addresses the questions that have gathered around that problem. In the case of Schlegel and chemistry, there can be no question of fielding all the questions in the history of Schlegel's reception. But one would wish the chemical conception to engage some of the main ways Schlegel has been read and, perhaps more important, misread.

Hegel's assessment of Schlegel is such a case, and it is all the more important to address because it is the most consequential example of both, of reading and of misreading, astutely focused, furthermore, on the very question of incomprehensibility. During his lectures on the philosophy of art, Hegel rebukes Schlegel for his ironic tone, for what Hegel calls a lack of "genuine earnestness."[22] If criticizing an adversary's tone, rather than the substance of his views, may have seemed like a trivial charge to the students assembled in Hegel's lecture hall, he quickly set them straight. Schlegel's devotion to irony is perilous, Hegel reasons, because when an ironic stance is taken to the extreme "whatever is, is only by virtue of the ego, and what exists by virtue of my ego, I can equally well annihilate again" (93/64). Since "anything and everything is only an insubstantial creature, to which the creator, knowing himself to be disengaged and free from everything, is not bound," he—Schlegel—"is just as able to destroy it as to create it," because—and the problem is finally given a name—"his attitude to it all is ironical" (95/66). The question of an attitude, then, is not incidental to a proper philosophical "position," but in fact crucial to it. With the right ironic attitude, a discussion of positions becomes superfluous, for any position that Schlegel might take one moment can shift in the next. It is for this reason that Hegel, rather than taking aim at any positively definable position (or even series of positions), directs his critique at what causes the shift itself, namely the ironic attitude. Put more generally: according to Hegel's logic, the *mode* of presentation, or—since we are talking about a writer—the *rhetoric* through which the world is made accessible, supersedes in certain cases the subject matter of the representation. The rhetorical means —the attitude, the tone—by which Schlegel writes of aesthetics does not merely influence his argument about aesthetics, but effectively takes its place; the rhetoric annihilates the argument. The form becomes the content.

The shrewd diagnosis that the shift in positions *is* the position serves Hegel as an occasion for unleashing a merciless attack on Schlegel. We need not follow him in this. Instead, we could attempt to take seriously his insight and analyze its mechanics and its implications. For if we wish to know how Schlegel transforms aesthetic thinking, we need to characterize the process of positing and annihilating that goes on in his writing; we need to follow the rhetorical turns that give rise to the incessant shifting that he himself labeled *Unverständlichkeit* and that so vexed Hegel. It is true that, even though Schlegel never composed a coherently articulated aesthetic theory, his writings do traffic in a conceptual language that challenges, modifies, and expands important aesthetic ideas; their argument does address a great number of issues arising from the aesthetic thinking of the late eighteenth century. But the reason his early work managed to irk contemporaries like Hegel, the reason it continues to irk many of us, lies not so much in *what* it says about the determination and judgment of the artwork as in *how* it says it. Hegel's vehement—and highly ironic—critique of Schlegelian irony may well be an irritated response to the fact that the formal ruses occurring in Schlegel's writings do not conform to the classical philosophical understanding of form and content, in which the form is a kind of jug holding thought and dispensing it as necessary. As I have suggested by way of the chemical allegory, in Schlegel's writings the formal elements coax the content into an incessant and rapid shape-shifting process, and vice versa, making it difficult to speak of "content" or "form" with any assurance of fixity.

Even if we preferred not to endorse the philosophical position that leads Hegel to his critique, we must admit that he identifies a reason for the vague feeling of dissatisfaction one often has when reading the early Schlegel. A strange impermanence of meaning seems to hang over his fragments. Meanings that the reader believes to have secured dissolve on further reading; others seem to be forever around the next textual corner, always apparently within grasp, but always just out of reach. It is hard to say what the fragments are *about.* This experience, not always pleasurable, is by no means confined to the fragments alone but can be encountered while reading much of Schlegel's early writings. The reader cannot quite shake the suspicion that what is being read may not be deeply ineffable but simply meaningless, that the texts refuse to submit to the hermeneutic categories of understanding, comprehension, coherence. They irritate in part because they mean to irritate.

Yet even when a certain rhetorical practice puts the validity of its stated content into jeopardy because an absence of meaning is at every moment a *possibility,* we are still not obliged, like Hegel, to equate such a possibility with the *reality* of meaninglessness. The very *fact* of that possibility, even though it is a possibility of meaninglessness, can itself yield a meaningful interpretation. Put differently: we need not collapse the result of an attitude with the attitude itself. Our doubt about the presence or absence of meaning in Schlegel's writings leads us into seeing, with Hegel, "the nullity of everything objective and absolutely valid" (96/66) only if we overlook the fact that doubt itself, what Schlegel frequently calls "hovering" (*Schweben*), carries its own form of positive consistency. The attitude that permits a process of untrammeled creation and destruction may nullify the validity of its *products,* but that does not mean that the *process* is therefore also null and void. On the contrary, we will see that in

Schlegel powerful claims about aesthetics are staked precisely in the very process that would seem to unhinge the conceptual solidity of aesthetic ideas. And since we have only textual material at our disposal, we must understand "attitude" or "doubt" not as psychological expressions of an empirical ego, but as effects entailed by particular rhetorical turns. Thus to learn anything more about a Schlegelian aesthetics than that it creates and annihilates at its own pleasure, we might look at how those turns imperil the validity of "everything objective."

Looking for Schlegel's aesthetics in those areas where a trapdoor can open up at any moment entails looking closely at formal mechanisms that have the potential to disturb the orderly progression of reasoning. Such a procedure admittedly runs the danger of undoing itself, for we have no guarantee that an investigation of trapdoors will itself be spared the experience of having the floor suddenly give way. Yet unless we want to follow Hegel in his curt dismissal of Schlegel, we can do little more than acknowledge the risk, then analyze how this process of the constitution and dissolution of content by form occurs.

We can see that, following Hegel's critique, we have encountered certain motifs—hermeneutic doubt, shift between positions, process versus product—that exhibit an affinity with many of the chemical motifs we discussed earlier. But before making the connection too quickly, we should continue the discussion in terms set up by (or at least recognizable to) Hegel. Of what, then, do the formal devices used by Schlegel to attempt a reformulation of aesthetics consist? Perhaps the most obvious lies in his choice of genres: he shuns the conventions of the philosophical treatise in favor of more volatile genres, such as the essay, the dialogue, and the fragment. Instead of a fully formed aesthetics, he offers us a group of texts—the *Lyceum* and *Athenäum* fragments (1797 and 1798), the "Conversation on Poetry" (1800), "On Incomprehensibility" (1800), among others—whose generic features tend to disorient a reader accustomed to the clipped presentation of systematic philosophy. They foster what their author calls a "sublime impudence,"[23] which gleefully mixes genres.

Among the many new genres with which Schlegel experiments in the last few years of the eighteenth century, the one that has given philosophers and critics the most trouble is what, in 1797, the twenty-five-year-old Schlegel brashly calls "an entirely new genre": his fragments.[24] Their novelty lies in their differences from the well-established aphorism (which I shall discuss in chapter 2), differences that open the form to a wide range of possibilities (including the already mentioned possibility of meaninglessness). Among the many strange features of this new form, Schlegel repeatedly mentions one that appears to be particularly contradictory and that crucially connects the fragment-writing project (which in the period that concerns us—1796 to about 1800—stands at the core of his interests) with the project of aesthetics. He claims to conceive of each fragment as an independent unit, "entirely separated from the surrounding world and complete in itself like a hedgehog,"[25] as he puts it in a fragment published in 1798 in the *Athenäum.* A year later, a fragmentary notebook entry puts the idea into philosophical language: "A fragment is a self-determined and self-determining thought."[26] And yet, in seeming contradiction to this mandate of self-sufficiency, Schlegel conceives of the ensemble of fragments as what he calls "a system of fragments."[27] "The encyclopedia," he contends, "can simply and absolutely only be presented in *fragments* alone."[28] How are we to think of the relationships among entities that are supposed to be absolutely unitary *and* absolutely multiple?

The interplay between part and whole that emerges from this brief sketch makes clear, even before we have said hardly a word about their content, that Schlegel's fragments address *in their form* the central problem of eighteenth-century aesthetics: how may individual and potentially unruly entities be brought into harmony with a coherent picture of totality? Even if Schlegel's fragments, individually or together, neglect to yield Hegel's "absolutely valid" truth, the truth of the genre of the fragment itself lies in the fact that it plays out—that it allegorizes—the negotiation between part and whole, both of which appear self-sufficient and not in need of the other, yet neither of which is thinkable without the other. The historical change signified by this concern—expressed both thematically and formally in the fragments—is that an issue that poetics and aesthetics previously formulated and adjudicated *for* poetry is taken up *by* poetry; an important distinction migrates from aesthetics into the realm of art itself. Self-reflexivity—being aware of its own operations—becomes with Schlegel a characteristic of the verbal artwork.

The question of what alchemy allows fragments to give rise to a coherent totality (or, in philosophical terms, to a system) has played a prominent role in the history of Schlegel criticism. Poets and philosophers of his time, as well as later critics of Schlegel's work (at least those who have preferred not to use the Hegelian method of summary dismissal) have had frequent recourse to a model that *advances* from part to whole, i.e., a model that is in essence teleological. This model can take at least three distinct forms: the first assumes a genetic and hence *organic* connection between part and whole such that the fragment would be thought of, for instance, as the germ out of which the articulated totality grows. The second relies on a *dialectical* motion between them; in this view the fragment inexorably entails and leads to the system from which it is thought to have been severed. And the third adopts the view of an *infinite progression* that, while never reaching its goal, nevertheless assumes the existence and, hence, the motivating force of that goal. Such teleological models hold not only for interpretations of Schlegelian fragments but guide more generally the conceptions of the artwork in eighteenth-century aesthetics. As we shall see in chapter 2, aesthetics moves from unconnected empirical phenomena to a total system of laws by undergirding its idea of the work of art with one or more of the models I have mentioned here. The consequence of employing such a teleological model, I argue, is that it tends to result, implicitly or explicitly, in a redemptive understanding of the artwork. The artwork not only leads somewhere, but it leads somewhere *good.*

While Schlegel's early writings (let alone those after 1804/5) exhibit all three models of the relationship of fragment and system, they also partake, as I have suggested, of a very different one that severely constrains the efficacy of the other three. If in what follows I focus on that counter-model to eighteenth-century aesthetics that calls our attention to the operational and material workings of texts, and if this model results in a nonredemptive notion of the artwork, it is not to deny the presence of traditionally affirmative features in Schlegel's writing, but merely to emphasize countervailing elements that have received less attention than they deserve. The chemical model permits us to conceptualize in positive form the very rhetorical process of unchecked creation and annihilation that Hegel criticizes as vacuous. This process behaves, in Schlegel's writings, much the way Hegel imagines the ironic attitude to function: once it is introduced, it begins to spread and infect everything else.[29] Thus instead of "creation and annihilation" we could read "synthesis and analysis," or better yet the process of "eternally dividing and mixing forces" (as Schlegel calls it in the already quoted *Athenäum* fragment 412), and we will have gained a measure of the distance separating Hegel from Schlegel: while "creation and annihilation" relies on an agent whose intentional integrity is so unimpeachable that it can only be compared with God (which is why Hegel identifies the attitude of the ironist with the power of a "divine genius" [95/66]), "synthesis and analysis"—understood chemically—allow only an ambiguous relationship between the maker and the process of making and unmaking. The relation of the process back to itself is marked by Schlegel's use of the reflexive: "*sich* ewig scheidender und mischender Kräfte," "eternally *self*-dividing and *self*-mixing forces." In folding back onto themselves, these forces redirect our attention away from the metaphysical source of the process and the equally metaphysical ends to which this process is presumed to be devoted, and toward the material manifestations of the process itself. Reading the chemistry in Schlegel allows us to switch the guiding distinction in our analysis: instead of the spent distinction of whole and part, which has guided the discussions of aesthetics since the late eighteenth century, the distinction of element and combinatorial operation allows for a more complex picture of the network in which the (verbal) artwork is produced and judged.

A certain suspicion may by now have formed in the reader's mind about what would appear to be an inconsistency in this project. Does my suggested reading not reproduce the flaws for which I fault other readers, namely the flaw of not being attentive to the fissures and contradictions in Schlegel's writings, the flaw of totalization? Am I not merely subsuming all the unruliness of the fragments and essays under yet another rubric, smoothing them out in a way for which I critique other readers (particularly in chapter 2)? I think not, and for a reason that goes to the heart of Schlegel's project. His fragments certainly display a lot of contradictory, bizarre, incomprehensible aspects, yet they do not exhaust themselves in sheer opposition to the idea of totality. (Such a position would be self-defeating, since it would require the solidity of the notion of totality as much as a position advocating it.) As we shall see, the oddity in Schlegel's work lies in aspiring to an account with claims to totality, while at the same time eschewing notions of coherence and unity. The early work that interests me here is not a mere record of miscellaneous thoughts suspicious of totality; it is sustained by and aspires to its own version of totality.

Proposing chemistry as an allegorical model of such a conception of totality seems to me to address the demands of Schlegel's project. Chemistry provides a conceptual frame for a notion of totality *without*, however, erasing (or being able to erase) the moments of contingency that interrupts a unifying conceptualization of totality. It is a model that accounts for the moments for which the theory itself provides no account, a model, in other words, that has built into it the areas of local incoherence—of incomprehensibility—that Schlegel's project contains.

2 The Fragment, Symptom of Aesthetics

In order to make the argument that the idiom of chemistry permits Schlegel to conceive of poetics in new ways, we need to look at how and where chemistry appears in his writings. It is thus significant that when in the well-known *Athenäum* fragment 116, often regarded as the key text of Jena romanticism, Schlegel writes of romantic poetry that "it wants to and also should now *mix,* now *fuse* poetry with prose, ingeniousness with criticism, art poetry with nature poetry," that romantic poetry should "*saturate* the forms of art with every kind of good, solid matter for instruction" (my emphasis),[1] many of his operative terms have specific chemical meanings. Note the choice of verbs when, more than once, he claims that "reason and unreason *saturate* and *permeate* each other" (my emphasis).[2] Indeed, as we shall see in the next chapters, the images and concepts of chemistry are borrowed and alluded to so frequently as not only to leave no doubt as to the importance of this theme in his writings, but also to put into question the notion of borrowing, of allusion, itself. Chemistry does not merely supply the metaphors for what Schlegel, referring to the innovations of romantic poetry, will later call "a *revolution* in the field of aesthetics,"[3] but in some ways it takes the place of poetry itself. Thus in his private lectures on *Geschichte der europäischen Liter-*

atur (History of European Literature), held in 1803–4 in Paris for an audience of four,[4] Schlegel maintains that "the Moderns have arrived at a higher view of nature through the investigations of chemistry, while the Ancients did so directly, namely through poetry and religion."[5] If for the Moderns chemistry supplies in mediated form the function that poetry and religion retained in immediate form for the Ancients, then the thesis that poetic production in Schlegel's work strives to *become* chemical by performing the logic of chemistry sounds less far-fetched already.

Yet merely adding up the chemical traces in Schlegel's work will not serve our purpose, even if the sheer quantity of evidence flips—through oversaturation, as it were—into a change in quality. By that avenue, we will arrive at little more than a demonstration of influence or of elective affinity between Schlegel's writings and the discourse of chemistry toward the end of the eighteenth century. We will merely have shown that Schlegel's thinking—more precisely: his prose—had *somehow* reacted with the chemical language swirling about him. That would hardly be a noteworthy insight. Since at the turn of the nineteenth century chemistry, and in particular chemical language, is roiled by radical changes (as we shall observe in chapter 3), it should come as no surprise if agile minds enlisted the new vocabulary for their own purposes.

In fact, chemical terms and metaphors do appear in the writings of many of the most important European writers of the time, but they are employed with differing intentions and serve very different textual ends. Thus years before Schlegel conceives of philosophy as "a sort of transcendental chemistry,"[6] the aphorist Georg Christoph Lichtenberg observes: "No matter how one looks at it, philosophy is always chemistry [*Scheidekunst*]."[7] This leads him, in another passage, explicitly to reflect on the kinds of links between writing and chemistry that we will also discover in Schlegel's work:

> How many ideas are scattered in my head which, if some came together to make a pair, could effect the greatest discoveries! But they lie as far apart as the sulfur from Goslar, the saltpeter from East India, and the dust of the charcoal kiln that together would

make gunpowder. . . . When while thinking we rely on the natural ways in which forms of the understanding and of reason join together, then the concepts often stick to each other too much, failing to unite with those to which they properly belong. If only there were something (like the solution in chemistry) where the individual parts could swim about in suspension and could thus follow the tug of every attraction. But since that is not possible, one must bring things together intentionally. One must experiment with ideas.[8]

At around the same time, Immanuel Kant, the same Immanuel Kant who will claim that chemistry can "never [become] a proper science,"[9] finds it advantageous to put precisely the innovations in his philosophical project in analogy with chemistry; in the *Prolegomena,* he claims that "critique stands in the same relation to the usual scholastic metaphysics as *chemistry* does to *alchemy.*"[10]

Chemistry performs distinct, at times contradictory, functions in the instances I have quoted (and more sources would simply increase the range of chemistry's metaphorical field). Since I do not mean to document Schlegel's relationship to science nor to reconstruct a buried natural philosophy in his work, but rather to gauge how chemical conceptions catalyze reactions in his writings that are of consequence for poetics and aesthetics, it would be useful to have a more precise idea of what inertia the reagent is deployed to overcome. What is the specific conceptual problem that chemistry is supposed to help solve? What are the textual and theoretical difficulties that invite a chemical intervention even as Schlegel, on the manifest level of texts, often embraces other solutions? To answer this question, we need to bracket chemistry (for the duration of this chapter) and articulate the poetological and philosophical project of the young Schlegel using the traditional concepts of philosophical and literary analysis, precisely to see where their shortcomings might lie. My claim will be that the project of writing fragments, and of conceiving of those fragments as a totality, bears directly on central issues arising from aesthetics and finds its most creative instantiation in the notion—and the practice—of chemical writing. Only when we observe the impasse into which Schlegel writes himself will we have gained a significant understanding of the new formulation (by no means the same thing as a new solution) that chemistry offers. We shall also see that this impasse has a clear philosophical pedigree: eighteenth-century aesthetic theories, above all Kant's, attempt to find an orderly place, within the framework of cognition, for a type of judgment that by definition evades determination by concepts. While respecting the freedom of aesthetic judgment from the rule of the understanding (which is to say: while acknowledging the ultimate unknowability of artworks), Kant uses thick strands of analogy to tether aesthetic judgment to a system of cognition, thus making it yield to rational communication. If what makes aesthetic objects *useful* to theoretical and moral considerations lies in the harmonious fit of part and whole, then a conception of art that reconfigures the work's relationship with totality (which as a consequence may have to undergo its own set of transformations) may not easily be harnessed to perform philosophical or political duties, even if those duties serve the noble purpose of free and universal communication. In short, the particular mode in which parts and whole are thought to interact has serious repercussions for the links the artistic sphere maintains with other social spheres.

The form taken by the relationship between fragment and totality —between part and whole—is not only important for the way Schlegel's work transforms aesthetic theories preceding his writings; it is also crucial for theories of art, indeed for theories of cultural production, coming after him. For even more powerfully than does the logical-cognitive model of aesthetics (which we can identify with Kant), the historical-cultural model that follows it (which, as a shorthand, we can call Hegelian) relies on an idea of the relationship of artwork and totality—now conceived as a historical progression—that permits the artwork to be both an expression and an allegory of its moment within that totality. Historicism (old and New), Marxism, economism, indeed any theory that regards cultural products as embedded in a social context assumes a theory of how cultural particulars relate to the historical totality. Otherwise, extending a claim from cultural particulars to the historical totality would be simply arbitrary. What is at issue in Schlegel's work is a profound, and profoundly consequential, rearticulation of this relationship between particulars and totality, one that shakes the artwork's seamless fit in a cultural and historical narrative.

Before attending to this negotiation in Schlegel's writings, two brief points need to be considered: one regards the history of Schlegel's reception(s), the other a methodological reflection on the role of philosophy in reading his work.

Reading Romanticism: 'Malaise Allemand' or Enlightenment of Enlightenment

The historical context in which my argument takes its place needs to be considered, for two reasons. The first derives from the fact that important strands of literary and intellectual history have rendered their verdicts on Schlegel with a shrillness that alerts us to the high stakes surrounding readings of his work.[11] When one and the same subject of an inquiry has been regarded by some as having stirred up an ideological brew from which Nazism drew nourishment and by others as an early practitioner of 1960s antiauthoritarianism, new readings of his writings cannot feign naiveté and present their findings in a historical vacuum. The second, related reason for including a discussion of the fluctuations in Schlegel's reception is that much of the shrillness I mentioned depends on how a question of intellectual history is answered: should Schlegel's writing be labeled as belonging to the "Enlightenment" or to "irrational reactions to the Enlightenment,"[12] (putting aside for the moment any qualms about the unsatisfactory nature of this dichotomy; what is crucial here is that the dichotomy has been operative for two centuries). The answer to this question is of interest because deciding whether Schlegel's work upholds standards of rationality or abandons itself to mystical irrationalism has serious consequences for a reading that attempts to establish an intimate connection between his writings and the scientific discourse of his day.

The most persistent and politically consequential charge against Schlegel has been that of irrationalism. It depends for its efficacy on a double displacement: first, his work is metonymically folded into a corporate entity called "early romanticism" or plain "romanticism," with which his fortunes are then permitted to wax and wane. Second, aesthetic questions—the specifically artistic ways in which Schlegel refashions problems of eighteenth-century aesthetics—are either hardly registered or else subordinated to philosophical or political questions. Hegel's judgment holding Schlegel to be unfit for "speculative thought"[13] is an early instance of the way in which nineteenth-century critics, literary historians, and philosophers—with the crucial exception of Kierkegaard and Nietzsche—denigrate the so-called Romantic School. As Karl Heinz Bohrer has shown in a meticulous account of the critique of romanticism, a long line of nineteenth-century writers—among them important figures such as Heinrich Heine, the literary historian Georg Gottfried Gervinus, and Rudolf Haym, author of the influential study *Die romantische Schule* (The Romantic School, 1870)—dismiss with varying degrees of intensity the most innovative elements in Schlegel's poetological writings in favor of a broad critique of his mysticism and piousness, thus projecting his conversion to Catholicism in 1808 back onto his work of a decade earlier.[14] As Bohrer demonstrates, such denigration continues in philosophical and critical traditions right through the twentieth century.

The point at which the charge of irrationalism carries maximum political baggage (and where a differentiation between Schlegel and "romanticism," let alone between the early and late Schlegel, vanishes) occurs right after 1945, when writers as ideologically at odds as Thomas Mann and Georg Lukács advance the thesis of romantic obscurantism as the intellectual parent of Nazism, a thesis that shows little sign of losing acceptance.[15] Jürgen Habermas, by characterizing important elements of romanticism as the messianic, philosophically unfounded celebration of Dionysian mythology,[16] has lent renewed intellectual legitimacy to the view of romanticism as an "annulment of Enlightenment" (as one widely used handbook of literary history calls it).[17] More recently, the eminent historian of Germany Gordon

Craig has identified "that peculiarly German sense of inwardness, or remoteness from reality" (which, in his view, typifies romanticism) as "the *malaise allemand,*" holding it responsible for engendering "forces of terror and violence and death."[18] By these he means not only Hitler[19] but also violent extremism in postwar Germany, notably the terrorism of the Red Army Faction (210). In all these cases, the motivation to speak, as Craig does, of a "familiar Romantic antagonism . . . to rationalism and progress" (206) may lie in part in the desire to shield rationalism and progress from any suspicion of complicity with the barbarities this century has wrought—to avoid, in other words, confronting the possibility that rationality and barbarism may be mutually entangled in what Max Horkheimer and T. W. Adorno have called the "dialectic of enlightenment."

Given such an assessment, it is all but inevitable that the relationship maintained by the main exponents of romanticism with the natural sciences is usually taken to be, at best, vexed. In an important article, Hans Eichner puts the matter bluntly: "Romanticism is, perhaps predominantly, a desperate rearguard action against the spirit and the implications of modern science—a rearguard action that . . . liberated the arts from the constraints of a pseudoscientific aesthetics but that was bound to fail in the proper domain of science."[20] This claim may or may not be right (it depends on one's understanding of "science"); what matters here is that it is quite irrelevant to our question. For we are not concerned with the question of whether Schlegel succeeds or fails "in the proper domain of science," but rather whether science succeeds or fails in the proper domain of poetry. Put less polemically: we want to know whether there are discursive practices—modes of reading and writing—that, at a particular historical moment, made possible the formulation of new configurations of well-known problems in science and poetics.

Typically, romanticism is thought to extend the poetic imagination to the entire world (in Coleridge's words, "we find poetry, as it were, substantiated and realized in nature").[21] Schelling, the main exponent of *Naturphilosophie,* a project meant to counter the perceived pernicious effect of Newtonian (i.e., mechanistic) science, imagines

43

the entire world as one giant organism, which as such is endowed with a soul, a *Weltseele*.[22] This view not only sponsors actual scientific research projects that have come to be known as "romantic physics," "romantic physiology," and "romantic biology,"[23] but also reflects (without being identical to) the romantic preoccupation with "poeticizing the world." But we may need to turn this classical understanding of the issue by 180 degrees: I will argue that, at least in a portion of Schlegel's writings, it is "nature," specifically the odd nature of chemical combinations, that realizes itself in poetry. Such a logic is not at all in contradiction with Eichner's judgment that romanticism is engaged in a "rearguard action against the *spirit* . . . of modern science," as long as it follows—if only despite itself—the *letter* of science. How literally the letter is followed in Schlegel's texts, we shall see in chapter 5.

The Philosophical Path

Defining itself in opposition to the charge of romantic irrationalism and conservatism, one prominent strand of the reception of romanticism since the 1960s attempts to enlist Schlegel in the very project of the dialectic of enlightenment that the other, older strand tends to shun. To do this, it regards romanticism, especially Jena romanticism, not as a foe but rather as an ally of the Enlightenment. Thus in his seminal study *Romantik und Aufklärung* (Romanticism and Enlightenment, 1966), Helmut Schanze pairs the two terms, emphasizing a continuum where other critics had seen an agon. Documenting the early romantic reliance on such Enlightenment mainstays as the aphorism, the idea of the system, medical models, and mathematics, Schanze discards the notion of romanticism as the dark side of reason and speaks instead of a "mimesis of Enlightenment."[24] A large number of studies follow that regard early romanticism's commitment to reason as a source of its socially productive, liberating energies. Schlegel and the Jena group are seen as "enlightening the Enlightenment about itself and saving it thus,"[25] in the nearly eschatological terms of the preface to a book whose title—*Romantische*

Utopie–Utopische Romantik—could well serve as the heading for a whole generation of romantic reception.

The most precise and at once suggestive description of Schlegelian writing around 1800 occurs, I think, in Maurice Blanchot's wonderful phrase "an excess of thought," applied to Jena romanticism as a whole.[26] Far from surrendering Schlegel to a mystical or emotive poetic tradition, Blanchot calls our attention to his uncompromising intellectualism. At the same time, his phrase alerts us to an imbalance, to an element of thought that exceeds thought itself, to "what is in thought that is more than thought" (as Slavoj Žižek might put it). We can see how thought may be compromised by affect or emotion, but how can it exceed itself *by means of itself?* In what might this excess of thought consist? We cannot address these questions at this point, but in later chapters I will suggest that one way of understanding this excess may be through a certain rational, albeit impure, automatism that insinuates itself into the operations of writing, an automatism modeled in Schlegel's writings by the chemical ideas of attraction and combination.

While in the hands of its severest critics romanticism is ultimately reduced to the status of an amorphous element of German mentality, the celebrations of utopian romanticism conceive of its achievements primarily in the language of philosophy. What is largely missing from both appropriations is an adequate reading of the artistic innovations of the early romantics. Even such shrewd and sympathetic readers as Philippe Lacoue-Labarthe and Jean-Luc Nancy, who acclaim the *Frühromantik* "without any exaggeration [as] the first 'avant-garde' group in history,"[27] maintain that "although it is not entirely or simply philosophical, romanticism is rigorously comprehensible (or even accessible) only on a philosophical basis [. . .] If romanticism is approachable, in other words, it is approachable only by means of the 'philosophical path'" (42/29). *Only* on a philosophical basis, *only* by means of a "philosophical path." As their quotation marks around "philosophical path" suggest, philosophy in Lacoue-Labarthe and Nancy's argument is by no means a homogenous intellectual practice that may be assured of its own orientation; the burden of their book,

The Literary Absolute, as of much of their other work, lies in throwing philosophy into a critical confrontation with literature that is not always productive or recuperable. Yet the writers who undertake this risky confrontation stand on the ground of philosophy—even as their work is designed to be, literally speaking, ground-breaking—and use the currency of philosophy—even when they insist on how worn-out it is. Lacoue-Labarthe and Nancy are by no means alone in this; some of the best recent work on early romanticism finds itself approaching the texts with philosophical questions.[28]

It may well be that for the purposes of asking certain questions—including questions that this chapter will attempt to raise—we have no choice but to stand on the broken ground of philosophy and to use its worn-out coin. Indeed, it may even be that literary criticism, if it wishes to avoid a rhetoric of appreciation, has little choice but to reach for philosophical tools. The predicament of criticism lies in the fact that even when it means to ask questions different from those posed by philosophy—questions of the aesthetic merit, historical context, formal structure, political relevance, or moral charge of works of literature—it remains bound to philosophical questions and premises; engaging in criticism of whatever variety with any degree of rigor entails an avowed or silent recourse to such philosophical queries as "what is . . . ?", "why . . . ?", or "to what end . . . ?" The entanglement with philosophy grows steadily knottier when the texts themselves directly engage philosophy. Thus it would seem that an alternative to the "philosophical path" is hardly imaginable.

My claim is that Schlegel offers us not an alternative to the philosophical path that would believe itself free of the paradox of asking about the relationship of philosophy and literature without already being on the side of philosophy (that would be a quixotic position), but rather a new mapping of that philosophical path. An aesthetically attentive reading of his early writings can find itself rewarded with insight into just how treacherous and impassable that path can be. Such insight hinges on a recognition of the formal innovation that his engagement with philosophical issues employs, i.e., the lexical, grammatical, and graphic presentation of his thinking. In this reading, the form of Schlegel's writings stands in an infelicitous relationship to the ends that the writings are said, by himself and others, to serve. Their form—the particular way in which verbal presentation occurs—is not (as classical philosophy would have it) a mere hull for disembodied thought material, but rather itself material and hence a source of meaning, however perplexing that meaning may turn out to be. Thus romantic writing would be more than a continuation of philosophy by other means, and this surplus can be located and named with some precision. It can be found in the materiality of the form, which takes such insistent shape that it exceeds the very category of meaning itself. If taken seriously, it refuses the attempt to bring the writing (now understood as the interplay of content *and* form) under the sway of philosophy, leaving a strange, fascinating, misshapen remainder. The very "philosophical path" that allows us to recognize the remainder is also severely hampered by it.

This is one of the senses in which Schlegel's work can be taken both to be, and to be about, aesthetics: if in aesthetics philosophy negotiates the relationship of concepts and those sensory phenomena (such as works of art) exceeding the reach of concepts, then some of Schlegel's writings offer an allegory of aesthetics by showing that the first point of negotiation occurs not between concepts and something lying outside of them, but between concepts and their own verbal presentation, in effect: between concepts and themselves. *Something* in the workings of Schlegel's model of poetic language—indeed, as we shall see, of all language—exceeds or evades maneuvers aimed at curbing or redeeming it—at comprehending it—by means of the philosophical path. Our task is to specify this something to the extent possible.

Will to Fragment, Will to System

Schlegel produced fragments at a furious pace and in astonishing numbers, especially in the decade between 1797 and 1806, publishing a few hundred in the journals *Lyceum* and *Athenäum* and scribbling thousands more in some 150 notebooks. (Even though some have been lost, the surviving notebooks manage to fill four thick volumes in the critical edition of his works [KA 16–19]).[29] We need to be cautious, though, about simply merging the fragments published under his supervision, in which their fragmentary nature (as both the title of the fragment collections and the structure of individual fragments confirm) is clearly intentional, with the jumble of witticisms, notes, and sketches published long after his death. The notebook jottings seem to have been meant for publication as part of a coherent whole (possibly even as an autobiographical bildungsroman modeled on *Wilhelm Meister*),[30] and are therefore, apparently, unintentional fragments. Furthermore, the heterogeneity of the fragments is not confined to the categories of intentional and unintentional fragments: even within each group, the fragments take on such protean shapes that one "genre" can hardly be expected to encompass them all. Yet, legitimate as such caveats are, they should not lead us to overemphasize the differences: there is a rich genetic link between the posthumously published fragments and those published in Schlegel's lifetime. Thus Schlegel draws many of the *Lyceum* and *Athenäum* fragments from his notebooks, sometimes with minor, sometimes with considerable revision. This turns out to be a two-way street: parts of many published fragments are echoed over and over in notebook entries years after their first publication. But there are, I will argue a bit later, even stronger reasons—reasons embedded in the very notion of the fragment—that will allow us to conceive of the posthumous work as fragmentary in the innovative, Schlegelian sense of the term.

Before we scrutinize the features that characterize the fragments' innovations, it would be useful to recall the philosophical context of their appearance. By this I do not mean a sort of philosophical ecosystem to which they "belong" or that will "explain" their appearance; I mean rather the way that late-eighteenth-century aesthetics—i.e., the conceptualization of art by philosophy—can be read as the situation within and against which Schlegel's fragmentary writing occurs. In Lacoue-Labarthe and Nancy's words, "it is because an entirely new and unforeseeable relation between aesthetics and philosophy will be articulated in Kant that a 'passage' to romanticism will become possible."[31] This passage to romanticism does not point to a historical-genetic account (Kant engendering romanticism) but rather to a theoretical account of the necessary conditions for reading romanticism in a philosophically consequential way. The *force* motivating the project of producing thousands of fragments, including many fragments about the idea of the fragment, becomes evident only when we consider the ambition behind eighteenth-century aesthetics, in particular as it manifests itself in Kant's *Critique of Judgment.*

Eighteenth-Century Aesthetics

Given that aesthetics, understood as a philosophical discipline, is usually taken to have been invented by eighteenth-century philosophy, it is remarkable what eighteenth-century aesthetics *cannot* be said to have achieved: the eighteenth century did not produce a philosophy of art (that accomplishment would be left to the nineteenth century); it did not render the separation of aesthetics and ethics, in Jean-François Lyotard's word, "irrevocable"[32] (a claim that has in any case turned out to be premature, since Elaine Scarry has recently set out to revoke precisely that separation);[33] nor can it lay claim to having provided us with the first significant philosophical meditation on beauty in the Western tradition. Its distinction is more profound and, therefore, less visible: not only does eighteenth-century aesthetics, the motley discourse stretching from Shaftesbury's 1709 *Sensus Communis* to the *Critique of Judgment* in 1790, bestow on the senses the dignity of philosophical attention (in Kant's case, by way of multiple layers), but it puts this bestowal in relation to a subject conceived as an agent of cognition and action. "Merely thinking about beauty does not produce an aesthetics," Alfred Baeumler has astutely argued. "Only when an absolutely independent aesthetic subject is presupposed can the idea of aesthetics as a distinct science arise."[34]

It seems odd to claim, as Baeumler does (ibid.), that the marker of this aesthetic subject is none other than the seemingly inconsequential concept of taste. But in its structure taste replicates precisely the philosophical gymnastics that the aesthetic subject is required to perform, namely reconciling and unifying the manifold particularity of experience with a standard assumed to be universal. Taste is intensely subjective, particular, and fused with bodily sensation, yet at the same time it makes claims to intersubjective validity, which is to say that it is socially motivated and to some extent abstract. The site at which the subjective and intersubjective claims of taste are yoked together with greatest force is called beauty. Thus Edmund Burke will claim: "I never remember that anything beautiful, whether a man, a beast, a bird, or a plant, was ever shown, though it were to a hundred people, that they did not all immediately agree that it was beautiful."[35] The condition under which such an observation (which is in fact a thinly disguised aesthetic norm) can be valid is that the subject manages to gather the manifold sensory data into laws and rules by means of taste, and of taste alone, i.e., *without* having recourse to external norms. For true taste does not of course consist in the mechanical application of law to sensory data, but in the far more complicated process of discovering the law, as it were, in one's own natural inclinations. It is precisely this recursive logic of aesthetic judgment that we find articulated in Rousseau's political philosophy. In his unforgettable phrase, the law is "not graven on tablets of marble or brass, but on the hearts of the citizens."[36] The "absolutely independent" subject is absolutely independent to the exact degree that it replaces its subjection to the coercive force of external laws (moral, logical, class based) with an internally produced coercion. The advantage of this form of legislation (not to mention the choice of the flesh as a medium of inscription) is, Rousseau adds, that it "insensibly replaces authority by the force of habit" (ibid.). Put differently: it internalizes and aesthetizes force.[37]

The most sophisticated and consequential version of a concept of taste as that which performs the strange task of judging *as if* following an external law is Kant's concept of aesthetic judgment. As Kant elucidates in the introduction to the third *Critique*, judgment plays an exceedingly important role in his philosophical project. At the outset, he reminds the reader of the non-negotiable abyss between the realms of necessity (under the purview of understanding [*Ver-*

stand]) and of freedom (under the purview of reason [*Vernunft*]) that the logic of the first *Critique* had produced: "An immense gulf is fixed between the domain of the concept of nature, the sensible, and the domain of the concept of freedom, the supersensible, so that no transition from the sensible to the supersensible . . . is possible, just as if they were two different worlds, the first of which cannot have any influence on the second" (KU 175–76). The relationship between the two worlds is, however, not symmetrical: "And yet [Kant continues] the second *should* have an influence on the first, i.e., the concept of freedom should actualize in the world of sense the purpose enjoined by its laws. Hence it must be possible to think of nature as being such that the lawfulness in its form will harmonize with at least the possibility of the purposes that we are to achieve in nature according to laws of freedom" (KU 176). I understand the problem that Kant describes to be this: in order for our free will to be able to act on the world ("nature"), this world must be structured to accord with our mental powers. If our cognitive powers are mismatched with the structure of the world, then we cannot hope to act on it meaningfully. The difficulty lies in the fact that we cannot be sure that nature is indeed thus structured. The template for comprehending nature that the understanding provides gives rise to laws that "concern only the possibility of a nature as such" (KU 179); they permit us to comprehend the world in general ways and produce a large number of particular empirical laws, yet fail to provide a way of integrating this manifold into a unity (KU 180, 183). But in order to make acts of free will in the world possible, the particular empirical laws "must . . . be viewed in terms of such a unity as if they too had been given by an understanding (even though not ours) for the benefit of our cognitive powers" (KU 180). This assumed, but never proven, fittedness of the structure of the world with our cognition is called purposiveness (*Zweckmäßigkeit*) by Kant. Something is purposive when its form permits us to conclude, though we may be unable to prove it, that a mind similar to our own has made it.

The task of fashioning a unity-in-diversity—i.e., of recognizing purposiveness, of detecting another understanding (even though not ours) at work—falls to the faculty of reflective judgment. While determinate judgment merely subsumes particulars under given laws, reflective judgment is operative when "only the particular is given and judgment has to find the universal for it" (KU 179), that is, when the law is produced by the activity of judgment itself. But in a circularity that is typical of reflective judgment, the purposiveness of the world that judgment is to *establish* must already be *assumed:* "Judgment must assume, as an a priori principle for its own use, that what to human insight is contingent in the particular (empirical) natural laws does nevertheless contain a law-governed unity, unfathomable but still conceivable by us" (KU 183–84). Judgment assumes what it establishes and establishes what it assumes: a self-founding, self-perpetuating process whose entire purpose lies in "making coherent experience out of a material that to us is so full of confusion" (KU 185).

To connect this process of the self-imposition of a law to aesthetics and to taste (as the agency of aesthetic judgment), Kant requires two further steps: the first is that the recognition of such purposiveness in nature fills us with delight: "We rejoice . . . when, just as if it were a lucky chance favoring our aim, we do find such systematic unity among merely empirical laws" (KU 184; see also 187). Put another way, the possibility of making a transition from free will (Kant's "second world") to the world of natural necessity (the "first world") registers itself in a bodily sensation. The second step consists in applying the logic of purposiveness to those objects that, in fact, have no purpose; or to be more precise: it lies in applying that logic to those representations that are made with complete disregard for purpose (for Kant's aesthetic theory concerns not objects but the internal state of subjects). Even though we have no interest in the ends (or purposes) to which the object is put, we recognize, because "a given presentation unintentionally brings the imagination . . . into harmony with the understanding . . . and this harmony arouses a feeling of pleasure" (KU 190), that it has the *form* of purposiveness. In short, we call it beautiful.

Even this simplified version of the Kantian concept of purposiveness makes evident how crucial aesthetic judgment is to making possible a coherent experience of nature and, as a consequence, of the actualization of the will in nature. It also makes evident that this zone "between understanding and reason" (KU 178) is only thinkable according to the logic we find in Münchausen's well-known tale: the hero gets out of a swamp by pulling himself up by his own collar. Here we have a law that has no firm ground to stand on and owes any stability it might enjoy to its own activity. This law given to the subject by itself is, furthermore, a result of a persistent activity of finding unity, coherence, synthesis in what is particular, confusing, manifold. When Kant applies the same agency of judgment developed to detect purposiveness in nature to the realm of art, it does not come as a surprise that he then conceives of art in analogy with nature (§ 45). In both, the condition of possibility of a successful aesthetic judgment—of pleasure—lies in the organic coherence of the manifold parts within a whole. Indeed, aesthetic judgment can be defined as the agency charged with crafting a coherent whole out of potentially incoherent parts. Only under this condition can the beautiful artwork hope to become "the symbol of morality" (KU 351).

Schlegel is clear about what sort of philosophical burden aesthetics has placed on the artwork. "The principle expressing the relationship of the whole to the parts and of the parts to the whole," he writes in lectures on transcendental philosophy held at the university of Jena in 1800–1801, "must be sought in art."[38] It is with this in mind that I suggest that the real site for artistic and theoretical innovation in Schlegel's writing is not to be found in those of his works conforming to obviously "literary" genres—lyric poems, a short novel, a play, none of them very distinguished—but rather among his experimental writings, above all the fragments. For we can read the genre of the fragment—always understood as part of what Schlegel calls totality (or system)—as a literal instantiation of the tension between parts and whole that we observed in Kant's aesthetics. The fragments not only deal with aesthetic issues (in the sense of containing information about the subject) but they perform, *in their form,* the play between manifold and unity. What makes them a significant intervention into aesthetics is that their position remains in play as much as possible, hovering *between* manifold and unity. It is evident that in such a case concepts such as taste, internal law, purposiveness, perhaps even aesthetic subject cannot remain unperturbed. To see how this play is enacted, we need to have a more detailed understanding of the fragments themselves, their generic features, and the conceptual innovations they introduce.

Fragment / Aphorism

How innovative the innovations in the form of Schlegel's fragments really are is not at all obvious, for many critics have tended to emphasize the continuities binding the fragments to the long-established aphorism. Far from working at cross-purposes with philosophy (as I claimed at the outset), the fragment is seen as a species of aphorism, which enjoys a distinguished career in philosophical writing. Do Schlegel's fragments not stand in the aphoristic—and very philosophical—tradition of Hippocrates, Erasmus, Bacon, Gracián, La Rochefoucauld, Pascal, Chamfort, and Lichtenberg?[39] In some sense they do. And Schlegel himself would seem to encourage such a historicizing move by calling his *Lyceum* fragments, with a nod to Chamfort's recently published collection of aphorisms, "a critical Chamfortade."[40] But an important critical tradition has relied so heavily on historical antecedents as to have weakened, perhaps unwittingly, Schlegel's stance against the established philosophical tradition. In a 1933 study, Franz Mautner, for all his erudite differentiations, ends up assigning Schlegel's work to the rubric of "aphorism," understood as the "sudden view of a totality of meaning" or the "discovery of the solution" to a question of which the mind was only half aware[41]—that is, to a genre that, while perhaps abrupt and uncompromising in form, engenders coherence and comprehension. Mautner's classification has allowed many critics following him to blur the boundary between the fragment and the aphorism by claiming the former to be really an instance of the latter. Thus one of the most thorough historical dictionaries of philosophy omits the entry "Fragment" altogether and subsumes Schlegel's fragments under the heading "Aphorism," which, in the history of philosophy, turns out to be rather old news.[42] In his landmark study of the genre of the aphorism in the late eighteenth and early nineteenth centuries, Gerhard Neumann proceeds from the potentially aphorism-breaking thesis that Schlegel's short writings present the *conflict* (rather than the mediated resolution) between the individual and the world.[43] Yet as I shall argue later, this insight is softened—and the fragment thus turned into the tried and true aphorism—when Neumann resolves the very conflict that the fragment, according to him, had laid bare. More recently, another wide-ranging study of the aphorism, noting that Schlegel's fragments are marked by a "productive reception" in the reader and an emphasis toward what is "integrating," blunts their edge and redeems them yet again for the genre of aphorism and, thus, for the cause of meaning, synthesis, and comprehension.[44]

Yet on closer inspection Schlegel's project turns out to maintain a complicated relationship with its presumed predecessors, a complication to which we are alerted by his choice of the term *fragment.* It will not have escaped the attention of Schlegel, the classical philologist, that the etymology of *aphorism* goes back to *aphorizein,* "to define," derived from *horizein,* "to bound" (whence our *horizon*), while *fragment* derives from *frangere,* "to break." And one of the first things the fragment can be said to break is the continuity with the tradition of the aphorism.[45] What at first sight seems to be a terminological quirk reveals itself to carry important generic and philosophical implications, for while the aphorism always contains the promise of autonomous comprehensibility by offering itself as a shrink-wrapped version of thinking, the fragment expressly calls attention to its own incompletion. If the aphorism attempts to bound the horizon of our understanding by offering a central point of focus, the very generic structure of the Schlegelian fragment aims at breaking such an understanding wide open.

The Displeasures of Reading Fragments

Even if Schlegel's fragments are *meant* to be aphorisms, we must admit that they avail themselves of this intention rather badly. Simply put, they do not offer enough of the right sort of pleasure to be good aphorisms. They rarely fill us with that rare moment of insight that sets in when (to borrow a pun from Mautner) the aphorism's often-used paradox jars our *doxa* with just the right balance of force and gentleness so that it feels like a moment of recognition, as though we had always known that our *doxa* had harbored that very paradox. With Schlegel, we rarely get aphorisms like these:

"The American who first discovered Columbus made a nasty discovery" (Lichtenberg).[46]

"My ambition is to say in ten sentences what everyone else says in a book—what everyone else does *not* say in a book" (Nietzsche).[47]

"There are two ways of disliking art. . . . One is to dislike it. The other is to like it rationally" (Wilde).[48]

Pleasures of the kind that these sentences set free is rare in Schlegel. Though there are a few marvelous aphorisms ("The historian is a prophet facing backwards"),[49] many of his attempts come across as labored ("Going to print is to thinking what the nursery is to the first kiss");[50] despite being structured like a witticism, as some of the fragments are, more often than not they turn out to be flat-footed or just puzzling ("A good preface must at once be the root and the square of its book");[51] "Wanting to judge everything is a great error or a small sin").[52] Moreover, many of the fragments are either too bulky (for instance in the *Athenäum*) or (in Schlegel's notebooks) so radically reduced to their essential logical relation that the use of German gives way to a graphical idiolect, consisting of Greek symbols and pseudo-mathematical notation that is too self-enclosed to be comprehensible to anyone but Schlegel scholars (if to them).[53] They are, literally speaking, unreadable. On a metaphorical level, this is also true of the published collections: the experience of reading them, and hence any pleasure that might motivate such reading, is constantly interrupted, dissipated, deferred, which is why the fragments often perplex, irk, provoke, and frustrate us, only rarely offering the pleasure that would give them the rounded isolation of meaning we seek in an aphorism. Unlike aphorisms (even aphorisms that appear embedded in prose, such as those by Wilde or, differently, by Bloch or Adorno), Schlegel's fragments depend far too strongly on an idiosyncratic network of meanings to be effectively quotable.

Historical Differences: Self-reflexive Discontinuity

But the fragments break their generic continuity with the aphorism in a still more far-reaching way: they articulate the mark of their historical distance from earlier works. "Many works of the Ancients have become fragments," Schlegel writes. "Many works of the Moderns are fragments the moment they are made."[54] Ancients and Moderns here are not (or not only) allegorical personifications of a philosophical issue (there totality, here fragmentation), but their relation is conceived by Schlegel in a genuinely historical fashion. Something has happened that has lodged brokenness (or, with less pathos, incompletion) into the very act of making. The condensed history of art that Schlegel offers here registers a caesura that sharply divides the old and new conceptions of the artwork. And this caesura is again not merely allegorical; Schlegel implicitly locates it with some precision in the second half of the eighteenth century: while Winckelmann, much-praised by Schlegel, still promotes an imitation of Greek art in 1755, Schlegel, forty years later, confines himself to its study (as the title of his major essay, "Über das Studium der griechischen Poesie" [On the Study of Greek Poetry], indicates). For Schlegel, the same circumstances that permit the Moderns to study, rather than to imitate, the Ancients, are also responsible for the entwinement of creation and fragmentation; indeed, he thinks of the two facets of modernity as being identical: "studying," he writes cryptically, "is [an] intentional fragment."[55] This shift from imitation to study, from whole work to fragment, is far more than a difference in emphasis, for implicated in the distinction between imitation and study are the completely different philosophical situations within which the two practices arise: Schlegel's position presupposes a historical perspective capable of registering that the conditions that allowed an imitation of the Ancients in 1755 have, in the intervening years, vanished.[56]

The Schlegelian fragment then fulfills a double historical task. First, through a process of historical self-reflection, it *diagnoses* incompletion as a crucial feature of the work of Moderns, of what we call modernity. Then, in doing so, it *exhibits* the marks of a break with an irrecuperable past. The fragment stands at one and the same time as a document of a radically new age (he is perhaps the first, Schlegel writes to Novalis, to do writing [*Schriftstellerei*] as art and as science [KA 24:205]) and, by virtue of that very self-conscious novelty, as a document of a time forever lost, a sign of mourning.

We can take this point one step further: the mark of the fragments' historical distance from their past consists of the notion of historical distance itself. The difference from the past is not merely a difference apparent to us, as we gaze down at romanticism from our allegedly Olympian perch, comparing its achievements with those of its past, but it is a difference registered in and by Schlegel's writings themselves. And it is a difference that makes a difference, for a reflected historicization—the awareness of an awareness of the impossibility of imitating the Ancients—distinguishes the modern conception of the artwork from the premodern one. This is not to say that artistic novelty is a Schlegelian or romantic idea: in Renaissance art, innovation, often conceived as an imitation of nature rather than of authority (for example by Leonardo), is clearly of crucial importance. What *is* a romantic innovation is that innovation is theorized there as such.

It may well be that, as Erwin Panofsky has argued, crucial concepts of romantic and post-romantic art—he names genius and artistic autonomy—were introduced in the Renaissance.[57] If so, they are present in the practice of art rather than in a theoretical apparatus accompanying it; the lag between practice and theory is plainly visible in the dearth of Renaissance texts we might put under the rubric of aesthetic theory, a situation to which Wladyslaw Tatarkiewicz has called attention in his encyclopedic history of aesthetics.[58] The romantic theorization of historical distance thus involves a redoubled innovation: conceiving of the artwork in terms of its difference from the past entails, along with the implicit act of mourning for a lost state, a recognition of the work's novelty, which is itself a novelty.

Thus Schlegel's insistence on the fragments as "an entirely new genre" is itself, as it were, an entirely new genre of self-description in which the reader is being prepared to look for and appreciate *dis*continuities with past experiences of reading. Indeed, we could say that the novelty in Schlegel's genre of fragmentation lies in inventing novelty as a literary norm; henceforth works of art will be judged by how far they differentiate themselves from their forerunners.[59] The historical perspective serves, then, not so much to revere the past as it does to validate and celebrate the innovations of the present.

The change in the meaning of the word *fragment* between its first and second appearances in the fragment about Ancients and Moderns—"Many works of the Ancients have become fragments. Many works of the Moderns are fragments the moment they are made"—nicely encapsulates the historical change from an ahistorical to a historical conception of the artwork. While the ancient fragment is a remainder, a document of the sudden intrusion of death or violence or accident—of history—into the work conceived as a notional totality, the modern fragment is *made* fragmentary; the first endures history's violence, while the second self-consciously produces a simulacrum of it. The fragmentation of the modern work is tragic and elegiac, certainly, but it is also the result of an engineered break with a notion of the timeless (i.e., unchanging) artwork. With the idea of a basic incompletion from the moment of creation, Schlegel replaces the self-enclosed and holistic artwork with an open one.[60] This necessitates a rethinking of the notion of "work": while for the older Schlegel his fragments, even those published in his lifetime, evidently do not qualify as "works" (for he included none of them in the edition of his "complete" works that he oversaw late in life),[61] the fragments have come to define Schlegel's "work" at least since Walter Benjamin's dissertation *Der Begriff der Kunstkritik in der deutschen Romantik* (The Concept of Criticism in German Romanticism).[62]

Mapping the two notions of fragment, and thus two notions of work, onto Roland Barthes's distinction between "writerly" and "readerly" texts[63] allows us to recognize another important innovation in the fragments' incompletion: in order for the fragment to be recognized and appreciated as "entirely new," it requires the active participation of a reader. It has no choice but to be "open," for without the work of the reader its very determination as a novelty would go unfulfilled. Thus Schlegel's picture of a "synthetic writer" who "constructs and creates for himself a reader as he should be"[64] is crucial to the project of innovating aesthetics; it also anticipates Barthes's writerly text in which the goal is "to make the reader no longer a consumer, but a producer of the text" (ibid.). For both Schlegel and Barthes, this reader is not, as it might seem at first, merely a narcissistic projection of the writer's fantasy of the sort that Italo Calvino offers in his clever novel *If on a Winter's Night a Traveler* (in which the—male—author observes how the—female—reader is thoroughly entranced by his book); Schlegel's reader is not imagined "as resting and dead, but rather alive and exerting a counterforce,"[65] a partner in a conversation who does not shy away from contentiousness. And it is with this active, critical, even resistant reader that the writer "enters into the sacred relationship of the deepest symphilosophy or sympoetry."[66] The "entirely new genre," then, entails an entirely new reader willing to enter into a new relationship in which the text emerges as the communal product of a conversational synthesis.[67]

Multiplicity

Earlier I remarked that most of Schlegel's fragments are curiously unquotable. What structural property might cause such an impression in the reader? One reason can be found in the fact that the fragments never appear alone, but always in what Schlegel calls "masses." If, as Blanchot states, "there cannot be a successful, a satisfactory fragment,"[68] it is because there cannot be *a* fragment; they always appear in the plural. This multiplicity is far from being a neutral medium in which fragments happen to be displayed; it challenges and, finally, renders impossible anything like the self-enclosed autonomy of each part. Every fragment looks (surrounded, as it is, by the white of the page) as though it should provide us with an aphoristic flash of cognition or recognition, yet in fact it always points elsewhere, at other fragments that presumably supply the missing meaning but which themselves, in turn, point elsewhere. In relying for their meaning on a (potentially endless) series of other fragments, the fragments anticipate in their structure an important characteristic of a conception of language that was developed by Ferdinand de Saussure more than a century later: no one element yields meaning by itself but rather each gains meaning through a differential relation to other elements that themselves remain ungrounded; just as uttering a meaningful word implies the existence of a *whole* language, finding meaning in one fragment requires assuming the *totality* of fragments.[69] This structure of deferral is one reason why Schlegel says of romantic poetry (which, if not identical with the fragments, at least shares the latter's salient characteristics) that "its proper essence" is "that it is eternally becoming, and can never be completed."[70]

Contradiction

The structural multiplicity of the fragments does not foster an ecosystem in which they live in harmony. On the contrary: contradictions—some subtle, some blatant—are rampant. Contradictions can be detected between far-flung fragments, but they occur even within the relatively homogeneous group of 127 fragments that appeared in 1797 in the journal *Lyceum.* A few pairings:

> A single analytic word, even in praise, can immediately extinguish the most astute witty idea whose flame, having lost its glow, was now supposed to give warmth.[71]

> If some mystical lovers of art, who regard every criticism as a dissection and every dissection as a destruction of pleasure, thought consis-

tently, then "Wow!" would be the best judgment about the worthiest of works.[72]

* * *

The concept of a scientific poem is strictly speaking as senseless as that of a poetic science.[73]

The entire history of modern poetry is a running commentary on the short text of philosophy: all art should become science, all science art; poetry and philosophy should be united.[74]

* * *

There is a lot of poetry, but nothing is rarer than a poem! This is due to the large number of poetic sketches, studies, fragments, tendencies, ruins, and materials.[75]

In poetry too everything whole may well be partial, and everything partial may after all be whole.[76]

The more fragments one reads, the more such conflicts, inconsistencies, and contradictions proliferate. And they occur not only *between* fragments but also very much *within* them. "It is equally fatal for the mind to have a system and to have none," a well-known *Athenäum* fragment begins. "It will thus just have to decide to combine the two."[77] (How can two mutually exclusive properties be combined? Does the mind, while combining the two alternatives, reside with the system or with its opposite? The same question also goes for the voice of the fragment itself: is it, while enjoining us to join the fatal options, systematic or nonsystematic? We shall return to this.) Schlegel scholars have expended an enormous amount of energy trying to make sense of such contradictions, which is to say inserting them into a system in which they can then release a productive energy propelling the project forward, toward a goal. Inevitably, I will end up doing some of this as well, but it is worth considering for a moment the prominent presence of conflict and contradiction as such, quite independently from the propositional content that is subject to this logical tug-of-war.

Far from being a regrettable side effect, the presence of contradiction is, within the logic of Schlegel's writings, a prized consequence of conceiving of the fragments in the plural. Unlike the aphorism,

which works by harnessing the power of paradox within each aphorism toward a higher truth, the Schlegelian fragment displays a contradiction—discernible only when the group of fragments is taken
together—that does not dissolve into a higher moment of harmony.
"Every sentence, every book, that does not contradict itself," Schlegel
notes at around the time that he was writing the *Athenäum* fragments, "is incomplete."[78] Such a requirement would seem to put the
project of writing fragments at odds with the enterprise of rationalist
philosophy. Schlegel not only posits the presence of contradiction in
every book and every sentence, but *requires* it as its condition of articulation, for without it the book or sentence "is incomplete." Thus contradiction is conceived of as a necessary feature of the entire system.

Polyphony

We may be able to approach this odd (philosophers might say:
monstrous) contraption—a system harboring necessary contradictions—by noting that in the fragments, contradictions serve not only
to effect a break with the classical aphorism and its reliance on the
pleasurably self-contained paradox, but also to signal a profound shift
in the conception of the voice permeating the fragments. In more
than one sense, that voice turns out not to be Schlegel's alone. In
contrast with the classical treatise, which relies heavily on the coherence of a single voice, a contradiction—*Wider-spruch,* literally
counter-speech—conjures up voices other than the single, uniform,
authoritative voice in which authors are usually thought to speak to
their readers. Many voices speak in the fragments, literally and figuratively. In the anonymously published *Athenäum* collection, there
are at least three authors besides Friedrich Schlegel: August Wilhelm
Schlegel, Friedrich Schleiermacher, and Novalis. Though the final
tally favors Friedrich Schlegel far too lopsidedly for the *Athenäum*
fragments to be an example of the communal intellectual production
that he calls "symphilosophy,"[79] both the collection as a whole and
the individual fragment are, according to Friedrich's idea, dialogic in
their very conception. Some of the fragments quite literally take the

form of a dialogue (for instance, KA 2:201, No. 221/PF 48 and KA 2:209, No. 259/PF 54–55); in one case (KA 2:211, No. 273/PF 56) Friedrich adds a few lines to a fragment written by his brother; that way "it is supposed to take the form of a small dialogue, a form to which the fragments are certainly no stranger."[80]

Yet the fragments do more than permit one or more voices to collide: they dissolve the coherence of the authorial voice as such. For layered over the authorial voices and at times drowning them out, a polyphony of a much stronger—and much stranger—kind pervades the fragments. The "motley heap of ideas"[81] that Schlegel amasses is far from inert; placed into such close proximity, the ideas begin to engage in a conversation by and with themselves, as it were. Schlegel imagines the ideas to behave "like the surprising meeting of two friendly thoughts after a long separation."[82] Dialogism is not merely an *effect* of the history of their writing, but it is lodged in the very structure of the fragment. There is a kind of endless chatter among these fragments (in the process of which the appearance of contradictions is as inevitable as it is necessary to keep the discussion going). If "a dialogue is a chain, or a garland of fragments,"[83] it is because the structure of conversation is embedded in the very form of the fragments. But unlike the essay "Conversation on Poetry," where it is at least thinkable (though highly unlikely) that the figures in the dialogue represent empirical persons (such as members of the Jena circle), in the fragments no such allegorical reading offers itself. Whatever transpires at "the surprising meeting of two friendly thoughts" cannot be traced back to the voices that put the fragments into circulation in the first place. This is not only because there is no reliable mapping between thoughts and sentences, but because the *encounter* between the two friendly thought-fragments produces effects controlled by neither. If there is a structural *doxa*, a communal project of thinking, embedded in the genre itself, then it is one that is in crucial respects *independent* of the authors' voices, independent even of human voices. The exchanges, meetings, conversations take place in a realm over which authorial voices and their intentions have less sway than they might imagine (or even wish), one in which "words often understand themselves better than those by whom they are used."[84]

System

I mentioned earlier that the dissolution of the authorial voice in favor of the autonomy of what Schlegel calls the "secret societies"[85] of words sharply accelerates the differentiation of the literary sphere from other discursive forms. The notion that a writer, far from controlling language, merely intervenes in the operations of a self-enclosed linguistic system has become a well-established idea not just in criticism but also among those producing literature in the late twentieth century; in this sense, Schlegel's work is, as Bohrer has argued, a forerunner of much of the most advanced (which is to say: elitist) literary movements in European literature (e.g., symbolism, modernism, expressionism, and surrealism).[86] Suspicious of anything that smacks of totality or systematicity, critics usually establish this genealogy by emphasizing the fragmentary, discontinuous, chaotic, incoherent aspects of Schlegel's work (Bohrer is no exception in this respect). Schlegel is claimed for modernity through fragmentation.

But claiming Schlegel for modernity via a near exclusive emphasis on the fragmentation of the fragments is not only reductive; it runs the danger of missing the ambition of Schlegel's poetics.[87] As the fragment that I quoted earlier indicates, having a system is not the only option fatal to the mind; not having one is just as bad. For this reason, Schlegel does not tire of voicing his desire to rally the apparently random snippets of writing into what he repeatedly calls "a system of fragments."[88] The "will to fragment" in his early work, to which Lacoue-Labarthe and Nancy, among many other critics, attest,[89] stands in tension with a powerfully expressed "will to system": "*I seek totality of knowledge,*"[90] Schlegel writes in 1796, at the very beginning of his most ardently fragmentary period. Shortly thereafter he adds: "Since everywhere in poetry and philosophy I have from the beginning and out of instinct steered toward the system, then I suppose I am a universal systematist."[91] The fragment, then, can be understood to partake of two radically distinct forms of temporality when it is brought in relation to a whole: as a part severed from something assumed to have been whole (thus making use of the logic of castration and mourning), or, reversing the order of part and whole, as a prospect of a future completion.[92] (I will propose a third possibility shortly.)

Part of what we would miss by overlooking the powerful presence of a will to totality is the close conceptual connection Schlegel's writing maintains, by way of the part/whole distinction, with central questions of eighteenth-century aesthetics. With it, we would also miss the manner in which he transforms the distinction. We can easily recapitulate the links with aesthetics if we render the confusing and melodramatic paradox of *Athenäum* fragment 53 ("It is equally fatal for the mind to have a system and to have none") in more familiar philosophical language. The dilemma the fragment articulates, the dilemma in which Schlegel and many of his contemporaries find themselves, is whether Enlightenment thinking, by questioning the transcendent claims of meaning-giving systems (chief among them religion), does not break the link between traditional explanatory accounts and the bewildering array of phenomena confronting human beings (now called subjects), whether it does not break it in fact in such a way as to make it impossible for a subject to fashion a totality out of the manifold. Put differently, the question would be: is it possible to maintain the coherence of metaphysical assurance, anchored ultimately in the idea of a benevolent God, given that it steadily weakens in the face of critique?

This is not just a question of grounding knowledge in certainty, the preeminent goal of Kantian critical philosophy and its Fichtean radicalization, but rather a question of how such a ground (assuming one is even found or established) can then support a coherent picture of the world, including a coherent picture of the subject. Put more pointedly: provided one accepts philosophical grounding as a point of departure, how can one get from its icy abstraction, bereft as it is of sensations and bodies and life, to an account of the sensory world that is built on that ground?

If aesthetics is the name that eighteenth-century philosophy gives to the negotiation every subject must perform in order to get from a fragmentary picture of the world to a coherent, total, and systematic one, then Schlegel's two fatal options of system and nonsystem entail an intervention in precisely this issue, an issue that makes aesthetics relevant for both the subject's access to the world and its connection to other subjects. At stake, therefore, are both cognitive and moral issues. But the question of the precise relation in which part and whole, fragment and totality, stand in Schlegel's writing, crucial as it is for our understanding of Schlegel's rewriting of aesthetic questions, is still unclear. It is worth knowing what solutions to this problem have been offered before we venture our own.

Mediating Fragment and Totality

Most studies concerned with Schlegel's aesthetic ideas have been dominated by the distinction of part and whole, fragment and totality. As Rodolphe Gasché has argued, "a concept of the fragment that merely emphasizes incompletion, residualness, detachment, or brokenness will not serve here,"[93] for such a mechanical fragment neither yields knowledge about the whole from which it is severed nor manages to challenge its concept. Instead of the mechanical link, many critics prefer to see an organic or quasi-organic connection of part and whole in Schlegel's writings, in which the whole determines its parts either by containing them or by being contained by them (as their essence, their telos, etc.). Either way, the relationship is temporally and structurally stacked in favor of the whole, for totality either dialectically dissolves the recalcitrant difference of the fragment, or else is organically implanted in the fragment's very core. Critics often work with an ontological conception of part and whole in which the whole exceeds the totality of parts, giving them their meaning in the first place. Here I do not mean those readings that, as Manfred Frank has put it, have "portrayed romanticism as so drunk with harmony and so enamored of the absolute that . . . one no longer sees how it has provoked the wrath of classicists like Goethe, Schiller, and Hegel

. . . nor what makes it radically modern."[94] Instead, I will focus on a few of the most important critics (Frank himself included) who have recognized that the deeply problematic character of the relationship of fragment and totality is precisely what energizes Schlegel's contribution to aesthetics, yet who proceed, in one way or the other, to redeem fragmentation for a higher totality.

As I noted earlier, Gerhard Neumann, for example, reads the fragments as presenting a *conflict* between part and whole. But the conflict itself is conceived according to a "dialectic of fragment and system"[95] in Schlegel's work, which is based, in turn, on an organically imagined homology between the two: "[The fragment] appears as a self-enclosed, unmistakable 'organism'; then . . . this 'fragment' as an individual comes into relation with the whole: to be sure, not by being subsumed within a rigid system, but through analogy; finally this model of the analogy of fragment and universe is transferred to the human being in his cognitive situation" (567). The narrative leading us from a short piece of writing to the universe and finally to the human condition, from "microcosm to macrocosm," as Neumann puts it (ibid.), offers itself so effortlessly only because all three structures are seen to stand in analogous relationships to each other. *Homologous* would be a more accurate term, for what guarantees the validity of Neumann's narrative is the assumption that all three entities— fragment, universe, and human individual—are organized *organically:* they are thought to have grown from the same seed.[96] The fragments, which set in motion this chain of recognitions, are permitted to be logically separate structures only insofar as they have always belonged to the "context of life" (568). Such an insight allows itself to be translated readily into the language of redemption: thus the fragments document the ruptured realities of life, yet also contain the seeds for overcoming the rupture: they are, Neumann declares, "mimesis *and* utopia" (569), broken *and* redemptive, indeed—relying on a Christian figure—redemptive because broken.

Other critics also generally disinclined toward an affirmative reading of texts have in Schlegel's case emphasized the dialectico-organic continuum between fragment and system. "Fragmentary totality, in keeping with what should be called the logic of the hedgehog," Lacoue-Labarthe and Nancy write, "cannot be situated in any single point: it is simultaneously in the whole and in each part."[97] How do we recognize this simultaneous presence? Again, through the homology of the organic. Thus, "the 'foundation' that fragmentation presupposes consists precisely in the fragmentary totality in its *organicity*" (65/44). And when the epiphanic flash of recognizing totality *in* fragmentation gives way to a historical account about the fragments, here as in Neumann's narrative the organic metaphor gives way to a dialectical conception.[98] Lacoue-Labarthe and Nancy remind the reader, through a reference to Heidegger's reading of Schelling, that *dialectical* is to be understood as covering "the thinking of identity through the mediation of nonidentity" (66/46); yet a dialectical analysis in this sense is inevitably undermined when it proceeds from an organic homology of the structures of fragment and system. Having thus established the organic matrix, the two authors can conclude: "Fragmentation is not, then, a dissemination, but is rather a dispersal that leads to fertilization and future harvests. The genre of the fragment is the genre of generation" (70/49).[99]

Pursuing this line of thought, Rodolphe Gasché argues that "a fragment, in the Romantic sense, is the only possible presentation [the romantics] could conceive of [for] the system."[100] They do so because "for the Romantics, the philosophy of the system is an aesthetic philosophy. For them the ideality and absoluteness of the whole, of the totality, are thinkable only in terms of an individuality, that is, as a sensible, and hence intrinsically plural, unity. For them the question of the presentability (*Darstellung*) of the manifold's gathering into one remains an irreducible question" (PF xiii–xiv). This characterization is as precise and concise as one could hope it to be: rather than being dissolved into the absoluteness of the system, fragments insist on displaying totality *in* their material fracturing. But how is this dialectic of identity through the nonidentity of fragments effected? To answer this question, Gasché has recourse to the by now familiar organic topos: "All fragments are systems *in nuce*. [. . .] Fragments are individuals, singular organic totalities, that is, systems in miniature. [. . .] They are the seeds for future systems. [. . .] [T]hey are only embryos of developing systems—isolated yet striving at a whole" (PF xii). The co-presence of identity and nonidentity, system and fragment, is only possible, it seems, because an anterior organic homology structuring both system and fragment guarantees its success.[101]

The conceptual difficulty of insisting on the particularity of the particular without, however, giving up on its relation to the whole and hence to meaning, i.e., the conceptual difficulty of thinking identity together with difference, also marks the work of Ernst Behler, the preeminent scholar of the *Frühromantik* of the past three decades. Referring to the fragmentary work of Schlegel and Novalis, Behler insists that "the claim to achieving systematic unity, . . . completeness, and totality in whatever form, is put into question by a mode of writing that from the beginning refuses any closure."[102] The crucial difference between Behler and the other critics I have cited lies in the last three words: the fragments' refusal, according to Behler, is not directed at the systematic totality itself, but rather at closure. Refusing totality, by itself, is not a very interesting gesture: unless the refusing agent wishes to remove itself from meaning-giving systems *completely* (and even choosing death does not necessarily accomplish this), it finds itself obeying, albeit negatively, all the determinations that it had meant to evade. Thus Behler maintains the link of the early romantic genre of the fragment to totality, but with the important proviso that this relation be marked by a *lack* of closure.

Behler offers two distinct avenues of conceptualizing such an open relationship between fragment and totality in Schlegel's work. One is to trace the fragment back through a German tradition (in contrast to the usual practice of pointing out its antecedents among the French moralists) consisting of Herder and Hamann and ending up in Luther's translation of a verse from the gospel of John (6:12) in which Christ admonishes his disciples, who stand in wonder of his miracle of feeding five thousand with a few loaves, to collect all crumbs (*fragmenta* in the Vulgate, *Brocken* in Luther) so that nothing may be wasted. Behler points out that because of the eucharistic interpretation offered by the gospel itself, in which (the body of) Christ is the true bread of life, a collection of *Brocken,* including an ensemble of linguistic *fragmenta,* acquires a deeply eschatological meaning (28). I see two problems with this way of linking the early romantic fragments to an eschatology and hence to a meaning-giving totality. One is the lack of textual evidence (Behler himself does not offer any). This problem cannot be circumvented by claiming that the genre itself participates in the tradition of the textual *Brocken* and therefore promotes, in its very form, a Christian eschatology, because, as Behler himself points out, "the fragmentary mode of writing appears . . . to announce a fundamental phenomenon in modern literature or even a turning-point in the history of writing" (28). If the fragments occasion a discontinuity, then the literary tradition preceding them can only offer a very qualified interpretive support. The second, more serious problem with reading fragment as *Brocken,* and thus as the promise of a future redemption, lies in the fact that Behler leaves it unclear how the assumed eschatological impulse in the fragments can be reconciled with their structural openness on which he also insists. Contending that "the reachability of the [eschatological] goal is decisively put into question by the 'infinity' of this procedure" (37) (presumably the procedure of producing fragments) does not resolve the quandary, for an eschatology *infinitely* deferred cancels itself. In order for the crumbs to gather into the bread that is the body of Christ, they must conform to the fixity of *symbol* and must ultimately foreclose the infinite openness required by Behler's reading of the fragments as *allegory.*

The other path Behler takes to conceive of an open relationship between fragment and totality involves the idea of infinite progress, a conceptualization that gains weight by the fact that Manfred Frank, the most knowledgeable reader of early romanticism among philosophers, has proposed it as well. The view of the essential perfectibility of human affairs had much currency in the wake of the French Revolution; in a review of Condorcet's 1795 *Esquisse d'un Table historique des Progrès de l'Esprit humain* (Sketch of a Historical Table of the Progress of the Human Mind) published in Friedrich Niethammer's

Philosophisches Journal, Schlegel himself professes to be "entirely convinced" of infinite perfectibility "as an idea."[103] Whether his poetological theory bears out this conviction is another question. For the notion that poetry is an infinite project (as *Athenäum* fragment 116 states) is not the result of a *historical* observation, but of a *philosophical* insight.

Much of the critical tradition since Walter Benjamin has recognized that Schlegel's idea of the infinite expandability of the field of poetry is indebted to Fichte's idea of self-reflection, an application of the analytic and synthetic powers of thinking to itself, resulting in what Hegel calls "a pure thinking of itself." The specific reasons why Fichte advances this notion need not concern us here, nor what he hopes to accomplish with it; for our purposes it is sufficient to note one salient feature: self-reflection constitutes a simple technique with huge, in fact infinitely large, consequences. When the distinction between thinking and its objects is introduced into thinking itself—put differently, when the differentiation between observer and world gives way to a differentiation *internal* to the observer—the potential forms of thought expand into infinity. The simplest possibility consists in applying the fact of thinking to itself: "I think X," I think that I think X," "I think that I think that I think X," etc. As the philosophy of mind since Descartes has demonstrated, an astonishing complexity emerges when one severs the combinatorial rules of rational thinking—synthesis and analysis, affirmation and negation—from the objective world and permits them to apply to thought itself.

Behler reflects a widely held belief among critics when he states that such "alternation of affirmation and negation, of stepping outside of oneself and returning into oneself, became the founding model of early romantic reflection."[104] If this is the case, if Schlegel spends his early years mining the theory of self-reflection for its artistic potential, then the first and immediate consequence is an explosive growth—into infinity—of the possible forms an artwork can take. But this infinity is not a totality that can be circumscribed, since the rate and direction of its expansion cannot be predicted; it is a "bad infinity," as Hegel would say, an exponential increase in the space of possibilities *without* relation to an absolute whole, hence without the safety net of being related to a *higher* truth.

Behler astutely registers the potentially uncontrolled proliferation of artistic objects, yet at the same time attempts to put a lid on it by pointing to a variety of goals toward which, he believes, the proliferation strives. One such goal is pedagogical: the mind matures, he contends, in following the infinite movement that the artwork performs. The "boundless reflecting in thinking and counter-thinking" (120) does not, he concedes, "consist for Schlegel in a mere synthesis or harmonious saturation, but lies in the movement itself, . . . in a 'hovering' between the antinomies, in forever switching between the antitheses, in which process *the life of the mind enfolds and enriches itself*" (134, my emphasis). How the movement *itself,* the hovering, the switching—empty, as they are, of a content one could name—furthers the enrichment of the mind remains unclear. Where Schlegel diagnoses the "life of the Universal Spirit [as] an uninterrupted chain of inner revolutions"[105]—a bizarre and deeply paradoxical notion to which I shall return—Behler sees a positive learning environment. "Without this contradiction, thinking would wither away," he maintains (135), when the real wonder is how thinking can possibly endure such a paradoxical stance.

Redeeming the fragments by harnessing them for a project of *Bildung* is part of a larger effort to rescue them from bad infinity and reclaim them for a good totality. The conceptual basis on which this attempt rests is precisely the classical aesthetic idea that the fragments are meant to put into question in the first place, namely the idea that, to qualify as artworks, objects must exhibit coherence, unity, harmony. As authentic works, Behler argues, fragments present even contradictions "as a *unity* of form and content, shape and statement, spirit and letter, in short: as a 'system of fragments'" (130, my emphasis). While Schlegel, according to Behler, recognizes that in philosophy bad infinity cannot be avoided once the recursive process of self-reflection begins,[106] "in poetry . . . the infinite thinking gain[s] unity and coherence" (126). Behler goes so far as to suggest that "the problem of the infinite process of thought solved itself [for Schlegel]

. . . on the aesthetic level" (ibid.). In this reading, then, Schlegel promotes the unbridled expansion of reflection in *thinking,* but not in
making. Indeed, the aesthetic is thought to solve the problem of the
absolute, insoluble by philosophy itself, namely the problem of how
to render—how to present—a finite version of the infinite.

The idea of art as the ultimate presentation of the absolute and
thus as the culmination of which philosophy itself is incapable goes
back to Schelling's *System des transcendentalen Idealismus* (System of
Transcendental Idealism) of 1800. There "the miracle of art" over-
comes the "infinite split" that plagues philosophy, the split that prevents it from fully presenting the absolute identity of unity and manifold.[107] This split is caused, according to Schelling, by the paradox of
reflection: in order to be thought in concepts (i.e., in order to be understood), the absolute needs to be reflected upon; but every act of
reflection puts its object at a distance (indeed, *makes* it into an object
distinct from the thinking subject). But the absolute, or as Schelling
often says, the absolutely Identical, is only absolute if it is neither
subject nor object, but a synthesis of the two. For Schelling, such a
synthesis is achieved in the "intellectual intuition" that art makes possible. Since art is able to present "the unconscious [*das Bewußtlose*] in
action and production and its original identity with the conscious"
(627–28 / 231), it is "the only true and eternal organon and, at once,
document of philosophy" (627 / 231). To the philosopher, Schelling
writes, art is "the Highest because it opens for him, as it were, the
holy of holies" (628 / 231). (In later writings, Schelling considerably
weakens this claim.) Art—here too conceived primarily as poetry
(*Dichtkunst*)—attains this position at the pinnacle of human consciousness by synthesizing what otherwise remains separate, (dis)solv-
ing the absolute, forging a bond between the identical and the nonidentical—in short, by serving as the supplement of philosophy.

There are no doubt important differences between Schelling's position and what we find among critics such as Behler or Frank, differences that Frank's reading in particular underscores emphatically.
In Schelling's construction, the synthesis is positively achieved by the
poem (to be precise: by the *totality* of all poems as products of the

"poetic faculty" [*Dichtungsvermögen,* 626 / 230]); we understand and intuit that the highest level of reflection has not only been thought but also realized in a sensible medium. Frank, by contrast, insists on the negativity of the relationship the artwork maintains with the idea of an absolute whole. Precisely because of its infinite extension, its discontinuities and contradictions, the artwork—and Frank very much has Schlegel's fragments in mind here—is read as directing our attention to the meaningful totality in its *absence*. The very failures at coherence, Frank argues ingeniously, give us a glimpse of the absolute: "The epistemic unpresentability of the absolute finds a complement in aesthetic intuition [*Schau*], which gives us the absolute by *not* giving it to us, which is to say *not* in a *reflexively* mediated form, but rather by presenting that which is itself *reflexively unpresentable*."[108] Were it not for the negation ("by *not* giving it to us"), this would be just another version of Schelling. But while, according to Frank, the latter's conception assumes a *symbolic* relationship between the artwork and the absolutely synthesized totality (293), Frank insists on an *allegorical* connection between the two.[109] An allegory, Frank explains, "is an artistic procedure that erases what is presented in its finitude as that which was not meant" (293); this self-cancellation of words and their meanings results in the production of meaning *elsewhere*. In contrast with the finality of the artwork, that elsewhere to which allegory points can be nothing but the infinite. "Allegory," Frank concludes, "is thus the necessary manifesto of the unpresentability of the infinite" (ibid.). Again victory is snatched from the jaws of defeat, for this unpresentability of the infinite is a failure that (miraculously, Schelling might say) reveals itself to be a success: it points us to the absolute. And if in this case it fails to open the door to the sanctum sanctorum, it can at least show us the way. For the unpresentability of the infinite, reasons Frank, is comprehensible *as* unpresentability only with reference to the idea of a *presentability* of the infinite (even if it is not achievable). We can only understand a door as closed if we assume the—infinitely deferred—possibility of its opening. Allegory, therefore, "is . . . the tendency towards the absolute within the finite itself" (291). Thus Frank accomplishes two things: he inserts the absolute as a "regulative boundary concept" (244)—as a limit, a goal—into the potentially infinite expansion of the artwork, regaining in this way a glimpse of the absolute in the midst of the chaos that the fragments present; and he characterizes the relationship between the fragmentary artwork and the absolute totality as *binding* ("the *necessary* manifesto of the unpresentability of the infinite").[110]

Despite Frank's insistence on a distinction between symbol and allegory, between a positively achieved presentation of the absolute and a negatively glimpsed manifestation of its unpresentability, a reading of Schlegel's fragments in terms of an "infinite approximation" to the self-identical totality arrives at some of the same redemptive conclusions we found in idealist aesthetics. Far from permitting the sphere of poetry to experiment with its own *artistic* version of self-reflection—a mode of experimentation that admittedly runs the danger of losing its way into a nonsense that proves useless to philosophy—such a reading attempts, as Frank's terminology clearly indicates, to regulate its boundaries by means of philosophical concepts prescribed as necessary. The negative approximation to the absolute turns out to be no less binding for the poem than is the absolute's positive presentation.[111]

One indication of how his interpretation couples the artistic performance of the artwork (here too understood as verbal) with a philosophical telos can be found in Frank's usage of *symbol* and *allegory*. For conceiving of allegory as *necessarily* referring to an absent meaning (the unpresentable absolute) turns it into a species of symbol. Indeed, allegory, as conceived by Frank, is an even more philosophical (and less artistic) trope than symbol, for he takes it to consist entirely in the gesture of pointing away from itself (or in telling it otherwise, as its etymology suggests).[112] It thus "erases what is presented" in favor of the unrepresentable. Paul de Man's essay "The Rhetoric of Temporality" of 1969 (not cited by Frank) is relevant here, for it develops a distinction between symbol and allegory precisely through a discussion of romanticism, especially Schlegel's early work. Symbol in de Man's schema is "the product of the organic growth of form . . .

since the material perception and the symbolical imagination are continuous."[113] Allegory by contrast is marked by a discontinuity and thus "appears purely mechanical" (ibid.); hence its meaning "is not decreed by dogma" (207). Instead of announcing the qualified, but still palpable, utopia in Frank,[114] allegory in de Man is an elegiac trope mourning the lost possibility of fulfilled identification offered by the symbol (207). It stands for loss and death, a very differently conceived version of the absolute.

In Frank's argument as in Schelling's, art is a vehicle—a metaphor—for a distinctly philosophical project (namely, being assured of the continued validity of a meaning-giving totality); as Frank, now sounding very much like Schelling, elsewhere bluntly puts it, "philosophy completes itself in and as art."[115] While the theory of art has ceased to prescribe specific thematic or generic features of the art work, it now lays down its norms via a purely formal account of the work. According it a place of honor may be philosophy's most sophisticated attempt at keeping art within its own sphere.[116]

It is true that there is evidence in Schlegel's work to support such a thesis. Much of the conceptual regulation is performed by Schlegel himself, who is not shy about using the organico-dialectical vocabulary, which the secondary literature could be said merely to systematize. "The more organic, the more systematic," declares a posthumously published fragment.[117] "*Systems* must grow; the seed in each system must be *organic*," another maintains.[118] He also seems to promote the notion that art continues speaking at the point where language fails philosophy. "Where philosophy ends," he notes in his *Ideas* of 1800, the same year Schelling's *System of Transcendental Idealism* is published, "poetry must begin."[119]

A few years later, Schlegel demonstrates more clearly than Schelling himself that the apotheosis of art entails not its autonomy but rather its strict functionalization: "Philosophy taught us that everything divine is only intimated and only to be assumed with probability, and that we must therefore accept revelation as the highest truth. But revelation is too sublime a cognition for sensible human beings. And thus art fittingly steps in as the medium in order to show human beings the objects of revelation in sensible presentation and distinctness.[120] The passage stems from lectures Schlegel held in Cologne in 1804–5 whose language frequently foreshadows the conversion to Catholicism that he was to undergo in the Cologne Cathedral in 1808.

Yet we are not obliged to read the logic of revelation and salvation back into the time of the *Athenäum*.[121] Indeed, there is plenty of evidence that right around 1800 the organic is no more than an unattainable ideal. Recall that in *Athenäum* fragment 412, which argues that "whoever has a sense for the infinite . . . thinks of his ideals at least as being chemical," concludes by cautioning that "only a perfect mind could conceive of ideals organically."[122] The organic conception is acknowledged here by Schlegel, but only as a desideratum for the future, a future that, moreover, is infinitely deferred. For the organic conception is specifically identified with "a perfect mind"—"the organic poetry [is] divine poetry," Schlegel elsewhere writes[123]—and for as long as our minds are not perfect, for as long as we are human rather than divine, an organic way of thinking remains closed to us. In contrast with divine organicism, the human option is to think one's "ideals at least chemically," to remain mired in the to and fro of open-ended division and fusion.

We certainly can read the later mysticism and organicism back into the *Athenäum*. But by doing so, while gaining a measure of coherence, we would run the risk of losing "risk itself," the very risk that Maurice Blanchot identifies as the defining characteristic of the incoherent, chaotic energy of fragmentary writing.[124] By resorting to a dialectic (even if a supposedly negative dialectic) that would allow us to redeem the fragments by taking their stark contradictions as a sign of absolute identity (present through its conspicuous absence), we give up the tension *within* contradiction. It is a tension that weakens markedly in Schlegel's writings as he gains distance from the *Athenäum,* but during those last few years of the eighteenth century, he attempts a breathtaking experiment in pursuing the internal logic of poetry to its ends. And he often does so *against* his own best intentions. This is why we find statements that point to a synthesizing project of aesthetics with other spheres of culture alongside statements that insist on poetry's difference. Thus, "where philosophy ends, poetry must begin," is the beginning of a fragment that closes a few lines later with a very different idea: "One should . . . oppose to philosophy not only un-philosophy but poetry."[125] Suddenly the field beginning where philosophy ends looks wholly altered: poetry is no longer Schelling's (and Frank's) *continuation* of philosophy by other means, but its opposite. Not *only* its opposite, to be sure, but *also* its opposite.

Between Chaos and System: Toward Chemistry

Providing an account of what Ernst Behler has called "the oscillating thinking between opposites"[126] *without* introducing too quickly the escape route of a telic resolution—providing, in short, an account of the impossible combination of the two equally fatal options of system and nonsystem that *Athenäum* fragment 24 demands—requires a different notion of system (or totality, absolute, absolute self-identity, etc.). It might be productive to give up distinctions such as organic/chemical/mechanical or part/whole (fragment/totality) to define both Schlegel's language and that of large parts of his critical reception. Rather than conceiving of the system as something distinct from, or even opposed to, the fragments, we might think of elements as being elements only insofar as they are subject to certain operational rules. The whole would then consist of the dynamic *process* governing the parts, a process involving an unpredictable movement *between* system and chaos; it would involve, in Schlegel's words, "changing between chaos and system, rendering chaos into system and then new chaos."[127] The system would no longer reside in the "elsewhere" to which the fragments would point—organically or dialectically or through infinite approximation—but like the romantic poetry of *Athenäum* fragment 116 "its true essence" would lie "in forever becoming, never being completed." (Its "essence" is not something we could grasp, but it would amount to a set of operations acting upon a set of elements.) Schlegel attempts conceptualizing totality as the very process of production when he says of his ideal poetry that it "would present that which produces with the product";[128] such a "poetry and poetry of poetry" would not find the "higher" truth of poetry elsewhere—the system, the absolute, the identity of identity and nonidentity—but in "that which produces" poetry, *poiesis* itself. And such a notion of writing operates according to a different model of temporality, one that is dependent neither on a narrative of loss nor on one of redemption, nor for that reason on the *absence* of narrative (which would be an absence of temporality), but rather on the interrupted temporality at the intersection of human and nonhuman processes. It involves the temporality of a material both internal and external to our consciousness, the temporality of *ver-*, a chemical temporality.

Conceiving of the system as the morphogenesis of its parts according to certain rules provides us with a powerful alternative to the idea of the system as an organically articulated body.[129] Philosophy, Schlegel writes, is "an epic, [and] begins in the middle."[130] And, we may add, it also ends there: read as an operational process, his idea of totality dispenses with both descent and ascent and consists of—better yet: exhausts itself in—the sheer process of dynamic interaction. Combinatorial change, without the sublating, recuperating, or elevating help of a consciousness reflecting on it, is all there is to totality. The system consists of nothing but interacting fragments. As Winfried Menninghaus has shown, we will look in vain for *a* ground, *a* point, *an* origin, since from the start we are dealt a multiplicity.[131] In his reading the concept of reflection operative in early romanticism implies that reflection is not a property that consciousness adds to its repertoire of cognitive skills, but constitutive of any cognition whatsoever. This Benjamino-Derridean insight, Menninghaus shows, is already fully anticipated in the manner in which the works of the early Schlegel and Novalis register *différance* in the doubleness inherent in any act of consciousness. If I prefer a *multiplicity* to the *duality* that is Menninghaus's focus, it is because I am interested in showing how Schlegel takes a further step by relying on a material model —chemistry—that allows him to offer his most trenchant critique of classical philosophy without recourse to the doubling figure of reflection.

The notion of totality as the set of combinations resulting from the application of combinatorial rules to elements (where neither rules nor elements are available prior to or independently of each other), the notion that takes the place of the metaphysical system, is one bereft of ground or goal. Because the infinitely large number of possible products—utterances, graphic signs—cannot be made available at once and hence a selection must be made, a powerful element of contingency enters the system, for the manner in which the act of selection (guided by subjective desires, appetites, anxieties, etc.) interacts with the mechanistic process of combining elements according to given rules is not one that can be predicted or controlled. It has built into it the possibility of promoting unintentional, accidentally generated signs that surpass a humanistically imagined human agency. This mingling of a formal system with an unformalizable remainder, which is how chemical reactions were imagined in the late eighteenth century, can yield beautiful shapes, but by the same token and following the same logic it can also give rise to chaotic, mad nonsense.

The transformation of aesthetic theory that we witness is all the more disturbing because Schlegel's writings retain concepts such as poetry, science, philosophy, and system, concepts that would seem to have been rendered obsolete by his experimentation. Certainly, in a sense these are conceptual leftovers. But precisely *as* leftovers they retain a peculiar potency. The shape these concepts take and the philosophical force they retain *after* their constitutive parts have been radically altered transforms their efficacy far more powerfully than would a critique that abandoned them for a new set of terms. Rather than breaking down and disposing of important elements of rationalist and idealist philosophy, his writings break them down to keep them *as broken*. We can take what Benjamin, in *The Concept of Criticism*, has written about romantic irony, whose determination he largely derives by way of studying the young Schlegel, to apply to

Schlegel's work in general: "It presents a paradoxical venture: to continue building on the formation [*Gebilde*] through demolition [*Abbruch*]."[132]

With a model in which the material mutability of literature *is* its totality, we are not obliged to read *process* as *progress,* for we would no longer compare the performance or achievement of verbal artworks to a yardstick outside of literature. We can dispense with the ritual of interpreting the determination of the work of art in terms of the needs or desires of other social spheres, and instead read the system as a system of literature, or, to unpack the word *literature:* as a system of letters. Literature thus understood would no longer serve a role (even as that of highest expression) and would thus cease to be conceived as a *medium,* as that which stands in the middle. For as we saw, even the "highest" role inevitably entails getting in the "middle," serving as a path to—or an expression of—something *else,* which is the true object of interest. (Thus in his Cologne lectures, Schlegel speaks of "art fittingly step[ping] in as the medium [*ins Mittel*]" between Man and God, a phrase that could also have been rendered as "into the middle.") In contrast with a functional notion of poetry, a system of literature takes the "medium" (in many senses of the term) as the end itself. Thus the proper focus of analysis shifts to the material practice of writing, since that is where the formal principles internal to the field of literature are used and abused (principles extending from grammar and morphology to conventions about meter, rhyme, metaphor, narrative stance, theme, etc.). This shift allows us to substitute a temporality of rhetoric for the organic, eschatological, or asymptotic temporality used in much of the critical tradition. As Paul de Man has observed, it is just this temporality that permits linguistic accounts of system and chaos to remain "an endless process that leads to no synthesis."[133] Rather than the redemption offered by apocalyptic temporal structures, de Man's temporality of rhetoric "dissolves in the narrowing spiral of a linguistic sign that becomes more and more remote from its meaning, and it can find no escape from this spiral" (222).[134] De Man calls this endless spiral "irony," a term he derives from none other than Schlegel himself.

Irony is one well-established way of describing the "risk" or the "chaotic energy" of fragmentary writing that we must contend with when we decline a synthesizing or integrating model of reading. This is not just Paul de Man's insight but also that of Hegel, who astutely recognizes the dangers lurking under the "ironical attitude" and thus wants nothing to do with it. If I propose a reading of this process by way of a detour through contemporary chemistry, it is in part because irony offers few advantages as a critical tool; there is little agreement in the critical literature—despite, or perhaps because of, its vast volume—about what constitutes irony and how its effects on the text or on the reader might best be described. This may be because irony is too familiar a rhetorical move to lend itself to an uncontested description (we cannot define it, but we think we know it when we see it). It may also be because, like Hegel, we often confuse a *textual* instance of irony with an *intentional* state assumed to be its cause; rather than limiting our analysis to rhetorical turns, we are tempted to speak of the "ironical attitude," a temptation that is understandable insofar as that attitude can be ascribed to a subject standing above irony and in control of it.[135]

Chemistry, by contrast, is unfamiliar enough to most of Schlegel's readers (both in his time and in ours) that long-held views do not tend to crowd in as soon as the word is mentioned. What is more, there is no intuitive way in which we connect any model of chemical reaction with our intentional states; if Schlegel proceeds to do so anyway, the analogy between chemical and mental states is far from obvious and requires imaginative and interpretive labor. Unlike written signs, chemical bonds are regarded by most of us as occurring outside of our consciousness. It is precisely this externality of the system of chemical combinations that makes it, for Schlegel, into an ideal model in his attempt at devising a system of writing indebted not only to intentional states or philosophical mandates but also to the logic of its own material. Underscoring its externality is eighteenth-century chemistry's entanglement with materiality, with the strange and unpredictable ways in which its material substances prevent a fully formal (which is to say: mathematical) description of the combinatorial logic guiding analysis and synthesis.[136] It is to the degree that late-eighteenth-century chemistry *fails* to master its material through mathematical abstraction that it becomes a rich model for the kind of poetics that Schlegel's writing encodes. The impurities in material combinations and imperfections in scientific understanding permit late-eighteenth-century chemistry to serve as an allegory for a poetics that does not abstract from what de Man has called "the prosaic materiality of the letter."[137] (Here Schlegel recognizes the potentials of a scientific discourse for poetic writing more adroitly than does the far more scientifically knowledgeable Novalis, who prefers mathematics as a model for language.)[138] Finally, because externality and materiality are features of a self-enclosed system, the system cannot make claims beyond its own boundaries. Applied to the realm of writing, this means: whatever wholeness, totality, or systematicity a chemically imagined system of writing manages to achieve is not transferable to other spheres—philosophy, psychology, political economy, etc.—that may imagine themselves to be suffering from a lack of wholeness. Here the difference in ambition and extension we find in the system of literature, compared with what, according to its traditional understanding, poetry is said to accomplish, can be made clear by way of a comparison with the difference between chemistry and alchemy. Alchemy attempted far more than the transmutation of metals: as the historian of science John Read has put it, it "sought to bring the microcosm of man into relation with the macrocosm of the universe,"[139] performing the sort of total synthesis toward which the organic-symbolic notion of poetry strives. Chemistry by contrast narrows its scope to a finite set of elements and combinatorial operations that, however, give rise to an infinity of possible objects. We could say, polemically, that alchemy is to chemistry what poetry is to literature. What is exciting and vexing about Schlegel's early writings is that they perform the move from one field to the other.

3 Chemistry in the Eighteenth Century

Mixing Metaphors

In the previous chapter, I attempted to do two main things: first, I tried to show how Schlegel's ambition in writing fragments that would, somehow, produce (or have as a consequence) a systematic totality is closely linked to central issues of aesthetic theory, issues clustered around the notion of the mediation between isolated particulars and coherent wholes. Second, I argued that the structure of Schlegel's fragments prevents them from closing in upon themselves, causing instead a basic openness—negatively understood: a rift or lack—in their very midst. This structural opening sets off interactions within and between the texts that at some point leave behind the author's motivations and wishes, producing their own uncontrollable effects. The link between these two arguments still needs to be explored, specifically the consequences the second argument has for the first: what does the idea of endlessly chattering, self-conflicted, and self-contradictory morsels of language, which nevertheless refuse to give up on the notion of totality, entail for aesthetic theory?

The project of writing a multiplicity of dynamically linked fragments whose completion remains forever deferred is linked to aesthetics and to the transformative critique of aesthetics, not by an agent external to the process (a goal, a motivating force retroactively posited, a will) but by the idea of linkage—of *Verbindung*—itself. Linkage can take many shapes in Schlegel's writing, yet most have something important in common: the terms he uses to describe the process—*verbinden, verschmelzen, durchdringen, mischen, kombinieren* ("binding," "melding," "permeating," "mixing," "combining") as well as their necessary corollaries *scheiden* and *trennen* ("separating," "dividing")—are taken from the lexicon of contemporary chemistry.

References to chemistry are ubiquitous in Schlegel's early writings. In his essay "On the Study of Greek Poetry," written in 1795, chemistry still carries the negative connotations one would expect to find in a text largely beholden to organicist wholeness: "When the critical anatomist first destroys the beautiful organization of an artwork, analyzes this elementary mass, conducts some physical experiments with it and draws from them proud results, then he palpably deceives himself: because the artwork no longer exists."[1] Yet a rich, complicated, mostly positively charged use of chemistry finds its way into his writing only about a year later, at the very time—August or September 1796—that Manfred Frank has identified as the beginning of Schlegel's disaffection with foundationalist philosophy and his resultant "conversion" to its critique.[2] The choice of metaphoric field and the doubts about the validity of philosophical foundations are not entirely coincidental, for, as we shall see, the very structure of eighteenth-century chemistry makes for an uneasy fit with the mandates of *Grundsatzphilosophie*.

But I will defer discussing the implications of Schlegel's adoption of a chemical vocabulary to the next chapter, and will first focus on how he deploys it. I have already mentioned the prominent occurrence of chemical metaphors in *Athenäum* fragment 116, in which Schlegel conceives of a notion of romantic poetry that "wants to and also should now mix, now fuse poetry with prose, ingeniousness with criticism, art poetry with nature poetry."[3] He imagines romantic poetry as a universal catalyst so powerful that having helped bring about the union of all the other isolated categories, it then catalyzes itself. In poetry, realism and idealism seem to be "fused most deeply";[4] "poetry and philosophy will permeate each other ever more deeply";[5] poetry is also the place in which "reason and unreason saturate and permeate each other."[6] "Where [poetry and practice] entirely suffuse one another and fuse into one, there philosophy is created,"[7] Schlegel writes. At times he imagines the entire project of early romanticism in chemical terms, for instance in the already quoted *Athenäum* fragment 412: "Whoever has a sense for the infinite . . . sees in it the product of eternally dividing and mixing forces, conceives of his ideals at least as being chemical, and when he expresses himself decisively, he speaks nothing but contradictions."[8] These "eternally dividing and mixing forces" permeate every corner of the Schlegelian text. Philosophy, "a sort of transcendental chemistry,"[9] is understood as "the science of all sciences that forever mix and again divide themselves, a logical chemistry."[10] Hence, "a completed critical philosophy would always only be chemically completed, not organically."[11] Put differently (and there are innumerable versions of this statement), "critique [is] the philosophical art of pure chemistry."[12]

Even more powerfully than philosophy, poetry (and literature) is imagined as a species of chemistry: "The chemical classification of dissolution into a dry and a wet variety can in literature also be applied to the dissolution of authors, who, having reached their zenith, must sink. Some turn into steam, others into water."[13] If this remark strikes us as more obviously ironic than some of the others I have quoted, that is as it should be, for irony itself is chemical through and through. "Irony is chemical ingeniousness,"[14] Schlegel writes, a "universal experiment."[15] And wit (*Witz*), which "is only the [external] appearance" of an irony imagined as "internal,"[16] is identified as "universal chemistry."[17] As with irony, here too it becomes clear that Schlegel has in mind an experimental, volatile, and hence potentially violent idea of chemistry. *Witz*, he declares, is an "explosion of bound spirit"[18] (and spirit—*Geist*—is not only the ghost that animates German idealism, but also a substance—present for example in *Weingeist,* spirits—well known to chemists). This explosive wit is the product of a "thick, fiery reason" (rather than the more usual "thin and watery" variety),[19] and it gives rise to an image of imagination, inspiration, and poetic production that could well serve as the description of a chemistry lab: "A witty idea occurs in the splitting of spiritual substances, which, before the sudden separation, must therefore have been thoroughly mixed. The imagination must first be filled to the point of saturation with life of all varieties before one can electrify it with the friction of free sociability in such a way that the stimulus of the softest touch, be it friendly or not, can elicit brilliant sparks and luminescent lightning, or smashing thunderbolts."[20] But it is not only imagination, philosophy, poetry—thinking and writing—that are described in the terms of chemistry. Schlegel extends the range of his extravagant metaphor to include economy, history, social relations, nations, and revolutions—everything, it seems, is chemical:

> It is natural that the French more or less dominate the age. They are a chemical nation. In them the chemical sense is excited more universally than in others. Even in moral chemistry they conduct their experiments always at a grand scale. Likewise, the age is a chemical age. Revolutions are universal movements, not organic but chemical. Large-scale trade is the chemistry of a large economy. . . . The chemical nature of the novel, criticism, wit, sociability, the newest rhetoric, and history thus far is self-evident.[21]

Of course, *none* of this is self-evident. What might such a promiscuous use of chemical metaphors mean? It is unclear to what degree of detail Schlegel understands chemistry; he is not as well-versed in the subject as is Novalis (who studied chemistry at the mining academy in Freiberg) or Goethe (who began with alchemical experiments as a teenager at home and pursued his interest in chemistry throughout his life)[22] or certainly Schelling (whose studies on natural philosophy display a remarkable knowledge of this as well as of other sciences).[23] It may well be that precisely because his knowledge is haphazard, gleaned most likely from secondhand sources, he is under less of an obligation to understand the science on its own terms (i.e., faithfully) and hence freer to experiment with its metaphorical range than are his better-informed contemporaries.

This does not imply, however, that his usage is arbitrary. Quite the contrary: chemical metaphors, deployed in wholly different contexts, cohere to a remarkable degree into one complex picture, for they draw their force not from a single point of comparison but rather from the logic of late-eighteenth-century chemistry as a whole. What renders Schlegel's use of chemical metaphors more than merely occasional or accidental, what pulls it together into a sustained allegory, is the fact that he imports into his writings an entire conceptual network rather than a series of isolated concepts. Terms such as *Mischung, Verwandtschaft* (or *Affinität*), and *Wechselwirkung* ("mixture," "affinity," "mutual effect") allude not only to a meaning that lies beyond their common range of significations but, because of the frequency, the prominence, and the interconnectedness of their usage, to a whole *system* of meanings. A sort of *Wechselwirkung* takes hold of the chemical metaphors themselves and infuses them with a dynamism that propels them beyond the limits of a local allusion. Thus when Schlegel uses the term *Mischung* ("mixture") he does two things at once in reference to chemistry: he alludes to a chemical meaning of *Mischung* (about which more below); and he activates an entire scientific and technical discourse in which *Mischung* is embedded, from which it draws, and, at the same time, to which it lends signification.[24] Allusion is too narrow a term, and intertextuality too vague, to designate the complicated way in which Schlegel's writings incorporate a whole discourse and the ways in which this discourse, transformed as it is in its new environment, continues to operate according to its own logic, transforming its host. I have preferred the term *allegory* to describe the way the numerous chemical metaphors and references are organized into a logic of chemistry. Since, in Paul de Man's words, the "secularized allegory of the early romantics . . . designates primarily a distance in relation to its own origin"[25]—since there is a space between the two strata of signification in allegory—a certain mobility, a certain shift, a certain degree of irony becomes possible in the way one thing tells the story of another.

When Schlegel claims that "the romantic imperative demands the mixture of all forms of poetry,"[26] we can read "mixture"—*Mischung* —in the technical sense used by contemporary chemists, i.e., not as an inert aggregation of substances but rather as a transformation in which the mixture of the heterogeneous substances yields a new homogeneous substance, what today we would call a chemical compound.[27] This is how the well-known chemist Friedrich Albert Carl Gren defines the concept in his *Systematisches Handbuch der gesamten Chemie* (Complete Systematic Handbook of Chemistry) of 1787: "The binding [*Verbindung*] of like parts into a whole is called gathering or joining together (*aggregatio*); the binding [again: *Verbindung*] of unlike parts into a homogeneous whole, however, is called mixture [*Mischung*] or combination [*Zusammensetzung*] (*synthesis, compositio, mixtio*). The former naturally does not yield new bodies . . . ; the latter by contrast yields one that is entirely newly made and different."[28] This terminology is widely shared among chemists of the time. In lectures on chemistry held in the winter of 1807–8 in Berlin, the very lectures that a few years later Arthur Schopenhauer would attend, the chemist and pharmacist Martin Heinrich Klaproth, who would be appointed to the first chair in chemistry at the University of Berlin in 1810, draws the distinction between the two sorts of mixtures along the same lines: "Mixture is the process of a close unification or permeation [*Vereinigung oder Durchdringung*] of two or more unlike substances such that they do not anymore occupy different spaces but rather one and the same space, and a newly created body arises. By contrast, when unlike substances merely touch without chemically permeating each other, this is called an aggregation [*Gemenge*]."[29] The process of mixing is of such consequence that Klaproth, like Gren and many other contemporaries, defines chemistry through it, calling it the "science of mixing [*Mischungskunde*]."[30]

But mixing is, by necessity, only half of the equation. In order to mix, one must first have in one's possession not only separate but, as Gren points out, heterogeneous entities ("unlike parts"). Indeed, Klaproth's textbook, essentially a series of recipes for making or isolating various substances, makes plain that the process of mixing not only requires but itself *produces* separations. The chemical process fuses, mixes, permeates, saturates, *and* it divides, separates, splits: synthesis *and* analysis both occur, often simultaneously. The two are thus not merely two sides of the same coin but generated by means of the same process: creations both. Thus, lectures Klaproth, chemistry "is also called the art of separation [*Scheidekunst*]" (1); Gren describes it as "the science that teaches us to know the mixture of bodies or their constitutive parts,"[31] while Johann Friedrich Gmelin, another well-known German chemist of the time, calls it, in a textbook from 1804, "the art of separation or the science of mixing [*Scheidungskunst oder Mischungskunde*]."[32]

Poetry and philosophy seem to be, in Schlegel's account, little more than versions of this "art of separation or science of mixing." He imagines each of them to operate according to chemical practices and principles, but as we shall see, Schlegel's most challenging conceptual innovations become apparent only when the common structure underlying both poetry and philosophy—namely writing—is understood according to the logic of chemistry. Before developing that argument (in chapter 4), it would be useful to take note of some of the main features of eighteenth-century chemistry.

The Other French Revolution

What sort of images and concepts energize the promiscuous use of chemical terms in Schlegel's writings? What is it about this particular science that predisposes it for use in a poetological and aesthetic context?

To say that chemistry is, at the time, one of the most exciting sciences,[33] begs the question, for we then want to know why it is exciting, and why exciting to Schlegel. We need to know more about chemistry, for otherwise the whole charge and ambition of Schlegel's deployment of the allegory will remain obscure. As we shall see, eighteenth-century chemistry is indeed an exciting endeavor, an investigative enterprise marked by a fundamental change that requires rethinking many large issues. These issues—the status of the experi-

ment, the combinatorial conception of matter, the position of chemistry between reductionist mechanism and organicism—are precisely
ones that allow chemistry to become a model capable of registering a
strange new idea of poetic production and reception. To be more precise: chemistry can become this rich model because of the particular
manner in which these issues arise. For chemistry in the eighteenth
century is a profoundly unsettled venture: it is torn between two major explanatory paradigms, between a claim to pure science and an
ancient artisanal history, between scientific rigor and the alchemical
practices that still suffuse it. It is a science in a state of thorough
chaos, of *Mischung,* of con-fusion.[34] Yet it is precisely this unstable
flux between stable positions that recommends chemistry as a model
for aesthetic practice.

"Flux" has seemed too weak a term to historians of eighteenth-
century chemistry; the transformation it undergoes is considered so
drastic that they routinely resort to the term "revolution" in describing it. For Thomas Kuhn the replacement of the phlogiston theory of
burning with Lavoisier's oxygen-based theory of combustion is of
such far-reaching significance that he uses it, along with the innovations of Copernicus, Newton, and Einstein, as an exemplary case of
a scientific revolution, of what in his idiom is called "a change in paradigm."[35] Kuhn insists throughout his book *The Structure of Scientific
Revolutions* that such a change becomes possible not through new
discoveries or new experimental techniques (these are, he shows, the
results and not the causes of a paradigm change) but rather as a consequence of "a period of pronounced professional insecurity"
(67–68), which finds its most persistent expression in an epistemological crisis. An "awareness of anomaly" (52) in the way experimental data fit a paradigm, leading to a "proliferation of versions of a
theory" (71), creates the sort of confusion that dooms one paradigm
and prepares fertile ground for another. For the chemistry to which
Schlegel is exposed it means an utter theoretical chaos in which there
are on the one hand, as Kuhn notes, "almost as many versions of the
phlogiston theory as there were pneumatic chemists" (70), and on
the other a new theory of combustion so novel and consequential

"that after discovering oxygen Lavoisier worked in a different world" (118).

There is an anomaly about the chemical revolution that Kuhn does not point out. For the first time in the history of scientific revolutions, it seems, there is not only an "awareness of anomaly," but an awareness of the awareness of anomaly. As I. Bernard Cohen points out in his vast study of revolutions in science, the chemical is distinguished from other scientific revolutions in this crucial respect: the man with whose name it has come to be associated, Antoine-Laurent Lavoisier, not only performed revolutionary scientific innovations but also made sure to identify them as such.[36] It is the first time, Cohen tells us, that a scientist describes his *own* work in these terms, a feat all the more remarkable in that Lavoisier does so in the form, as it were, of a prophecy; when he notes that his work is destined to unleash "a revolution in physics and chemistry,"[37] the year is only 1773 (and Lavoisier only thirty), and his revolutionary work still lies almost entirely in the future. What interests me is not the impressive immodesty displayed by Lavoisier, but rather the fact that performance and self-description are as much a feature of the chemical revolution as they are of the "*revolution* in the field of aesthetics"[38] that Schlegel perceives himself as promoting. Quite apart from the substance of this chemical revolution, we find that the structure of its own historical self-assessment recurs in the poetological field, specifically in the way Schlegel conceives of his fragments as "an entirely new genre."[39] There is in both cases a self-conscious effort at marking an innovation *as* an innovation, a move that in its self-reflexivity is itself innovative, both in chemistry (as Cohen shows) and in poetics (as we saw in the previous chapter).

The identification of certain innovations in poetics and chemistry in the late eighteenth century as revolutionary gains in weight—or at least in ambition—when they are linked with the other, far better known French Revolution. This is precisely what Lavoisier does[40] (though it does not save him from being guillotined during the Reign of Terror for the crime of being a landowner). Even though the evidence for a link between chemical and political ferment in France is inconclusive, many of Lavoisier's contemporaries, Schlegel among them, assume it: the combination of chemistry and revolution, mediated by gunpowder, is simply too potent to be resisted.[41] Thus when *Athenäum* fragment 426 (quoted more fully above) suggests that the French "are a chemical nation," that revolutions are consequently "not organic but chemical," Schlegel is making a point neither obscure to his contemporary readers nor particularly original. The asserted bond between the political and scientific projects allows him silently to align his "*new School,*"[42] via the analogy to chemistry, with a political revolution. The way this alignment operates, and the consequences it has for a (often silently held) political conception in Schlegel's work, will concern us in chapter 6.

In what does the chemical revolution consist? The answer given by traditional historians of science[43] is that while Georg Ernst Stahl, the inventor of the notion of phlogiston, and his followers believe that substances *release* phlogiston while burning, Lavoisier would have burning substances *bind* oxygen, discarding phlogiston on the dustbin of the history of science. This does not sound like much, but in effect it occasions a complete reconceptualization of the notion of matter itself. (Lavoisier may have been immodest, but he was certainly not mistaken about the impact of his theories.) The new view turns the conception of simple and compound substances on its head: a substance that Lavoisier (and we) would call a metal is to the supporters of the phlogiston theory a compound of what they call calx and phlogiston; burning causes it to be purified. Lavoisier by contrast proposes the opposite: a metal is a simple element that is turned, in burning, into a compound he calls an oxide.

The reinterpretation of the process of combustion requires the very elements of chemistry—literally and figuratively—to be ordered anew. For the new conception no longer permits the notion, maintained by philosophers, alchemists, and chemists since antiquity, that all matter consists of admixtures of four elements joined by attraction and sundered by repulsion (or, as Empedocles would have it, by love and hate, thus anthropomorphizing matter in a way that turned out to have great resonance for Goethe). In fact, demonstrating that the ancient elements are really compounds becomes in the latter part of the eighteenth century a spectacle with important repercussions: on June 24, 1783, an august gathering in Paris, including the king himself, witnesses how Lavoisier and a collaborator open the faucets on a hydrogen and an oxygen tank, allowing the two "airs" to mingle, and then proceed to collect a few drops of water in a funnel. Far from being considered a gimmick, synthesizing water becomes "the decisive element" in winning skeptics over to the new theory.[44]

Yet Lavoisier puts more on display than merely an experiment demonstrating the fact that water is not an element but a compound; in a sense he also demonstrates the very demonstrative power of experimentation as such. For the epistemological force of the experiment is only as great as the willingness of observers to accepts its results as evidence. No doubt such force of evidence owes a great deal to improvements in the technical control of reactions. Thanks to more acute experimental technology, two other elements besides water held to be indivisible since Hellenism—earth and air—are shown to be compounds; only fire (now called caloric) is still considered an indivisible substance. Its improved experiments force chemistry to take a path not usually associated with scientific progress: rather than ending up with fewer elements, researchers keep coming up with more: Lavoisier lists thirty-three in his main work, the *Traité élémentaire de chimie* (Elementary Treatise on Chemistry), published in 1789;[45] two years later, in one of the early examples of how a German audience was introduced to the advances in France, the young chemist Christoph Girtanner names thirty-six "undivided bodies";[46] in 1807, Klaproth already claims fifty-one elements, albeit some with question marks.[47] As a result, for Lavoisier and his like-minded contemporaries there is nothing ontological about the notion of an element. An element is an element when chemists fail to divide it further; it is as simple, and as pragmatic, as that. When confronted with the issue of the "real" elements of matter, Lavoisier displays the impatience typical of a true empiricist:

All that can be said upon the number and nature of elements is, in my opinion, confined to discussions entirely of a metaphysical nature. . . . [I]f, by the term elements, we mean to express those simple and indivisible atoms of which matter is composed, it is extremely probable we know nothing at all about them; but if, by contrast, we apply the term elements, or principles of bodies, to express our idea of the last point at which analysis arrives, all substances that we have not yet been able to analyze [*décomposer*] by any means are, for us, elements.[48]

Elements, then, are no longer deduced but rather *made* through experimentation—which implies that through further experiments they may also be *un*made. On this point too, Lavoisier is abundantly clear, for he continues:

Not that we are entitled to affirm that these substances we consider as simple may not be compounded of two or even a greater number of principles; but, since these principles are never divided, or rather since we have no means of dividing them, they act with respect to us as simple substances, and we ought never to suppose them compounded until experiment and observation have proved them to be so. (1:xvi–xviii / xxiv)

The experiment—rather than theological or philosophical authority—becomes the ultimate arbiter of what is considered to be an elementary substance. Thus when Girtanner calls elements "undivided" (*unzersetzte*)—as distinct from indivisible—bodies, he quietly substitutes for the ontological claims about primary substances in natural philosophy the epistemological modesty of empirical chemistry: *thus far* they have remained undivided, but what the future holds nobody knows. By the turn of the century, this view has become largely entrenched among German chemists. "The only referee [in the question of elements] is experience, and we must stop at its judgments," Klaproth declares in the *Chemisches Wörterbuch* (Chemical Dictionary) he published together with Friedrich Wolff in 1807. "It is important, however, to regard this side of our edifice of research as open."[49] (And rightly so: the number of elements keeps climbing;

by June 2001, 112 had been shown to exist, some of which occur only in laboratories for fleeting fractions of a second.)[50]

The concept of the experiment—of *Versuch* or essay—plays a crucial role in Schlegel's reconfiguration of poetics. It permits him to develop a conception of (poetic) language that is not anchored in ontological certainty but is, like the elements of chemistry, constitutively open to expansion. New linguistic arrangements arrive not ex nihilo, but as the results of new combinations (which can occur in unpredictable and spontaneous ways). But Schlegel's experiments engage not only poetological or aesthetic questions; they can be understood at the same time to intervene in the philosophical discourse of German idealism. And here, as I shall argue in the Afterword, the effects of introducing the allegory of chemistry is as corrosive for *Grundsatzphilosophie* as it is energizing in the artistic realm, and largely for the same reasons. For a reliance on experiments involves two features that must appear highly suspect to a philosophy bent on establishing foundations. First, far from anchoring itself in a single starting point, chemistry in practice begins with a multiplicity that, moreover, threatens continually to proliferate. Second, and worse still for idealist philosophy, elements are not understood ontologically but rather, as the historian of chemistry William Brock has remarked, "pragmatically and operationally";[51] they have no more than an ad hoc status, for they can lay claim to primacy only until the next experiment manages to separate them into even more basic units.

To see how the eighteenth-century conception of the element is as ill-suited as a model for foundationalist philosophy as it is well-suited for poetics, we need to look at the self-understanding and self-constitution of chemistry as a science. In an important sense the scientific breakthroughs in the late eighteenth century do not constitute a revolution *in* chemistry but a revolution *of* chemistry. They found modern chemistry in the sense of constituting an interruption in the progression of chemical knowledge: while post-Lavoisier texts are comprehensible to modern chemists without great difficulty, considerable hermeneutic labor is required for earlier works. But this perceived break (largely a result of the success in the reform of nomenclature) masks the profound *continuities* between the old and the new chemistry. It hides and is thus a symptom of the fact that "the question of the 'alchemical origins' of chemistry haunts the memory of chemists."[52] For even more important than the change of paradigms that has been the focus of theoreticians and historians of chemistry is the permanence of practices and conceptions that marks even post-revolutionary chemistry.[53] For chemistry struggles with a choice not merely, as Kuhn argues, between two *scientific* paradigms, but also between two paradigms belonging to entirely incompatible orders, one technical (artisanal, artistic), the other scientific. As the historians of science Bernadette Bensaude-Vincent and Isabelle Stengers demonstrate, the "authoritative division into two periods—the pre-scientific and the scientific ages—has not stood up to detailed analysis."[54]

We are alerted to the shadow that alchemy throws on chemistry by an imprecision (or flux) in the self-understanding of chemistry, which I glossed over earlier. While chemistry in the late eighteenth century attempts to gain equal footing with other disciplines by insisting on its scientific status, it cannot quite shake the fact that it has been and to some extent remains an art.[55] Thus, as we saw earlier, Gmelin equivocally characterizes chemistry as "the *art* of separation [*Scheidungskunst*] or the *science* of mixing [*Mischungskunde*]." Klaproth too uses precisely these terms, explicitly calling attention to the dual character of chemistry: "Chemistry is no mere speculative science but at the same time an art."[56] Wavering between these two designations is not characteristic only of chemists' own self-understanding: Johann Christoph Adelung's dictionary of 1793 defines chemistry as "the art *or* science of dissolving natural bodies . . . into their components and combining these into new products" (my emphasis).[57]

Some chemists in France boldly claim for their field the title of a science in clear contradistinction to art. Thus Lavoisier's collaborator Fourcroy declares in 1800, "Chemistry is a science distinct and separate from all others: it can no longer be mistaken for alchemy, which, even if successful, would be only one of its experiments; nor metallurgy . . . pharmacy . . . natural philosophy . . . medicine . . . nor, in short, can it be mistaken for any art."[58] Yet one cannot quite shake the impression that the fervor of this assertion signals just how mingled the two orders still are. Lavoisier himself remains far more circumspect in his assessment of the status of chemistry, venturing that only one part of chemistry is "the most susceptible, perhaps, of one day becoming an exact science: that which deals with chemical affinities or elective attractions."[59] (It was of course precisely the theory of elective affinity that was "overthrown" two decades later, in 1808, by Dalton's atomic theory.)[60] It is, above all, the failure of chemistry to submit to a mathematical model (or the failure of chemists to submit their unruly material to such a model) that leads Lavoisier to admit to confusions and contradictions in his science: "This science still has many gaps, which interrupt the series of facts, and often render it extremely difficult to reconcile them with each other. It has not, like elementary geometry, the advantage of being a complete science, whose parts are all closely connected."[61] Far more than French chemistry, German chemistry finds itself uncomfortably perched between, on the one hand, an art—a craft, a *techne*—with deep roots in alchemy and pharmacy and, on the other, a science interested not in particular products but, as Klaproth would have it, in "dividing natural bodies into their components and investigating their properties, effects and relationships against one another."[62] Thus, as the historian of science David Knight has observed, "in the 1790s, the situation of chemistry in Germany was chaotic."[63] At this point the "confused interregnum"[64] in which chemistry finds itself is thus not limited to the question of what scientific theory it should pursue but stems at least as much from the fact that it finally cannot quite extricate itself from its own history.

Between Mechanism and Organicism

The confusion in eighteenth-century chemistry—theoretical, terminological, and disciplinary confusion of the most acute sort—lends enormous mobility to the allegory of chemistry in Schlegel's writings. Yet it would be a mistake to credit chemistry merely for its failures to erect a coherent and consistent theory of matter. It seems to me that crucial conceptual achievements in eighteenth-century chemistry are as important as its failures in making the science into a reservoir of images and concepts from which Schlegel's poetics can draw. I have in mind here the series of theoretical and experimental steps that distance eighteenth-century chemistry from vitalist conceptions, on the one hand, and from reductionist mechanics on the other. This is an achievement at a theoretical level so deep that it remains largely untouched by the battles raging around the chemical "revolution"; it marks a slow shift in practices and attitudes that takes most of the century to achieve.

Because the spectacular scientific successes of the sixteenth and seventeenth centuries—those of Copernicus, Kepler, Galileo, and Newton—involve a redescription of what was once a divinely animated universe in terms of what Newton calls "celestial mechanics" (in other words, a universe ruled purely by mechanical laws), the conception of a reduction of the picture of the world to springs, levers, and pulleys becomes the ideal of scientific explanation. It is to be applied not merely to falling apples and rotating planets but also to plants and animals, even to the human body itself (in 1682, the aptly named botanist Nehemiah Grew speaks of nature as "one Great Engine"). The earliest "fully and consciously developed" application of the technological model to the human organism is performed by Hieronymus Fabricius ab Aquapendente in his 1603 study *De Venarum Ostiolis* (On the Valves of the Veins).[65] It is soon extended to other features of the human body: for instance, in Harvey's mechanistic conception of the heart and the circulatory system in the early seventeenth century and culminating in La Mettrie's fully mechanized *L'Homme machine* of 1747.[66] The exemplary metaphor for this epistemological view is the clock, a device that, despite its staggering complexity, can be explained down to its last cog wheel. Thus the explanatory ideal of chemistry, like that of every other domain of knowledge, is expected to conform to the model of the clock.[67]

Robert Boyle, the great proponent of the application of the mechanical standard to chemistry (as well as to alchemy, for Boyle practiced both), seizes on the image of the clock: the world, he declares, is comparable to "a rare clock such as may be seen at Strasbourg."[68] In place of occult or hermetic accounts, he demands explanations in terms of matter and motion, for "mechanical principles and explications are for their clearness preferred."[69] To accommodate such a demand, Boyle proposes, in his *Sceptical chymist* of 1661, a conception of matter that rings remarkably modern: "I now mean by 'elements' . . . certain primitive and simple, or perfectly unmingled bodies; which not being made of any other bodies, or of one another, are the ingredients, of which all those called perfectly mixt bodies are immediately compounded, and into which they are ultimately resolved."[70] Some historians have taken this to be a "revolutionary reconceptualization" of the notion of the element.[71] As Boyle himself notes immediately after the lines just quoted, however, his conception of it remains in effect empty: "Now whether there be any one such body . . . of those, that are said to be elemented bodies, is the thing I now question." For in order to be "primitive and simple bodies, or perfectly unmingled bodies," in order to conform to strict reductionist prescriptions, Boyle's elements cannot display any qualitative differences (for then the question would arise of how those qualities would be accounted for in an indivisible body); he imagines his elements, or corpuscles, as a uniform and simple matter, bereft of differences. The historian of science William Brock has made the distinction between Boyle's conception of the element and the modern one admirably clear: "To Boyle, materials such as gold, iron and copper were not elements, but aggregates of a common matter differentiated by the number, size, shape and structural pattern of their agglomerations."[72]

In the absence of a sophisticated theory of atoms, such a view leads to odd ideas about how matter is ultimately constituted. Descartes, for example, whose ideas, while mechanistic, differ from Boyle's, imagines that indivisible particles come in three shapes, massive and solid, long and thin, and irregular.[73] The seventeenth-century chemist Nicolas Lémery similarly conceives of acids, for example, as being composed of sharp-tipped particles; the more pointed the tip, he argues in his *Cours de chymie* of 1675, the more sharply the particles will prick the tongue, hence the more acidic the substance will seem.[74] To twentieth-century observers who have come to see scientific reductionism as the quintessence of rigor it may seem odder still that the corpuscular (or atomistic) idea of matter is—and is understood by many of its proponents to be—perfectly compatible with alchemy. Boyle's and Newton's extensive alchemical work is often treated as an embarrassment by many historians of science, yet it certainly does not violate their atomistic conception of matter. For if all matter is made of the same basic particles, arranged differently, then no fundamental reason would seem to militate against their rearrangement. It is a question of practicability whether the "primitive and simple bodies" in a piece of lead can be coaxed into a new arrangement that would give us gold.

The very reasons that make the mechanistic theory of corpuscles or atoms useful to alchemists render it almost utterly useless to eighteenth-century chemistry.[75] Thus various versions of the Aristotelian theory of the four elements and the Paracelsian theory of three principles, though having been shown inadequate by Boyle, survive in the work of chemists for almost a century after the *Sceptical chymist* is published. And for a good reason: chemists are interested in the very differences of quality between substances that Boyle's matter, being "catholic and universal," cannot accommodate. In order to conduct meaningful *chemical* experiments, scientists in the eighteenth century have to give up on a program that would have reduced chemistry to a form of mechanical physics. Thus Klaproth, having provided his listeners with a list of elements, goes on to warn them that "we may not . . . regard these as physical primary substances [*physische Urstoffe*] or elements of nature. Those exceed our concepts and can therefore not be objects of chemistry."[76] Lavoisier, as we have already seen, dismisses all talk of an unchanging and uniform primary matter as being "entirely of a metaphysical nature." Chemists in the eighteenth century neither doubt nor assume the existence of atoms (their version of the *Ding an sich*); they simply ignore them, because as an explanatory tool they are ineffective. Since they are interested in the distinct *qualitative* properties of substances, "the idea of elements rather than atoms was what came to work for chemists and separated their science from mechanics."[77] The real differentiation of chemistry as an independent science thus occurs, long before Lavoisier, in its persistent rejection of mechanism, with its assumption of a homogeneous simple matter, in favor of a (chemically) irreducible heterogeneity.[78]

Long before the eighteenth century, chemists used two different analogies for the composition of matter: substances, natural or artificial, were made of things resembling either building blocks or the alphabet.[79] These two analogies reflect two fundamentally distinct philosophical assumptions: the building block analogy assumes the ultimate sameness of the smallest particles of matter (even granting differences in geometry), while the alphabet analogy assumes their ultimate and irreducible difference. As we have seen, the increasing reliance on experimental techniques promotes the idea of material difference, for otherwise one would have to assume, as Boyle himself recognizes, "that all words consist of the same letters."[80] The steady migration of chemistry, in the course of the eighteenth century, toward a theory assuming that matter is heterogeneous as far down as the eye of the experimenter can see, as it were, strengthens the alphabet analogy, thereby moving the enterprise of chemistry closer to the verbal arts and making the former more readily available as an allegory of the latter than the mechanistic building-block theory could ever have permitted. The *tertium comparationis* around which chemistry and the alphabet pivot is the idea that a very small number of distinct entities (elements, letters) can, by means of selection and permutation, potentially yield an infinitely large number of products. While the starting point of the system (elements / letters and operational rules) may be limited, it is designed in such a way that its results are limitless.

Eighteenth-century chemistry arrives at the model of irreducibly heterogeneous elements by way of asking about the rules that operate on matter, i.e., the rules that join the letters of the chemical alphabet into word-substances. Here the crucial impetus that excites eighteenth-century chemists comes not from Boyle but, improbably, from Isaac Newton. He succeeds in asking the right—which is only to say: scientifically productive—question because of a certain slippage in his conception of mechanism. To critics such as Leibniz and Fontenelle, his "celestial mechanics" are simply not mechanical enough: instead of explaining planetary motion in terms of bouncing billiard balls, Newton introduces strange "forces of attraction" acting over vast, empty space. Yet persisting with his forces, Newton proposes to extend them from the heavenly bodies to the materials found on earth. In an appendix to his *Opticks* of 1717 he demands: "We must learn from the Phaenomena of Nature what Bodies attract one another, and what are the Laws and Properties of the Attraction, before we enquire the Cause by which the Attraction is perform'd."[81]

Attraction, also called affinity, turns out to be something chemists can work with. They had noticed sudden recombinations when two substances were mixed. Thus when (using modern terminology) two solutions of barium chloride and sodium sulfate are mixed, the substances enter into a new chiastic arrangement: barium sulfate precipitates, leaving sodium chloride in the solution.[82] To explain such behavior, the concept of attraction appears promising, provided that it is not understood in its gravitational sense: unlike physical attractions (such as gravity) that apply uniformly and evenly, chemical attractions turn out to be temperamental, unpredictable, and puzzling. The recombinations between substances occur with varying degrees of intensity; they can be observed between some substances but not between others; at times the recombination is complete, at other times there are substantial leftovers from the original combinations. In other words: attraction describes substances *chemically,* expressing all their qualitative idiosyncrasies. It is with this special understanding of attraction that the Newtonian program sets into motion a century-long quest to identify "the Laws and Properties of that Attraction," a quest that both predates and survives the chemical "revolution" (recall Lavoisier's hope of rendering the theory of affinity into an "exact science"), because it permits a specifically chemical (i.e., nonmechanical) research project.

This brief historical review not only provides us with a more nuanced view of the development of the sciences, but, more important, allows us to glimpse chemistry's suitability as an allegory of poetics. Such suitability must remain suspicious for as long as *any* commerce between romanticism and the sciences is seen in the context of the deeply held—and largely correct—idea, articulated by the historians of science Andrew Cunningham and Nicholas Jardine, that many of Goethe's contemporaries "turned against what they perceived as the soul-less mechanical natural philosophy of the Enlightenment."[83] This claim varies in one minor but crucial respect from a view widely held among literary scholars, a view lucidly and forcefully advanced by Hans Eichner, one of the foremost scholars of romanticism in general and of Schlegel in particular. Recall that for him, "Romanticism is, perhaps predominantly, a desperate rearguard action against the spirit and the implications of modern science."[84] While Cunningham and Jardine speak of romanticism as a turn against "*mechanical* natural philosophy," Eichner makes a far more general claim about romanticism as a turn against "modern science" *tout cours.* For Eichner, as for many other (nonscientist) critics, science *is* mechanics, and all science, ultimately, a version of physics. Thus, he claims, "biology has been reduced almost entirely to a subbranch of physics and chemistry, and chemistry, where it is more than a craft or a collection of rules of thumb, *is* mathematical physics" (10). This assessment, which would come as a surprise to most contemporary biologists and chemists, rests on the belief, advanced by logical positivism, that the only good explanation of the world is strictly mechanistic, which is to say reductionist.

Once the only legitimate form of science is taken to be mechanics, any anti*mechanistic* turn immediately becomes guilty also of being anti*scientific,* a "rearguard action against the spirit and the implications of modern science." Thus the romantics, having been shown to have rejected the only tenable scientific program, i.e., mechanism, have no choice in such a narrative but to propose mechanism's opposite number, namely organicism. Eichner is again admirably explicit: "Machines do not grow, organisms do. Schelling and other Romantics not only replaced the 'static' world of earlier thought by an evolving one but exchanged the mechanistic assumptions associated with modern science for an equally sweeping organicism" (15). My point here is not to contest that (the young) Schelling and certain romantic scientists (men like Oken, Carus, Ritter, and Steffens) view nature as an organism—they plainly do—nor that this view can be found, often in less coherent forms, in the writings of Goethe, Novalis, Coleridge, Keats, Wordsworth, and Schlegel—it can—but merely that organicism does not offer the only possible alternative in a turn against mechanism.

As we have seen, eighteenth-century chemistry constitutes such a non-, even antimechanistic practice. It does so not because of an inherent irrationalism or animus against science, but precisely insofar as it founds and differentiates itself *as* a science. It is, in other words, possible to give up an adherence to mechanism without therefore having to embrace its "opposite," organicism. It is also, by analogy or by allegory, possible to give up a rule-bound and mechanical poetics (such as, for instance, Boileau's) without therefore being obliged to defend a view of the artwork as an organism. Chemistry—and this, I believe, is the main attraction it holds for those parts of Schlegel's writings that experiment with a new conception of the artwork—provides the concepts and images that situate it just *between* mechanism and organicism: the theory of attraction, anthropomorphic and unevenly applied as it is, breaches a gap with mechanism, endowing the elements with a simulacrum of life and volition. At the same time, mechanism has not been entirely evaded, for the manifestations of attraction—combination and recombination—ultimately rely on a process of mechanical substitution, even if its precise logic remains shrouded in mystery. Combinatorial logic—separation and recombination—is conceptually antithetical to organicism, for it permits no passage of time for growth and development, for *Bildung*.[85] Notionally, combinations are instantaneous and, as we shall see, to some extent chaotic, which is why they stand in sharp contrast to the organic notion of metamorphosis.

Eighteenth-century chemistry, then, whether pre- or postrevolutionary, harbors at its core two linked concepts—attraction and combination—that refuse to be fit into either mechanical (soulless, dead) or organicist (vital, "poetic") accounts of nature. They are chemistry's own, permitting it to move precariously between the two older, philosophically well-entrenched realms. Attraction and combination are the concepts that, as we shall see, energize Schlegel's poetological experiments.

4

"Theory of the Combinatorial Method" of Poetry

Experimental Art

In chapter 2, I argued that Schlegel's early writings—in their themes, but also and far more urgently in their formal arrangement as self-declared fragments—carry on a sustained discussion and transformation of key aesthetic concepts. In chapter 3, we saw how the same writings—again both thematically and, to a far more pertinent degree, formally—emulate a process and a logic found in eighteenth-century chemistry. We can now begin to join these two strands and consider how, once it has been invoked as an allegory, chemistry acts upon self-descriptions of the poetic process, of the writing and reading of verbal artworks. As we shall see, *combination* and *attraction*, encouraged to unfold their force within the frame of the *experiment*, are the ways that chemistry exerts its effects on poetry. It is in the peculiar mixture of these concepts that we find the most innovative features of Schlegel's poetic theory, features that anticipate later developments in poetic theory by many decades.

Schlegel himself is quite aware of the connection between innovation and chemical metaphors. "I must constitute an entirely new method," he notes, and specifies it as a "theory of the combinatorial method."[1] He may have failed at explicitly constructing such a method (or theory of method), yet I believe that we can glean such a method—and not merely its outlines or traces—from his writing practice, which is most vividly experimental, as I have noted, not in those instances in which it conforms to genres traditionally taken to be poetic, but rather in the odd in-between cases where a genre is, as it were, created for the purpose: the fragment, the notebook entry, the essay. The chemical model turns out to be particularly well-suited to providing both a description and an explanation of many of the idiosyncratic features of Schlegel's fragmentary writing noted earlier: its willful incompletion, the strange link it maintains to what Schlegel calls the system, the coyness with which it withholds meaning (and pleasure), its habit of appearing in the plural, and the strange way it is permeated with voices—authorial voices but also disembodied, ghostly voices. These seemingly disconnected elements gather into a form, I think, if we understand them as being effects of a large-scale process of experimentation in combinatorial writing, one of whose features is admittedly to undo the consistency of form itself. In this sense, chemistry is not presented here as a new all-encompassing hermeneutic model, replacing models such as organicism and infinite approximation, but is rather an account of the very appearance of hermeneutic failure in reading Schlegel. It attempts to describe the incomprehensibility in *ver-*, and in describing it, comprehend the operational mode of incomprehensibility.

To what extent Schlegel intentionally sets out to perform his own writings as experiments cannot be said. There is certainly a lot of evidence that he regards the experiment as a crucial procedure in implementing what he calls the combinatorial method in both philosophy and in poetry. During his Jena lectures on transcendental philosophy in 1800–1801, for example, he claims: "The sphere of the combinatorial spirit is quite undetermined. But there must be a method according to which one can proceed. This method will be experimentation. Whoever proceeds according to this method can permit himself to perform the most daring experiments [*Versuche*]. He will certainly encounter reality."[2] The term *Versuch* appears frequently in his early writings; as I noted earlier, its polysemy (*experiment,* but also *essay*) implicitly—at times even explicitly—links experimentation with the practice of writing. That Fichte's *Wissenschaftslehre* (Science of Logic) is thus "nothing but an experiment" Schlegel considers to be "very true."[3] Or rather it, like every essay worthy of its name, is not one experiment but a whole series of experiments, indeed the process of experimentation itself, for "the essay [is] not *one* experiment, but a constant experimentation."[4] Thus his own writings in the *Athenäum* are "the whole chain of my experiments,"[5] which address, as we by now know, among other issues the question of whether "this reciprocal communication of ideas . . . is at all possible": "Where would one have a better opportunity of conducting some experiments about the possibility or impossibility of this matter than when writing a journal like the *Athenäum,* or taking part in it as a reader?"[6] Conducting experiments, then, is a possibility open to writers *and* readers. Schlegel provides us with a quasi-scientific account of what earlier I vaguely called the "openness" (or, even more vaguely, the "infinity") of the artwork. The poem can now be imagined as a textual laboratory in which both writer and reader are permitted (indeed, required) to conduct experiments. Even if we cannot be certain what sort of experiments the writer has in mind, we have his explicit permission to conduct our own. What follows, then, is an experiment in reading some of Schlegel's writings as elements of "eternally dividing and mixing forces." I shall begin at a high level of textual organization, that of genre, and steadily tighten the focus of my analysis, from fragment collections to the individual fragment to show the strange workings of his combinatorial experiments. In the following chapter, I will telescope things down to the smallest unit of writing, the level of the letter, where Schlegel's laboratory of poetry attempts what I take to be its most daring experiments.

We have seen how metaphors of mixing and of dividing pervade Schlegel's prose. But of far greater consequence, I want to argue, is the point at which the *metaphoric* employment of these key chemical operations folds back, as it were, upon the writing itself, when the operations find their *literal* realization in Schlegel's words and sentences. In short, I am interested in those areas of Schlegel's work where the logic of chemistry becomes an allegory not only of the ostensible *topic* of the writing but of its very *form,* the practice of writing itself. Yet imagining the mixture of poetry and philosophy as chemical does not necessarily mean that texts aspiring to such mixing—such as Schlegel's—would themselves act chemically. A self-*description* is not the same thing as a self-referential *performance.* The latter is more ambitious and more difficult; it runs a far greater risk of failure. It is at such a performance that Schlegel's writing aims.

One of the places where the model of contemporary chemistry can be said to motivate Schlegel's writing practice is in his choice of genre. Before 1804, he rarely wedges his writing into a strictly delimited genre, preferring instead elastic forms that permit the motley presence of fictional and nonfictional, imaginative and intellectual elements. "The romantic imperative demands the mixture of all genres,"[7] he declares importantly, and, mixing his chemical metaphors in his enthusiasm for mixtures, adds: "In true romantic prose all elementary parts must be fused to the point of mutual saturation."[8] His reviews, essays, "characteristics," and fragments of the *Athenäum* period willfully violate the neat categorizations of classical and neoclassical poetics.[9] A crucial reason why the novel enjoys such high standing in much of his poetological writings is that he "can hardly imagine a novel as anything but a mixture of narration, song, and other forms,"[10] as a character remarks in the "Conversation on Poetry," itself a text that straddles the divide between fiction and truth, literature and philosophy. (Schlegel's own work amply demonstrates that mixing genres does not in and of itself make good literature: his novel *Lucinde* is a thoroughly mixed, and wholly wretched, piece of writing.)

The countervailing forces of bonding and of division come to a head with maximum intensity in the "entirely new" genre Schlegel invents for his work, namely the fragments. Fragments of course result from a process of division, partly understood as a willful removal of everything that is not ab-solutely—which is to say indissolubly—essential, and partly understood as an accidental fracture from a whole (the fragments as "chaos").[11] Yet for all their singular separateness, they cannot be imagined in the singular, and we know why: if their structure is to correspond "very precisely to natural philosophy"[12] so that they become "chemical fragments,"[13] they must engage in constant commerce with one another.

For Schlegel this means an almost obsessive interest in the material form of the fragments on the printed page. Having implored friends and relatives to produce fragments by plundering their store of letters, essays, and notes (KA 24:67 and 91), he insists that what appears to be a hodge-podge somehow forms itself into an indivisible ensemble. Such an ensemble, he reasons, stands in no need of explanation or transition to guide the reader, for it will yield a readily discernible unity by itself (KA 24:97). He repeatedly argues against splitting up the collection of fragments into two issues of the *Athenäum* (e.g., KA 24:64), warning that it would result in the "dismemberment of *a whole*."[14] "The epideixis of universality," as he likes to call the presentation of the romantic ideal that the fragments aspire to, "and the symphonism of the fragments would suffer formal destruction through the real abstraction . . . of the Whole into two parts,"[15] he writes his brother, a proponent of spreading the fragments over several issues of the journal, lest the reader find them too much.[16] Friedrich is driven by two impulses that are doubtless contradictory, and, given the logic of chemistry, necessarily so: on the one hand, his interest lies in pure numbers, in the sheer quantity of the fragments—"How beautiful they are one by one, and how much more so the whole mass,"[17] he exclaims about a new batch of fragments from August Wilhelm. On the other hand, the result of this open-ended, entirely fluid process of mass production (which is also the production of a mass) becomes, once bonded, a Whole. Some of his fragments are "member[s] of a mass that cannot be divided," he writes, and adds in exasperation: "These damn things really do hang together."[18]

Objective Irony

The elective affinity that Schlegel registers in the fragments derives not merely from a vaguely felt certainty that his writings, deep down, form a unity, but from the way in which the chemistry of analysis and synthesis operates on the syntactic structure and semantic composition of the fragments. We have noted that many of the fragments, especially those found in the posthumously published notebooks, follow the syntax "x is (or is a version of) y," where y neither belongs to the familiar range of the meanings of x, nor entails it, nor is entailed by it. One example (and not an entirely innocent one, as we shall see): "Irony is the form of what is paradoxical. Paradox is everything that is at once good and great."[19] The fragment's entire force is drawn from the juxtaposition—Schlegel would say: the combinatorial quality—of the terms *irony, paradox, good and great,* and, to a lesser extent, *form.* If the juxtaposition is experienced as unexpected yet fortuitous, the newly joined terms will release in the reader a perceptible amount of cognitive energy—a quickening of attention, a ripple of pleasure, heightened curiosity. If it jars, however, the reader might experience a negatively charged energy, an irritation or exasperation, and might look elsewhere for an answer to his or her bewilderment. The fragments are indeed, as Gerhard Neumann has said, "experiments in definition,"[20] especially if we take the notion of "experiment" literally.

But is Schlegel's poetic-philosophical experimentation, his knack for putting oddly matched ideas into a sentence and shaking vigorously, structurally different from what any writer of good aphorisms does? I think it is, and for one simple reason: almost all of his experiments, taken in isolation, fail. Rarely in the fragments do we hear the satisfying sound of two unrelated ideas clicking into a new and surprising shape. Since this pleasure is not (or is only infrequently) provided within each fragment, we can look outside, extending our search—and the chemical account—beyond the individual fragment to the whole ensemble. For the Schlegelian peculiarity—and the feature that makes aphorisms into fragments—lies in the fact that the combinatorial method operates not only horizontally but also vertically, both within and between units of writing. There may be various ways in which we understand the idea that "irony" is the "form of what is paradoxical"; whatever those different ways may be, they will not remain unchanged once we recognize that both elements in the statement stand in a long series of equivalencies. Irony, for example, is also "logical beauty,"[21] and beauty is identified as "one of the original modes of action of the human spirit,"[22] which in turn is nothing but "inner sociability."[23] Sociability, we know from the already quoted *Athenäum* fragment 426, has "a chemical nature" which it shares with "the novel, criticism, [and] wit." A chemical nature is not the only thing that sociability and wit share, for wit itself is defined as "absolutely sociable spirit,"[24] or (as we already know) "an explosion of bound spirit."[25] We could continue this series, and we would keep finding ways in which one side or the other of the same equation ("*x* is *y*," or "*x* has *y* as its essence") is filled with different semantic content, as if to test, as in the experiments of combinatorial chemistry, whether perchance what Schlegel, referring to witty bons mots, calls "surprising contingency"[26] might yield a pair that releases a new meaning or forms a new stable connection. We can also find the reverse experiment: the same word or group of words is plugged repeatedly into different syntactic forms, trying out new configurations.

Without stretching the usefulness of these concepts too much, we can say that the combinatorial logic of chemistry, as used by Schlegel, is isomorphic with Roman Jakobson's notion of *selection* and *combination* as the two cardinal features of linguistic structure. Selection runs along the paradigmatic axis of language and operates according to similarity (hence the basis for metaphor), while combination moves along the syntagmatic axis and operates according to contiguity (hence the basis for metonymy).[27] In chemical writing (as in Jakobsonian language), each term derives its significance *both* through the series of other terms that could take its place (selection) *and* from its place in the configuration to which it belongs (combination), both of which are subject to constant change. The analogy between the two models becomes even more strikingly evident when we consider the special treatment that Jakobson accords poetic language, the area of language that attracts Schlegel's greatest attention. In Jakobson's view, a poetic effect is created when the criteria usually reserved for the paradigmatic axis of selection are projected onto the syntagmatic axis of contiguity, when, in other words, it matters greatly which of the many possible terms that can occupy a syntactic slot is chosen to take its place next to a word chosen with equally great care.[28] When discussing the criteria according to which poets make such selections, Jakobson resorts to interestingly vague language. He detects "a semantic propinquity" between rhyming units that exceeds their similarity in sound (367), a propinquity that cannot be quite explained, except in an anthropomorphic vocabulary by now well familiar to us: "In a [poetic] sequence, where similarity is superimposed on contiguity, two similar phonemic sequences near to each other *are prone* to assume a paronomastic function. Words similar in sound *are drawn together* in meaning" (371, my emphasis). What do we have here but a linguistic theory of elective affinity, a thesis about the strange chemistry between words that has led some to believe that "words often understand themselves better than do those by whom they are used."[29]

Having concluded that the one true sentence, the *Grundsatz* sought by philosophy, cannot be uttered, Schlegel maniacally produces more and more elements and tries more and more new combinations, not so much in the hope of finding the One valid definition that will anchor everything else, nor in the belief that the truth would, as it were, bubble to the surface by itself; rather, the entire energy of the writing is channeled into the *process* of "persistent experimentation" itself, where (if anywhere) the truth would be found.

But what of the definitional experiment with the concept of irony? The fragment promising a definition—"Irony is the form of what is paradoxical. Paradox is everything that is at once good and great"—did not, it seemed, get us any closer to an understanding of the idea. Nor did the equivalencies or near-equivalencies ("logical beauty," "inner sociability," "chemical nature") throw light on what irony might be. And we have reason to suspect that continuing the series by sub-

stituting ever more terms would not help. For the series takes us neither backwards nor, for that matter, forward to a gold standard of
meaning. All we find is more fragments, more experiments, more
provisional definitions. And each new experiment can either plug a
new element into the initial syntactic structure (i.e., substitute z for
y to yield "x is z"), or it can attempt to vary the syntax itself ("x depends on y when z is the case"). Since the shape of each configuration
is endlessly malleable (changing as elements are added or subtracted),
the meaning of its elements remains in flux.

Has the entire exercise of writing and reading fragments about
irony and the series of terms with which it has reacted been pointless?
Are we where we started? Not quite. To say that "irony is chemical ingeniousness"[30] or a "universal experiment,"[31] while not offering a definition we could take home, points exactly to the *operational* aspect
of irony. It shows us not what irony *is,* but what it *does:* to defer the
achievement of meaning by at least one step, to send us down a false
semantic path, to introduce a swerve or interruption in the path leading from statement to meaning. We have, without perhaps realizing
it, learned quite a bit about irony. It seems we were looking in the
wrong place: we were searching vainly for the concept of irony in the
semantic content of the definitional series, and now find that the operation of irony was on display in the weird progression of the series
all along. The copula "is" in the "x is y" syntax of Schlegel's "experiments in definition" does not quite reward us with the certainty of
essence we expected of it, for the "definition" of irony resides not in
the predication ("is y") but rather in the skewed and unreliable manner in which "is" itself works. But we cannot claim Schlegel did not
warn us: "Irony is the form of what is paradoxical." The trouble is
that we cannot *grasp* this form but can merely observe the process by
which it eludes our grasp. And *that* turns out to be the best definition
of irony we can hope for: one that speaks of the operation while performing it on itself.

This operational aspect is true not of the definition of irony alone,
but, in Schlegel's account, of definitions per se: "A definition that is
not witty"—i.e., chemical, combinatorial, surprisingly contingent—

"isn't worth anything, and for every individual"—we might substitute: for every substance that cannot further be divided, for every element—"there are infinitely many real definitions."[32] Which is to say: instead of finite definitions, we can only hope for bon mots, "the best [of which] are *echappées de vue* into the infinite."[33] Since it is impossible to define irony positively—since, in Paul de Man's words, "irony is no longer a trope but the undoing of the deconstructive allegory of all tropological cognitions, the systematic undoing . . . of understanding"[34]—Schlegel defines it via the irony in the form of definition itself.

Syntax and semantics, process and elements, then, are not separable; they fold into one another, they affect each other. Schlegelian definitions do not consist of a syntactic algorithm that processes a particular semantic content, but present us with an operation that performs the definition as it spells it out. Thus we find that the very form of definition has been skewed by the idea—irony—that is to be defined. When syntax and semantics cannot be neatly held apart and the operandum begins to operate on the operation, furnishing a strictly formalist account of a system is rendered impossible, for it is irreducibly infected by its own materiality.[35] In the terms of *Athenäum* fragment 238, we are given "that which produces with the product."

The meaning of irony we find in the process of material coupling and uncoupling that frustrated our original search for meaning consists of a constant movement *away* from where we would expect the process to go. (Here we find the very sort of mobility to which Hegel objects with such vehemence.) This is what I take Schlegel's strange phrase "irony of irony"[36] in the essay "On Incomprehensibility" to mean: irony (like *ver-*) not only *participates* in the infinite chain of witty definitions eluding us, but also, doubling back on itself, *names* the strange path taken by this chain. It is not the sort of irony an author can decide to employ or omit; rather it is what Walter Benjamin in his *Concept of Criticism* has called the "ironization of form."[37] Benjamin distinguishes this form of ironization, which "presents an objective moment in the work" (ibid.) and "stems from the spirit of art, not from the will of the artist" (85/164), from the subjective form of irony which is indebted only to the artist's intention. The objectivity in the form of irony that Benjamin emphasizes coincides precisely with the external, unpredictable, contingent logic of writing that the present analysis has been foregrounding in the chemical allegory.

Thinking of objective irony as an effect of a materially imagined chemical system (in which the material elements of the text are agents of division and mixture) makes a redemption of such irony difficult, if not impossible. Far from emanating from a higher spirit, it simply results from a system with certain rules of operation, a system, furthermore, that can at any moment go awry (as the attempt at producing a definition of irony demonstrates). Yet redeeming it is precisely what Benjamin proceeds to do. His "spirit of art," from which the ironization of form stems, turns out to be another will, indeed a will of a higher kind, thanks to which "the relative unity of the individual work is thrust back deeper into the unity of art as universal work" (86/164). An ironic artist might seem to destroy the very coherence of his work, but that is only an illusion; on a higher level, Benjamin believes, this incoherent, shattered, fragmentary work "draws its indestructible subsistence" (ibid.) from the sphere of objective irony: "The ironization of the form of presentation is, as it were, the storm that raises [*aufhebt*] the curtain on the transcendental order of art, disclosing this order and in it the immediate existence of the work as a mystery. The work is not, as Herder regarded it, essentially a revelation and a mystery of creative genius . . .; it is a mystery of order, the revelation of its absolute dependence on the idea of art, its eternal, indestructible sublation [*Aufgehobensein*] in that idea" (86/164–65). With his storm announcing the day of revelation, his disorder sublated into a higher, transcendent, and eternal order, his disclosure of mystery, Benjamin broaches the sphere of religion long before the Schlegelian text does so. The real mystery and revelation lies in the ready availability of his dialecticizing move. For as we have seen, on both metaphoric and literal levels (as allegory and as performance), the model of romantic poetry with which Schlegel experiments at this time does not require a dialectical sublation; understood in its most far-reaching implications, it does not even permit one. Not only does it not produce a "transcendental order" capable of revealing a mystery and guaranteeing the indestructibility of art; it is capable of the most thoroughgoing *dis*order. There is no evidence of a higher spirit guiding the eternal forces of division and mixture, and were there one, it would be as likely to be a demon as an angel.

If the "revolution in the field of aesthetics"[38] that produces romantic poetry—and the blueprint for all literature committed to artistic innovation—lies in this mix-and-match technique, then we could not have moved further away from the conventional notion of romantic poetry. Instead of the genius in whose generous light the poem grows like a flower, becoming the symbol for the ineffable absolute, Schlegel presents us with a model in which the poet's quest for meaning can only find expression by means of a disembodied combinatorics. Because expressions are not generated by the data processing system alone, but rather by an intervention of embodied thought (itself formed and deformed by external symbolic systems) in that disembodied order, the result is subject to "surprising contingency," to what Schlegel calls "the glimmer of error and of madness, or of obtuseness and of stupidity."[39] If romantic poetry consists of an overflow, then it is not Wordsworth's spontaneous overflow of powerful feelings, but an overflow of selections and combinations. Is this not an instance of the "excess of thought" that Blanchot has ascribed to Jena romanticism?[40] Does it not arise when the machinelike mechanism of the "combinatorics of thought" (e.g., language) intrudes upon our most private thoughts, an alien thought whose position we could never occupy but whose operations drive our process of intellection? And does this externality of thought within thought (which psychoanalysis has termed the unconscious) not get exacerbated when thought means to express itself? For to be communicated, it must again interact with an abstract and external system (e.g., writing). This combination of human and nonhuman elements (which themselves are not strictly distinguishable) gives rise to that unpredictable excess of which Blanchot speaks.

The logic of chemical writing does not render the genius and his flower impossible, only incomplete; at any moment, the two can find themselves in an altogether different configuration that they have neither anticipated nor intended. Indeed, rather than discarding the notion of genius, we may prefer to think of it as the capacity of exposing one's writing to the hazards inherent in writing. Blanchot's sentence that "fragmentary writing is risk, it would seem: risk itself,"[41] may be less bathetic than it first seems if we understand it to describe the sort of exposure to contingency and meaninglessness that Schlegel's early writings constantly court. Combinatorial chemistry, far from canceling the possibility of the poetic work, provides the means for imagining it in new and vastly amplified ways. "Through the chemical view, nature turns into appearance," Schlegel notes; "at first glance, this puts a stop to the enthusiasm of poetry. Looked at more closely, it provides a great foundation."[42]

Combinatorial Chaos

Schlegel's name for the agent that is responsible for the task of mixing—of combining—writing at all levels is *Witz,* wit. Etymologically related to *Wissen* (knowledge) and thus to *Wissenschaft, Witz* is the agency of this haphazardly knowledge-producing method. In his lectures *Die Entwicklung der Philosophie in zwölf Büchern* (The Development of Philosophy in Twelve Books), Schlegel defines wit as "the faculty of discovering similarities between objects that are otherwise independent, different, and separate, thus binding"—or bonding, *verbinden*—"what is most manifold, what is most different into a unity," calling it simply "combinatorial spirit."[43] But this spirit, far from being quietly methodical, does its work with a good deal of violence. Since wit is an "explosion of bound spirit," its occurrence in the mind "can elicit brilliant sparks and luminescent lightning, or smashing thunderbolts."[44] If Schlegel identifies it with the *ars combinatoria*—and he does[45]—then it is a thoroughly chemical combinatorics he has in mind, for "wit is universal chemistry"[46] because it makes use of a combinatorial method tainted by the force of chemical bonding. If "the true method of philosophy were a combinatorial analysis"[47] (a richly paradoxical notion, as we shall see in a moment), then Schlegel makes clear that this combinatorics is nothing but a more generalized, abstracted version of the chemical model of eternal division and fusion. In a book on Lessing he writes: "It is this combinatorial quality that I . . . have called scientific wit. Without universality, it cannot emerge, for only where a plenitude of heterogeneous substances are united can new chemical combinations and their permeations occur."[48] Choosing chemistry as the guiding metaphor for this sort of combination—sudden, violent, unpredictable—will no doubt seem melodramatic to professional chemists, yet it expresses, perhaps in somewhat exaggerated form, the essential characteristics of chemical bonding as it is understood by the late eighteenth century. For as we have seen, the only reason chemists require the notion of chemical, or elective, attraction is because they are deeply puzzled about why substance A will bond with B but not with the seemingly similar C (or with B only in the presence of D, or in the absence of E, etc.). This unaccountability, while preserving the basically mechanical logic of selection and substitution that defines combinations, is what is fruitfully deployed in Schlegel's poetological theory.[49]

Should we conclude that Schlegel's true innovation in aesthetics lies in bringing to bear on poetry a combinatorial method gleaned from chemistry, then we will only have repeated what he himself diagnosed in hindsight. I cite more fully the notebook entry of 1812 that I briefly quoted above: "The new poetry or so-called *new School* corresponds very precisely to natural philosophy. It was a *revolution* in the field of aesthetics. This is where romantic poetry as a combinatorial and universal kind belongs."[50] Here Schlegel identifies and interconnects the crucial elements of what I have been arguing: that what is truly new in the "new School" of romanticism derives from the allegorical relationship poetry maintains with "natural philosophy" (which not only includes chemistry but is in his work best exemplified by chemistry); that such innovation reverberates in aesthetics; that the quality leading to such a "revolution" is to be found in the combinatorial process borrowed from chemistry, which in turn entails poetry's universality. Schlegel's assessment is all the more valuable for the fact that it does not occur in the heady days of the *Athenäum* (the days of "sublime impudence," of the "entirely new genre," of the ambition to become, along with his brother, "the critical dictators of Germany"),[51] but comes, in a private notebook entry with no need for public posturing, more than a decade later, long after his conversion to Catholicism and after he has jettisoned many of the very advances he judges here.[52]

The idea of an incessantly fusing and self-dividing work of art itself results from Schlegel's belief that not just art but the totality of our knowledge—in his fluid terminology: the *system* or *encyclopedia*—consists of nothing but such ceaseless couplings and uncouplings, of a chemistry reduced to its absolutely basic operations, what he calls "the combinatorial."[53] In the few short years around 1800—precisely at the time when the metaphors of chemistry command the most urgent presence in his work and before the increasing dominance of religious, particularly mystical, language—combinatorial logic is of such importance to him that, as he notes, even "the encyclopedia must experiment."[54] A notebook entry from 1799 claims: "The true standpoint is the central or encyclopedic one. The method perhaps transcendental or combinatorial. For both method and standpoint a certain tendency is required to get off the ground[.] This tendency is the combinatorial."[55] Regardless of starting point, the only sort of *motion* possible for an extension of knowledge, be it poetic or prosaic, consists of a process of combinations and separations.

The logic (Schlegel says: magic)[56] of a combinatorial textual system lies in a feature that we identified also as crucial in the theory of chemistry, namely that it can produce its infinite series of possibilities through a recursive application of a few operational rules to a finite number of basic elements. "The one great advantage of poetry" vis-à-vis the other arts, as Schlegel already claims in 1795, is its "*unlimited range*,"[57] unlimited by virtue of the fact that its self-enclosed operations have entirely open-ended effects. And among those effects many configurations can be found that have never been seen before. Thus the demand that "poetry and philosophy should always deeply permeate one another" can be followed by the statement "this will produce completely new phenomena"[58] only if we understand the process of permeation to follow a chemical logic. This is another way of saying that the permeation of philosophy and poetry occurs on poetry's terms.

While new phenomena rapidly expand to endow writing with an "unlimited range," the direction in which such expansion occurs remains indeterminate; unlike developmental narratives that guarantee a steady perfectibility by relying on a telos (approached organically, dialectically, or through an infinite progress), here any prospect of betterment is accompanied by the possibility of setbacks, even annulment.[59] If this is a defect, it is one inherent in experimentation. The Schlegelian artwork can go awry not only because it is badly executed, but also because precisely when it is well executed it contains at every moment the possibility of laying bare, to quote more fully a passage we already know, "the old nature and force . . . where naive profundity permits the glimmer of error and of madness, or of obtuseness and of stupidity to shine through."[60] The potential presence of error, madness, and stupidity—of an experiment run amok—foils any aspiration that the work of art may dependably fulfill the glorious ends that philosophical aesthetics has in mind for it. Simply put, the artwork has no ends because it can have no end. Its structural open-endedness bars it from reliably serving philosophically or socially useful functions. Once it is imagined as contaminated by chance and shaped by a self-driving dynamism, the artwork becomes unfit for the redemptive tasks dreamed up by philosophies and political ideologies, no matter whether they aim to fetter or to unleash liberty.

The claim that the artwork is unsuitable for tasks brought to it from outside can also be reversed: it is only suitable for tasks brought to it from *inside*. We can think of these tasks as potential combinatorial states available within a certain conception of writing: by allowing rules governing the poetic writing process (rules that can be grammatical, generic, historical, etc.) to rub against each other, as it were, new possible formations arise from inside the material of writing itself, including formations containing areas where the reader must contend with what Roland Barthes has called a "systematic exemption of meaning."[61]

It may have become clear how Schlegel's efforts distinguish themselves from the long tradition of combinatorial efforts—some systematic, some playful—preceding him: while the traditional combinatorics relies on a mathematical model, which goes back at least to the *ars combinatoria* of the thirteenth-century Franciscan friar Ramón Llull, Schlegel, as we have seen, prefers chemistry. Llull's is a strange and complicated system in which the nine essential qualities of God (goodness, truth, glory, etc.) are assigned to the letters *B* through *K* (skipping *J*) and then combined and recombined to produce all propositions that are true of God. In his 1666 dissertation *De arte combinatoria,* Leibniz develops the Llullian scheme into a project that would occupy him throughout his career, namely the invention of a "calculus of concepts" based on an "alphabet of thought."[62] In essence, this is an attempt to render language in mathematical terms: if thoughts could be reduced to their simplest elements, if those elements could be assigned to signs (letters or numbers), and if, moreover, the combinatorial rules governing these signs could be laid out completely, then a calculation would reveal the truth or falsehood of a proposition. What is more, an infinity of completely new propositions could be derived by nothing more complicated than applying the combinatorial operations to the elements of the system.

I would like to set aside the many fascinating features of Leibniz's stupendously ambitious, and utterly mad, project to focus attention on two aspects that it shares with all mathematically based combinatorial systems: first, such a combinatorial system is universally applicable in its domain, that is, it produces *all* combinations and permutations of a set of elements with complete regularity. Thus a system with three elements *A, B,* and *C* yields (assuming that repetitions are not allowed and the order is insignificant) three, and only three, two-letter combinations: *AB, AC, BC.* To Leibniz and its other practitioners, the chief attraction of this combination-generating system lies precisely in its reliability, for it allows, they believe, the creation of a language that is universally comprehensible. (Llull invents his to convert the many infidels in his Judeo-Muslim-Christian Majorca; Leibniz is interested in establishing peace between nations.) But for this feature of the *ars combinatoria* to function properly, a second must obtain: the system must be entirely formalistic. It must yield its results in a predictable, algorithmically unimpeachable—which is to say: mechanical—fashion *regardless of its content*. No matter what may be understood by *A, B,* and *C,* the fact that, given the formal constraints I mentioned earlier, there are exactly three ways of pairing them up remains true. It is because of the radical formalism of the system that, lest his system refer to nothing but itself, Leibniz is required to assume a preexisting harmony of the order of signs and the order of things: "There exists," he writes, "between signs . . . a relationship or an order that corresponds to the order of things."[63]

John Neubauer, to whose informative book *Symbolismus und symbolische Logik* (Symbolism and Symbolic Logic) I owe this last passage from Leibniz, uses the idea of combinatorial art to establish a continuity of practice from the hermetic work of Ramón Llull via the playful combinatorics of Baroque poetry to the writings of Schlegel and Novalis and, finally, the "poésie pure" of the French symbolist poets, notably Stéphane Mallarmé and Paul Valéry. It is his contention that the *ars combinatoria* is an attempt "to help poetry out of its crisis by means of a mathematical form," a crisis provoked by the "jolting consequences of scientific discoveries."[64] What on his account makes combinatorics useful for romantic and post-romantic poetic practice is the willingness of poets *not* to make the Leibnizian assumption about a preestablished harmony of signs and things, to sever instead the presumed link between signifiers and signifieds; thus Valéry's pronouncement: "It is the faculty of speech that speaks."[65] Once released from the necessity of reference, poetry can devote itself entirely to pure language, to exploring its breadth and depth by means of mathematical techniques.

This reading, while suggestive and original, strikes me as problematic, certainly with regard to Schlegel. The problem lies not merely in the paucity of evidence provided by Schlegel's writings for such a reading, especially in comparison with those of Novalis and Valéry (Mallarmé's case is again more ambiguous, I think). A far greater difficulty lies in the inadequacy of the mathematical model of combinatorics in describing the innovative features of Schlegel's—and not only Schlegel's—poetic practice and poetological conception. It stands in violation of the two crucial features of Leibnizian mathematical combinatorics that I mentioned a moment ago: the universality in the application of operational rules and the strict formalism separating the rules from the material upon which they act. His combinatorial conception does *not* function homogeneously, but is rather, as we have seen, contaminated by strange and unaccountable forces of attraction and repulsion. Its material—words, syllables, and letters—can never be fully abstracted, but always infects the formal rules—its syntax—with semantic remainders. And it is precisely the strength of this method that combinations *cannot* always be controlled and, hence, predicted. In short: the system behaves far too bizarrely and chaotically to comply with the mandates of variation, permutation, and combination inherent in a mathematically combinatorial system.[66]

Instead, Schlegel's combinatorics inhabits the dubious region of eighteenth-century chemistry, with its mysterious forces of affinity and repulsion that attempt to regularize the otherwise unaccountable behavior of the elements. It is this unaccountability, rather than the clockwork mechanism of mathematics, that appeals to Schlegel. "The most important scientific discoveries are *bons mots* of the [Leibnizian and Baconian] kind," he writes in an *Athenäum* fragment. "They achieve that through the surprising contingency of their formation, through the combinatorial quality of thinking."[67] Far from approaching the Truth with the help of a machine that generates well-ordered combinations, his science—*Wissenschaft*—moves by leaps and bounds, by small and large eruptions of combinatorial contingency, by the explosions of wit. Thus "the encyclopedia can simply and absolutely only be presented in *fragments*," which Schlegel glosses as "combinatorial ideas."[68] The mathematically inspired model of combinatorics has no room for such contingency; it is methodical and dull (which is precisely why Leibniz favored it) and hence ill-suited as a model for both the excess of sense produced by a genius-poet and the excess of "error and of madness, or of obtuseness and of stupidity" that can shine through poetic language. I suspect that this inadequacy also applies to the other modern writers discussed by Neubauer. Does the line from Valéry, quoted with a bit more context, not point to this excess from the strictly mechanical in mathematics? "It is the faculty of speech that speaks; and speaking gets drunk, and drunk dances."

This hybrid logic powerfully describes the ambiguous relationship of part and whole that we observed in the fragments, a relationship that is crucial as an allegory for aesthetic theory. The chemical model of constant combination and separation allows for a notion of fragments whose sheer numerical plenitude plunges them into a force field of reciprocal attractions and repulsions that, *as such* and without dialectical sublation, constitutes a whole. Schlegel himself offers a conception to distinguish this form of totality from the organicist totality prevalent in the writings of his contemporaries: "Where one attempts to form elements not merely *homogeneously* but also heterogeneously, there one strives for *totality* not merely for *unity*."[69] Totality —*Ganzheit*—achieves its infinite reach precisely by abandoning unity in favor of the nonidentical, combinatorial, differential system that requires heterogeneity. The insertion of *merely* (*bloß*) before *homogeneously* and *unity* makes amply clear which term Schlegel, at this point, prefers. How clear his preference is becomes even more evident when we consider the way he maps the distinction between heterogeneous totality and homogeneous unity onto the historical axis of Ancients and Moderns that we encountered earlier: "The Classical poetic genres have only *unity;* the progressive genres alone have *totality*."[70] While *Athenäum* fragment 24 ("Many works of the Ancients have become fragments. Many works of the Moderns are fragments the moment they are made") registers the discontinuity between Ancients and Moderns with an equanimity that at least permits us to imagine hearing a faint longing for a lost wholeness, the fragment just quoted—probably written in 1797 or 1798, almost coincident with the *Athenäum* fragment—polemically favors the romantic Moderns. And it does so because of the *lack* of homogeneous unity exhibited by their works. The logic that governs much of the essay "On the Study of Greek Poetry," published in 1797 but largely completed in the autumn of 1795, is turned on its head: if there the advantage that Classical works enjoy lies in their organic articulation, here, merely two or at the most three years later, it is precisely chemical fragmentation that has been turned into the distinguishing feature of Modern works. Fragmentation is the mark that lifts Modern texts above the "mere" unity of the Classical, because fragmentation—and only fragmentation—offers the possibility of totality. As Schlegel sharply recognizes in lines I quoted earlier, universality is a function of fragments imbued with "combinatorial quality . . . for only where a plenitude of heterogeneous substances are united can new chemical combinations and their permeations occur."

This idea of a nonunified totality relies on difference even when it coheres into a temporarily stable configuration (such as a fragment); it is indebted neither to a mystical immediacy, nor to the implacable teleology of a dialectic, nor to the seemingly natural developmental narrative of an organism. Its spatial and temporal structure is very different from all of these. Rather than a unity guaranteed either through the assurance of immediacy (where the temporal vector would be zero), or by endless progression (where the temporal vector would be infinite), the chemical system is the expression of a series of oscillations of "part" into "whole" and "whole" into "part." I put "part" and "whole" in quotation marks because logical chemistry is not a form of philosophical alchemy; Schlegel does not offer us a series of distinct entities whose essence might consist of "partness" (say, the fragments) and whose destiny (their *Bestimmung,* in the language of *Athenäum* fragment 116) would lead them to a distinct entity whose essence in turn might be called "wholeness" or "totality." If instead we speak of element and combinatorial operation, we will more easily grasp that this notion of totality consists of the sheer process of transformation. And since the fragments offer no progression—either up or down—nor a fixed beginning or end, their totality lacks the two crucial mainstays of the metaphysically imagined system: motivating force and telic movement. In other words, it lacks center, ground, axiomatic beginning, seed, what Schlegel calls the "big lump in the middle."[71]

In this context, the prescription of *Athenäum* fragment 53 to combine the deadly alternatives of system and nonsystem ("It will thus just have to decide to combine [*verbinden*] the two")[72] begins to make sense. In effect, eighteenth-century chemistry accomplishes precisely such a combination of system and nonsystem, and it does so along the axis of time. While the mastery of the totality of possible combinations of matter, natural or artificial, is a promise for the *future,* chemistry around 1800 is marked as we have seen by methodological and terminological confusion, by an unsystematic pluralism of approaches. In this sense, eighteenth-century chemistry *is* the bond between the two "equally fatal" alternatives of system and nonsystem. Schlegel locates the process that is neither dead nor alive— we might imagine it as consisting of activity *as such,* of pure expenditure—in the endless and vigorous movement *between* life and death, much as chemistry stands between the mechanical and the life sciences, while straddling both.

Once we recognize that the fragments as a whole are subject to the logic of textual chemistry, we begin to see how the features we had noted in the fragments in earlier chapters—incompletion, multiplicity, polyphony, and a persistent evasiveness in their meaning—derive from this logic. Willful fragmentation is a Schlegelian idiosyncrasy mainly because he deliberately calls attention to the rifts and gaps— the discontinuous heterogeneity—of a writing that works by mixing and dividing. But in principle *any* text engaged in the combinatorial game will by definition lack completion (for example, because the reader may always perform further combinations). This lack of completion is not to be seen as only a loss, but is at the same time the condition for the infinite development of the artwork, which is to say, of the infinite process of interpretation.

We can translate this language steeped in idealist jargon into terms much more familiar to us. Mallarmé has defined the verbal artwork as an *enigma,* in other words, by way of the puzzlement it generates in the reader. In an interview on the question of "literary evolution," he states apodictically, "In poetry there must always be an enigma, and that is the goal of literature—there is no other one—to *evoke* objects."[73] This is a definition Foucault seems to have in mind when, letting modern literature begin with Mallarmé, he takes the production of "a pure language that had become . . . enigmatic" as the advent of "something that has been called, since that time, *Literature.*"[74] In both cases, conceiving of poetry or literature (Mallarmé slides from one to other in his definition) as an enigma has at its core the idea that the poet, rather than bringing forth a perfectly coherent work, sets into motion the play of "a pure language," and that this barely controlled play gives rise to a hermeneutic excess, which in turn triggers a bewilderment that the reader finds, or is expected to find, pleasurable. In order to be properly enigmatic—Schlegel might say, infinite—the modern work has little choice but to consist of detached elements innovatively rearranged. Thus "many works of the Moderns are already fragments when they are made," for they could otherwise not partake of the project of chemical writing and reading.

A work thus defined requires not only readers but a multiplicity of other fragments, for otherwise it would have nothing with which to enter into commerce. As I have argued, chemical experimentation is operative not only within each unit of writing, or between that writing and its reader, but also within various pieces of writing. The game of substitution and combination, skewed by Jakobsonian propinquities, can be observed at every level of the composition of writing, from the individual letters to the entire essay. At no level of organization does the text reach a state of inviolate completion, but is rather attracted and repelled by other textual elements, both inside and outside itself. Schlegel by no means confines the effects of this game to his own production; his tireless effort at "bringing into contact"[75] with one another more and more masses of writing extends to the writings of friends and collaborators and even includes, in breathtaking ambition, the entirety of great modern European literature (the canon of Dante, Shakespeare, Boccaccio, Cervantes that he repeatedly invokes). All of them become fair game for textual chemistry.

When we place the multiplicity and willful incompletion of the fragments into a chemical context, the fragments' polyphony emerges, as it were, by itself, but with an important modification. For this polyphony, this "symphonism of the fragments" leading to "symphilosophy," does not produce harmonious sounds alone; it is shot through with noise. The reason is by now familiar to us: a chemically imagined formation will never progress to ever greater smoothness but contains, necessarily, divisions and differences; it promises perfectibility but at the cost of corruptibility. *Athenäum* fragment 412, which I will quote one last time, points in this direction: "Whoever has a sense for the infinite . . . conceives of his ideals at least as being chemical"—this much we know—"and when he expresses himself decisively, he speaks nothing but contradictions." Getting from chemical *thinking* to decisive *expression*—i.e., translating the logic of chemistry into language—calls forth contradictions, *Widersprüche,* a form of polyphony so radical that it breaks the controlled bounds of polyphony; for here voices move not side by side but against ("contra" [*wider*]) each other. The naked juxtaposition of terms may have left us at a loss on a first reading (why would chemical ideals lead to contradictions?), but we are now in a better position to supply the conceptual transition that Schlegel omits. Since a chemical system fails to function without internal heterogeneity (as the theory of elements demonstrates), its verbal counterpart too requires internal differences; in the most radical—"decisive"—case these will consist of "nothing but contradictions." The insistence on contradiction, then, is not proof of Schlegel's want of skill in "speculative thought" (Hegel), nor is it another example of Schlegel's irksome or perverse predilections that we may ignore in favor of his nobler tendencies. Rather, it is entailed by the lofty ideals of "universal poetry," which are infinite *because* they are contradictory.

The profusion of contradictions, pulling the reader's hermeneutic attention into opposite directions, certainly heightens the sense of perplexity that the fragments' strangely elusive meanings leave in the reader. Yet I think there is a stronger reason for why Schlegel's fragmentary writing—and since it serves as a model for the romantic poem, that poem itself—is unable to offer its readers a closure of meaning. For we need to be clear that not only is the conception of science at work here different from what is usually held to be the romantic one (namely a "poetic" interpretation of organic nature), but, more important, that Schlegel's "romantic poetry" refers to something very different from what is usually understood by the term. Wordsworth's view that "all good poetry is the spontaneous overflow of powerful feelings," often taken as a description of romanticism in a nutshell, can hardly apply here.[76] The combinatorial method does not consist in combinations alone; it does not bring forth ever more ample syntheses, nor does it engender a smooth and steady enlargement of the range of poetry. Contrary to appearances, Schlegel's demand "that everything should be poeticized"[77] does not imply that an ugly and unruly reality should be covered with the patina of harmonious poetry. If anything, the opposite is the case: poeticizing reality entails the possibility of cracking the polished manner in which an *un*poeticized world appears to us, of introducing "surprising contingency" into our unruffled worldviews. There can be little harmony in a notion of poetry modeled on the combinatorial method, for in order to function, the latter, like the chemistry on which it is modeled, requires separation, analysis, breakage. As we have seen, eighteenth-century chemists insist on this, as does Schelling; Schlegel himself registers this fact with the seemingly paradoxical term "combinatorial analysis," which would, according to him, be "the true method of philosophy." Just as the "chemical process of philosophizing" consists in the fact that "philosophy . . . must always organize *and disorganize* itself anew" (my emphasis),[78] poetry, as imagined in this constellation, must continually form *and deform* its aesthetic products. The two opposed tendencies, Schlegel notes, are inherent in poetic language, "whose tool, the arbitrary language of signs, is man-made and therefore infinitely perfectible *and corruptible*" (my emphasis).[79]

Thus the combinatorial logic of chemistry calls not only for a concept of "progressive universal poetry" that opens "the prospect of a boundlessly growing classicism"[80]—thus promoting the apotheosis of art that is so often laid at the door of romanticism—but also for one that "permits the glimmer of error and of madness, or of obtuseness and of stupidity to shine through." Indeed, the two can be nothing but one and the same, each calling forth the other as inexorably as synthesis requires analysis. "[Romantic poetry] alone is free" precisely because it is free to lead to both the capacity for "the highest and most versatile formation" *and* to "the *combinatorial chaos* in the fragments."[81] If it is free of the rigid norms promulgated by classicist theorists such as Boileau, Dryden, or Gottsched, it is also, to an important extent, free of the volition of the poet.[82] That the force of norms is replaced not by a cult of genius but rather by something that evades both norms and genius is what I take to be the real innovation in Schlegel's work. It yields beauty and sublimity of the loftiest order and *for that reason* is also capable of producing the basest forms of ugliness and disgust.

The Gold Standard

We can measure Schlegel's commitment to a poetry driven by chemical experimentation by his response to an alternate model of chemistry, one not consisting of couplings and uncouplings with no end in sight, but promising, rather, to bring all the mixing and matching to a close. This other, redemptive chemistry is mentioned as a counter-model in the essay that I discussed early on. I never got much beyond the second syllable of the title word, *Unverständlichkeit,* but there is more to this ambitious essay than that. "I wanted to show," Schlegel writes about the texts he has published in the *Athenäum*, "that words often understand themselves better than do those by whom they are used, wanted to call attention to the fact that there must be secret societies among philosophical words, words that, like a host of spirits sprung forth too early, often confuse everything in their writings and exert the invisible force of the world spirit also on those who try to deny it."[83] It would be a stretch to claim that

Schlegel sketches a structuralist picture of language in which laws internal to the linguistic system remain independent of its users' intentions; he does not quite anticipate Saussure, Hjelmslev, and the entire "linguistic turn" (though he prepares the ground for them). Instead of a proper theory of language, he offers us premature spirits, invisible forces, and secret societies. (But does the *Verbindung* holding together the secret societies—*Ordensverbindungen*—not perhaps follow a scientific logic all too familiar to us?) His conception of the autonomy of the linguistic sphere, however indistinct and tentative it may be ("words *often* understand themselves better," "there *must be* secret societies among . . . words . . . that . . . *often* confuse everything"), undergirds the idea of a poetic autonomy along the lines I have been discussing: this autonomous work of art is not one that the artist can claim for himself against social pressures and historical changes, as the idea is often (mis)understood, but one that to an important extent disenfranchises the artist himself. The secret bonds Schlegel detects between words—the contingently combinatorial game that words play—confirm his often repeated anti-foundational stance: that "there are simply no principles of philosophy and poetry outside of themselves."[84]

"On Incomprehensibility" is an essay in which Schlegel goes further with irony and "sublime impudence" than in anything else he published during his lifetime; yet it is also a remarkable document of Schlegel's ambivalence vis-à-vis the "revolution in the field of aesthetics" that he finds himself unleashing. For even here, at his most audacious, Schlegel harbors doubts about a world of words run amok; he seems almost startled at his own daring, as though the responsibility rested with *him* for the fact that "the glimmer of error and of madness, or of obtuseness and of stupidity . . . shine[s] through" words. Thus he announces his wish for "a real language, so that we might stop rummaging about for words and behold the power and seed of all activity,"[85] for a "holy, delicate, fleeting, airy, fragrant, as it were imponderable thought."[86]

For a few sentences, the essay perches between two views of language: both noninstrumental, nontransparent, self-enclosed, yet one playful and tricky, the other mystical and sublime. The first encourages the sort of fearless experimentation that I have been trying to document here, the other the exhalation of imponderable thought in a wordless language ("that we might stop rummaging about for words"), which becomes a romantic cliché (and has made romanticism itself into a cliché). At one point, little more than two pages into the essay, Schlegel finds a way of negotiating the impasse that permits him to pursue, for the rest of the essay, the path of irony, play, and experimentation. It will not come as a surprise that this negotiation is conducted through the medium of chemistry.

> It was only quite recently that this idea of a real language was stirred in me again. . . . In the nineteenth century, [the physician and chemist Christoph] Girtanner assures us, . . . we will be able to make gold . . .: "Every chemist, every artist will make gold; kitchenware will be made of silver, of gold." . . . I had often quietly admired the objectivity of gold, I can even say I worshipped it. Among the Chinese, I thought, among the English, the Russians, on the island of Japan, among the inhabitants of Fez and Morocco, even among the Cossacks, Cheremis, Bashkirs, and Mulattoes, in short: wherever there is some education and enlightenment, silver and gold are comprehensible and, through gold, everything else. Now when every artist possesses these materials in sufficient quantity, then he may only write his works in bas-relief, in gold letters on silver tablets. Who would want to reject such a beautifully printed text with the vulgar remark that it is incomprehensible?[87]

One of the versions of contemporary chemistry, the very discourse responsible for the sort of experimentation that results in incomprehensibility, promises a redemptive end to the havoc that the science has wreaked. A well-known German popularizer offers the gold standard of comprehensibility to "every chemist, every artist."[88] Yet Schlegel, though "stirred" by this potential realization of his wished-for "real language," recognizes it for what it is, namely "just phantoms or ideals."[89] After this, there is no further mention of real language or imponderable thought. We could conclude that Schlegel knew his chemistry better than some of the scientists of the time (an unlikely possibility), or that he was less susceptible to the hyperbolic claims of science than scientists themselves (just as unlikely). A more plausible conclusion would be that, at this point, Schlegel is so committed to a model of chemistry bereft of an anchoring gold standard—committed because it serves as the right allegory for his conception of poetic experimentation—that he brushes aside any alternative model of chemistry offering a return to alchemy, brushes aside any notion of synthesis without further analysis, of closure, the absolute, comprehensibility.

5 αβ & LMN

In Schlegel's early writings, I have argued, chemistry effects a significant change in the conception of the artwork, specifically of the verbal artwork, by working at cross-purposes with some of the most crucial concepts employed in eighteenth- and early-nineteenth-century aesthetic theory. The idea of artistic totality—a totality whose significance lies in mirroring two other totalities, namely that of nature and that of the individual subject—is diminished by a productive principle that relies neither on epiphanic illumination nor on organic *Bildung,* but on the process of dividing and mixing. This process, I have also attempted to show, interrupts the passage from nature, through art, to a redemption of art (in ethics, in politics, in metaphysics), for it vitiates the homological relationship of part and whole. A fragment does maintain a relationship to a notional totality, but in a chemical conception such a fragment cannot symbolically *represent* the totality of which it is a part. The fragment merely points to it as an entity that has suffered a loss, that consists of the process of combination and recombination without succeeding in—or even aiming at—filling the loss. It has seemed to me that such a conception, which Schlegel's experimental writings both describe and perform, marks not only an important departure from classical aesthetic accounts but points toward conceptions of literature that we think of as having been developed only much later.

To gauge what sort of a relationship this quasi-scientific notion of writing ("quasi" because the science itself hardly qualifies as more than a quasi-science) may have with later ideas of literary writing, we need to apply the method of dividing and mixing at an even lower threshold of textual analysis. Thus far in this study, chemistry has played itself out on the level of syllables (*ver-*), of words, of groups of words such as fragments, and of groups of fragments. But Schlegel's writings appear to seek the elective affinity between language and chemistry at far greater depths, for in some ways the most consequential instance of the operations of combinatorial logic occurs when the alphabet is made to behave like the elements of chemistry. If it can be shown that not only some philosophical and poetic utterances but also language itself is imagined according to a discursive model perched between alchemy and chemical automatism, then we will have gained a better understanding of just how far-reaching Schlegel's poetological innovations are. If language is not understood as a tool of communication but as an autopoietic system, a generator of utterances and meanings, and a generator, furthermore, that is subject to "surprising contingencies," then we will have a measure not only of the distance we have traveled (with Schlegel) from organicist and teleological notions of the artwork, but also of our proximity to modernist conceptions of poetic experimentation and linguistic unreliability.

As Friedrich Kittler has argued in his *Aufschreibesysteme 1800/1900* (Discourse Networks 1800/1900), the most significant media history of modern literature to date, the manner in which a text or group of historically proximate texts (a "discourse network") conceive of the relationship between the letter and larger linguistic units is crucial in determining how much a text or textual network takes its own material basis into account and how tolerant it is of the aberrations of meaning. Because texts are, as Kittler claims, materially speaking no more than the permutation of twenty-six letters, and because letters are furthermore inherently meaningless marks, the degree to which the letter is acknowledged or disavowed indicates the degree to which a text is prepared to admit the intrusions of meaningless materiality.

Language as the Prototype of All Artistic Media

In considering the letter, we have arrived at a point where we can begin to consider why, in Schlegel's work, the verbal artifact comes to stand for the work of art as such. Responding to the question, "Is, then, everything poetry?" one of the speakers in the "Conversation on Poetry" maintains: "Every [art and every science], even if it does not traffic in the words of language, has an invisible spirit, and that is poetry."[1] In the peculiar shape that it takes in Schlegel's work, the operational field of the chemical allegory is first *reduced* to the workings of specifically poetic—and thus linguistic—signs, only then to be *extended* to all sign systems, an extension that is not explicitly performed but merely assumed by Schlegel, since the linguistic sign is the "invisible spirit" even in the nonverbal arts. It is thus in language that eighteenth-century chemistry unfolds its full allegorical force, even when Schlegel has the full aesthetic field in mind.

We have seen how chemistry's methods—combination and division, substitution and permutation—serve as a model for the combinatorial operations of language on several levels. In the previous chapter, we observed its mix-and-match workings on the level of syntax, where chemistry permits Schlegel to perform writing experiments that reveal the dual selection process in the making of utterances. Just as the bonding of two substances restricts choice in successfully adding a third, every new word in a syntactic sequence narrows the choice of the following word. At the same time, the strange and unexplained affinity of substances—i.e., the "secret societies" among words—opens the door to sudden substitutions and wonderful rearrangements of the elements in a configuration. We have also seen how Schlegel applies these principles to language on the level of the syllable, probing the range and the limits of the game of combination and substitution. In both cases, we noted how the volatility and flexibility of the combinatorial system is accompanied by odd restrictions and puzzling, at times incomprehensible, results that hold at bay the possibility of a willful and predictable manipulation of the process. If it is Schlegel's aim to show that artistic production moves between senseless mechanism and soulful organicism (and we shall see in a moment why the adjectives are distributed the way they are), then chemistry provides a rich model for capturing this in-between-ness: a formal mechanism that is, however, very much adulterated by nonformalizable matter, a system of combinations unable to rid itself of the strange material demands—the affinities and aversions—of its elements. And the artistic medium that Schlegel finds to be most congruent with this model is (poetic) language.

Since the particular qualities of the chemical model encourage Schlegel to favor language as the template of all systems of semiosis, since they lead him to embrace poetry as the quintessence of all art, we need to ask to what extent this view overlaps with, or differs from, the belief, widely held in eighteenth-century aesthetics, that poetry stands at the summit in the ranking of the arts. The hierarchy of the arts arises from and entails complex aesthetic and metaphysical conceptions, and a detailed analysis would go beyond what can be performed here,[2] but for our purposes we can say this: when Kant claims in the *Critique of Judgment* that "among all the arts *poetry* holds the highest rank" (KU 326), this ranking, far from being traditional or gratuitous, emerges from the deepest levels of the very structure of aesthetic judgment. Poetry is not merely given preference because it shares a medium—namely language—with philosophy,[3] but because it emanates, in Kant's construction, from the same organ—the larynx—that also gives rise to aesthetic judgment. For the *voice,* according to Kant, not only animates poetry but also motivates the very specificity of aesthetic judgment, namely the fact that it is subjective and intersubjective (Kant says: universal) at one and the same time. We are able to "lay claim to everyone's agreement" in judging something to be beautiful (and that claim [*Anspruch*] is already an act of speech, of *sprechen*). We are justified in this because "we believe we have a universal voice [*allgemeine Stimme*]" in us according to which we make such judgments and thus such an *Anspruch* (KU 216). Indeed, the voice (*Stimme*) that permeates poetry reappears in every aspect of the process of judging aesthetically. We listen to nature, which on Kant's account is the template according to which art is made, expecting to recognize "a lawful harmony [*Übereinstimmung*]" (KU 300) in its products, yet invariably fail in this endeavor (for the recognition of such a harmony exceeds the cognitive powers of mortals). Since the grounds for such harmony cannot be found in nature itself, "we naturally look for it in ourselves, namely in what constitutes the ultimate purpose of our existence: our moral vocation [*Bestimmung*]" (KU 301). It is for this reason that an "agreement [*Einstimmung*]" (KU 216) about aesthetic judgments can be and is required of everyone. *Stimme, Übereinstimmung, Bestimmung, Einstimmung, Beistimmung* (KU 216), *Anspruch:* the *Critique* reverberates with voices. It thus has little choice but to accord the highest rank to "the arts of speech" (KU 321), at whose summit Kant places poetry.[4]

In contrast with Kant's gesture of identifying poetry as an entirely oral activity, the most innovative aspects of Schlegel's poetic theory do not erase the traces of written marks, indeed often direct our attention to them. While the promiscuous recombination of fragments and fragments of fragments—phrases, words, syllables—could conceivably be also performed in spoken language, the chemical combination of *letters* with which Schlegel plays is imaginable only in or as a consequence of writing. (In fact, there are reasons to think that even combining and substituting what we think of as phonetic units becomes possible in a programmatic or artistic way only in writing. For as soon as the number of basic elements exceeds a certain small number, say four or five, it becomes difficult to remember and manipulate *all* possible combinations and permutations of which they are capable. In that sense, the mnemonic device of writing—indeed of alphabetic writing—appears to be the condition of possibility of combinatorics.) When the chemical model is allowed to play itself out on the level of graphemes—the letters of the alphabet, mathematical symbols, idiolectal marks and abbreviations—we get a glimpse of a poetics that differs sharply from its organicist predecessors. Schlegel's is a theory of the production and consumption[5] of poetic texts that distinguishes itself by affirming the material medium in and through which such texts take place, at a time when its denial is ubiquitous. While poetological efforts around the turn of the nineteenth century aim, as we shall see in a moment, to disavow all traces of the medium of literature (i.e., the written and printed text) in order to imagine a voice sounding through the letters, Schlegel directs our attention precisely to the material and its combinatorial properties.

Such a move involves, once again, the double motion of contraction and expansion. For limiting the operational field of what can hardly still be called "poetry" to two or three dozen elements, acted upon by a few combinatorial rules, steeply increases the complexity of the system. Suddenly, a vast number of letter combinations become available, such that no oral tradition and no dictionary could possibly contain. Thus opens an avenue of analysis, which, though it cannot be followed here, is worth alluding to: a theory of poetry that takes seriously the medium of its object and has the potential of revealing analogies in other artistic media. Schlegel does not wonder how his chemical combinatorics might play itself out in media other than language, yet it is not difficult to see that important currents in twentieth-century visual arts (abstraction, montage, collage) and music (twelve-tone composition, let alone compositions employing seemingly random combinatorial principles) self-consciously rely on applying a combinatorial logic to the material elements at their disposal.[6]

But to anticipate an argument I will make more fully in the pages to come: experimenting with the external material of poetry and its combinatorial possibilities is not therefore modern or modernist, if by that we understand the program, identified by Friedrich Kittler as that of the "discourse network around 1900," of "writing and writers as accidental events in a noise that generates accidents and thus can never be overcome by accidents."[7] The material model that interests me in Schlegel's work maintains a subtle elective affinity with the production of random writing and, hence, of nonsense, without however giving itself over to this randomness. That model, I would argue, describes the workings of modern literature far more richly than Kittler's random utterance generator.

In Kittler's historical narrative, there is no place for such an ambiguous formation, for his account of the switch of the "discourse network around 1800" to that around 1900 is digital: plenitude of sense in one, "the great Kingdom of Nonsense" in the other (56/42). Nonsense simply cannot be a feature of the earlier discourse network, for this network's entire motivating force consists in suffusing all utterances—poetic or not—with the One unifying Sense. This production of sense on all discursive channels involves a vast cultural change, precipitated in Kittler's view by advances in technology and literacy: it requires changes in pedagogy, in the status of civil servants, in the role of mothers, and, of course, in literature and its criticism. Or rather, with Foucault we could say that the shift around 1800 toward sense does not so much change criticism as necessitate its founding;[8] criticism displaces commentary because now the task of the reader not only includes *finding* sense but also, and above all, *making* it. Thus the importance of the new field of hermeneutics (to be developed into a science by Schlegel's Berlin roommate Friedrich Schleiermacher), which gathers the scattered elements of semiotic systems into a coherently signifying body. In contrast with this organic organization of meaning, Kittler's discourse network around 1900, prominently represented by Nietzsche and Mallarmé, contends with and even encourages the production of nonsense, which consists of "the mathematical manipulations of permutation and combination" (246/195).[9] Here again technology both drives and allegorizes the change, for instead of the continuous motion of the pen around 1800, writing around 1900 happens through the discrete serial selection of typewriter keys.

The originality and perspicuity of Kittler's account is made possible by its admirably tenacious adherence to conceptual pairs: here sense, there nonsense; here spirit, there letter; here organic, there mathematical: there is no third. Yet just such a third possibility is available in some—quite important—strands of the discourse network around 1800, and its name is chemistry. Here, the mechanicomathematical and the organic do not represent two irreconcilable alternatives; we find, rather, that one infects the other: smooth growth is interrupted by the automatism of combinatorics, which in turn is constrained by elective affinities not to be accounted for by the system. As a result, the spirit is unthinkable—unrecognizable—without the letter(s), and nonsense is always not merely an event at the outer limits of sense but right in its midst: as we by now know from Schlegel, "the purest and most splendid incomprehensibility" can after all be obtained "precisely from science and from art, whose very aim is being comprehensible and making comprehensible."[10]

Saying that the discourse network around 1900 is, as it were, already woven into the network around 1800 is not merely to say that the earlier discourse adumbrates the writing practice of the later discourse, that it is a more limited version of a later practice taken to be far more adventurous. It would be reductive to regard the in-between motion, the hovering, of Schlegel's chemical experimentation as a movement leading from the organic romanticism of 1800 to the mathematical modernism of 1900. I would claim, *pace* Kittler, that this in-between motion already characterizes what we most prize about literature, modernist or not: that it probes the range—the breadth and the depth—of the logic internal to its material. This logic is not exhausted by a reference to a seemingly radical notion of pure contingency (Kittler's random word generator), but must include the strange, neither contingent nor deterministic, relationship that connects *Rate* to *Ratte* and *stehen* to *verstehen* to *Unverständlichkeit*. Some have termed this relationship, using a psychological metaphor, the "unconscious in language," while I, using a scientific metaphor more applicable to a material practice, have called it the chemical.

It seems to me that we are interested in entering the great kingdom of nonsense only if it is somehow contaminated by sense (and the manner of this contamination matters greatly to the degree of our interest). This is *not* to say that all nonsense ought to be sublated into a higher sense (for that would amount to no more than an apotheosis of nonsense), but rather that our curiosity—our desire—is roused by disturbances of sense in the field of nonsense and, conversely, of nonsense in the field of sense. (Nothing else is meant by the appearance of the unconscious in language.) It would require a separate study to show that the work of Kittler's main exemplars of the network around 1900, for example Mallarmé and Morgenstern, depends not on accepting or even embracing the accidental generation of words by means of a blind combinatorics, but rather on the excess of *sense* that such a combinatorics generates. In this regard, chemistry is an allegory of a form of textuality neither suffused with one self-same meaning nor cleansed of meaning entirely, a form of textuality that is between those states; a form, in short, that evokes in its readers doubt about the degree to which authorial control or literal contingency has shaped the product, and, with doubt, desire. It is a form of textuality we simply call literature.

Writing Life

The voice that sounds through poetry in its Schlegelian conception, I have claimed, suffers interference from writing. This insistence on the written mark is not a philosophical desideratum alone, but is reflected in Schlegel's daily life. His voluminous collected works document an almost unbroken trail of writing beginning in his student days and leading up to the hour of his death. Early on January 12, 1829, the fifty-six-year-old Schlegel was preparing what would have been the tenth in a series of lectures on the "philosophy of language and of the word" in a Dresden inn, when he was stricken, literally, in mid-sentence. "The wholly complete and perfect comprehension itself, however, . . ."[11] is the last and, in a sense, only authentic fragment he ever produced, if by that we mean a fragment shaped not by an author but by a stupid and contingent occurrence like death. (Though logic tells us otherwise, it is next to impossible not to read death as a stamp of authenticity, hence impossible not to give in to the temptation to take Schlegel's last written words as the summa of his work.)[12] He is far too self-aware a writer not to have noted and reflected on his severe—and ultimately fatal—case of graphomania.

"I am a grammatical nature," he, twenty-six-years-old, writes in a letter to Novalis, "and I understand you better written than while speaking."[13] That such a condition is not necessarily experienced as pleasurable becomes evident in a letter Schlegel writes his brother August Wilhelm two years earlier; fired by republican enthusiasm, he writes of one day entering politics: "Then I shall also live with you and write no longer what does not say itself [or: which does not go without saying], but can again learn to talk. It will be a happy, blessed, wonderful time."[14] A few years later, in 1799, he offers a public self-description of his devotion to the written word in an essay composed in the form of a letter to his lover and future wife Dorothea Veit, the daughter of Moses Mendelssohn:

> I have come to keep my promise . . . even if only to tease a woman so determinedly contemptuous of all writing and the world of letters with my love of these things. You would most likely prefer a conversation. But I am an author through and through. Writing holds for me I don't know what secret magic, perhaps because of the glimmer of eternity that hovers around it. Yes, I confess to you, I wonder what secret power lies hidden in these dead pen strokes. . . . I would almost say, in the somewhat mystical language of our H.: Life is writing; the sole purpose of mankind is to engrave the thoughts of the divinity onto the tablets of Nature with the stylus of the formative spirit.[15]

It is a strange thing to say: life is writing. If that is the case, then biography does not, as I just put it, "reflect" the prominence writing is given in Schlegel's work. Writing would in fact be nothing but biography, for it would mark the exact place at which *bios* and *graphe,* life and writing, become one. Thus biography would cease to be a belated written record of an expired life, a document of death consisting of dead letters, and would instead be the name for a process of writing imagined as alive. But how can we imagine such a thing? How would "dead pen strokes"—results of a purely mechanical process—metamorphose into "life," an organism believed to exceed mechanism? We know the answer provided by Kittler, who cites the same passage from the essay to Dorothea: the source that gives meaning to those arbitrary signifiers engraved into nature by the erectile stylus is Dorothea herself, more specifically the *Muttermund*—literally the mother's mouth, catachrestically her cervix—which through speech gives birth to writing.[16] The entire discourse network around 1800 is conceived to be permeated with meaning at every level because its origin is the meaningful and meaning-giving mouth of the mother. In a strange closing of the loop, woman is not only the source of the writing but also its ultimate destination: once writing has been processed by male hands, women, who teach writing but do not themselves write, become its main consumers.[17] The speaking mouth of the mother is, as it were, the matrix for a written language; it naturalizes the mechanics of writing. "Writing had been made effortless and reading silent," Kittler remarks, "in order to confuse writing with nature."[18]

But writing in Schlegel, even in the passage I just quoted, is not as effortlessly submerged by the category of nature or of life as it may seem, nor is the division of genders as clearly marked. Take the following passage from *Lucinde*, which echoes the lines from the essay to Dorothea with high fidelity:

> It was good we finally talked with each other again. I am also contented that you were reluctant to write and scolded the poor innocent letters of the alphabet, because you really do have a greater genius for talking. But I still have a few things on my mind that I could not talk about and that I will try to indicate to you in writing.
>
> Why in writing? Oh my friend, if I only knew of a finer and more subtle element of communication . . .[19]

The logic here is identical to that above—an addressee who prefers speech, a writer who extols the excellence of letters—with one crucial difference: this is a letter from man to man. This is not the place to speculate why Antonio, the addressee, can be put into the same position as Dorothea; but we can see that the gender distribution among the correspondents blurs the clean dichotomy set up by Kittler.

Even in its own terms, the open letter to Dorothea complicates the logic of the signified. Though Schlegel resorts to the language of "magic" and "secret power," we need not jump to the conclusion that a sort of mystical union is at work between writing and life. For one thing, the identity of writing and life—of the letter and the spirit, of the signifier and the signified—is not quite achieved: Schlegel "would *almost* say" that life is writing; and since that near-claim is made in the name of another, Schlegel puts the copula "to be" in the subjunctive—"Leben *sei* Schreiben"—thus draping a veil of uncertainty over an utterance that could well be read as direct speech (in that it follows a colon), hence could have been put in the more resolute indicative voice. The status of the near-assertion about the near-identity of writing and life is made even more uncertain if we consider who this other is in whose name it is almost made. All we know is that it is "our H." When reading the passage, we are likely almost unconsciously to expand H. into a name, say "Hardenberg," and the name into the person Friedrich von Hardenberg (and him back again into a (pen) name, "Novalis"). But the text itself never decodes H., and for most readers of the *Athenäum* it would have been impossible to guess H.'s identity (assuming H. has an identity). Despite our wish to see a person—a human voice—speaking through the letter, part of what gives the passage its peculiarly ambiguous force is the fact that H. is not entirely reducible to a voice, that on the manifest level of the text it is ultimately nothing more than a letter—which is to say: an element of writing—and that this written mark itself writes: life is writing.

Reading the letter *H* as an author no doubt seems a bit forced, for surely its use in Schlegel's open letter to Dorothea is in keeping with the eighteenth-century convention of identifying (real or fictitious) characters with (real or fictitious) initials. Its occurrence here would indeed be incidental, even accidental, did it not echo an idea, expressed all over the work of the young Schlegel, that the letter, long maligned and subordinated to the spirit, should rise to eminence in both poetic practice and poetological theory. His work sets out to offer an "*apology for the letter,* which as the only authentic *vehicle of communication is very venerable.*"[20] The letter, he declares, is the "principle of art and science"[21] and hence "must be active, alive, agile, or progressive."[22] Once the letter is revalued, it becomes imaginable to recast the difference between Ancients and Moderns in new terms: "In the Ancients we see the perfected letter of all poetry; in the Moderns we suspect its growing spirit."[23] Far from conforming to their classical image of childlike naiveté, the Ancients that Schlegel gives us here are grown-up enough to *write* their poetry. But the perfected letter is not, for that reason, bathed in the hazy light of inaccessibility reserved for those entities that are thought to signal classical excellence. The "dignity of the letter" is to be observed even and especially by the Moderns, for that way, Schlegel writes, "the seed of the new philosophy could be placed close to the border of the old one."[24]

We will look in greater detail at how the "dignity of the letter" is to be restored, but before doing so it is worth considering to what extent Schlegel's very search for the conceptual charge of the letter, regardless of the particular strategies it takes, defies the standard treatment the idea of the letter receives in the aesthetic and poetic discourse of his time. The force of Schlegel's "apology for the letter" becomes palpable only when we see how habitually it is insulted, and the strangeness of his conception becomes all the more remarkable when we keep in mind under what unlikely and hostile conditions it comes about. For the letter serves as the negative member of a pair of concepts whose positive member—the spirit—is hailed as the true text of poetic production. Precisely because it is zealously, almost religiously, demonized, the letter constitutes a poetological category of great consequence.

The Debasement of the Letter around 1800

The debasement of the letter, always in the service of the elevation of the spirit, is so rampantly and successfully effected in the literature of the late eighteenth and early nineteenth centuries that it is almost unrecognizable as a motif. Apart from reasons of ubiquity, we have trouble seeing it because in many ways our own "discourse network around 2000" still powerfully adheres to it. When, for example, an interpretation of the United States Constitution seeks to establish "original intent," i.e., what its framers "had in mind," it is guided by the asymmetrical distinction of letter and spirit that the late eighteenth century so vehemently insists upon. In one sense, this distinction is, as Schlegel notes, "a religious difference";[25] it attempts to reach an anterior and immaterial consciousness by means of an avenue of access that does not rely on mere textual evidence; in other words, it demands belief in a transcendent will. (Accordingly, the Constitution is usually treated as an essentially sacral expression of the will of a collective divinity known as the Founding Fathers, rather than as the outcome of a messy and contingent negotiation of conflicting interests and ideals among a varied yet historically specific group of men.) The aesthetic and poetic texts around 1800 are fully aware of the religious legitimation for their condemnation of the letter; their source is the well-known passage in Paul's second letter to the Corinthians: "The letter killeth, but the spirit giveth life" (3:6). But already in Paul the religious issue—the difference in the ways Jews and Christians maintain their respective relationships with God—is not purely religious but also hermeneutic: the religious prescription is sustained by an implicit theory of interpretation that the literature and philosophy of Schlegel's time articulates and formalizes. Paul's theory replaces the (Jewish) obedience to the letter, which often results in perplexity, with a (Christian) belief in a securely transcendent knowledge. Instead of being detained by the particular arrangement of black letters, the reader is now called upon to read beyond—which is to say: between—the lines so as to glimpse the light of the animating spirit. The radically new relationship to God depends upon a radically new relationship to the text.[26]

When late-eighteenth-century literature adopts Paul's letter-spirit distinction, it draws, to be sure, on its religious authority, but it also removes the distinction from the theological domain and makes it into a generalized principle, a distinction governing the relationship with *all* texts, including and particularly fictional ones.[27] It is one of the accomplishments of Kittler's "Discourse Networks" to have made the appearance of the spirit in the literature around 1800 literally audible. He traces the opening gesture of a hermeneutics of the spirit—of a signifying system beholden to the signified—to the sigh with which Faust's *Geist* interrupts his speech at the beginning of the tragedy: "Habe nun, *ach!* Philosophie/Juristerei . . ." ("I have, alas! studied philosophy/Jurisprudence . . ."). But Faust does not achieve the establishment of the hermeneutics of spirit by himself. Before the spirit made itself heard through the welter of his words, the letter had already been stripped of its dignity. It had been rendered invisible and transparent, a diaphanous garment for the spirit. This is not a feat that can be accomplished once and for all (not even by an Apostle), but must be repeated over and over. Paul's words are thus echoed and repeated by Luther,[28] and Luther's by Lessing: "Luther! Great, unrecognized man! . . . You have saved us from the yoke of tradition: who will save us from the still more unbearable yoke of the letter! Who will at last bring us a Christianity that you would be teaching *now,* that Christ himself would be teaching now!"[29]

Lessing's amplification of the signal coming from Paul via Luther resounds throughout the institution of German letters—better: of German *Geist*—for decades to come.[30] Herder and Heine, the two bookends of the *Goethezeit,* echo the denigration of the letter not by repeating Paul and Luther, but by repeating *Lessing* (indeed the very lines I just quoted).[31] Thus by the late eighteenth century, the motif of the empty, dead letter as the mere shell of the ascendant spirit derives its legitimacy among writers not only from religious authorities but also, indeed primarily, from literary ones; it is an issue that is adjudicated by and for literature and thus becomes virulent in it. "This is what she said! O Wilhelm, who can repeat what she said!" young Werther burbles, having just repeated, verbatim, what she, Lotte, said. "How can the cold dead letter convey this heavenly expression coming of the spirit!"[32] For Werther as for Lessing, a copy of whose *Emilia Galotti* lies open by Werther's side as he heaves his last sighs, the questions surrounding the letter (Who will save us from the yoke of the letter? Who will bring us a new Christianity? Who can repeat what she said? How can the letter present the spirit?) have ceased to be questions and have been turned into exclamations ("Who will save us . . . ! Who will at last bring us . . . !" etc.). *Werther,* like much of the literature of the time, is certain enough of the basic incongruity of letter and spirit that the novel closes its eyes and ears to any possibility of finding an answer to the question of how the spirit might be presented in letters. Were it not bemoaning the inadequacy of the letter with such clamor ("O Wilhelm"), it might have been able to register the fact that the quarrel between the spirit and the letter had become a matter *internal* to letters—to literature—itself. For conjuring the heavenly expression of the spirit is nothing but an artistic device of the cold, dead letters of which *The Sorrows of Young Werther* are composed; the more artful the latter, the more convincing the former.[33]

Far from hobbling the topos, the very mysteriousness of gaining access to the spirit in the letter (or enlivening the latter with the former) appears to guarantee its success. In a letter of September 1787, fully thirteen years after first publishing *Werther,* Goethe avers that in his published works (still only "four slender little volumes," as he puts it) there is "not a letter [*Buchstabe*] of them that is not lived, felt, enjoyed, suffered, thought."[34] Yet how precisely a letter can be felt or enjoyed or suffered or even thought remains unexplained (which may be why the sentence reports these sentiments, presumably felt with urgency, in the tentative and impersonal passive subjunctive ["nicht gelebt . . . wäre"]). But such inscrutability does not undermine but rather bolsters the idea of a signified beyond all signifiers. Thus when her father has just intercepted a crucial missive, threatening to open it, one of Schiller's tragic heroines can think of nothing better to say than, "As you wish, Father, but you won't understand it. The letters [*Buchstaben*] lie there like cold corpses and come alive only to the eyes of love."[35] An ineffective intervention: not only does it fail to keep him from opening the letter, but its prediction proves egregiously incorrect, for father is of course capable of understanding it all too well.

Despite such failures, the idea that there are, in effect, two radically incommensurate ways of reading—a blind reading going no further than the letters, a visionary reading bypassing them and beholding the spirit directly—remains powerfully operative. Sometimes, Schiller writes, "the dead letter of nature becomes a living language of spirits [*Geistersprache*], and the outer and inner eye read the same writing of appearances in entirely different ways."[36] Doubling the forms of reading—a mechanical form (through the "outer eye") and a spiritual form (through the "inner eye")—in effect means reducing the forms of writing to zero. Because the inner eye can make direct contact with the spirit lurking in the letters, it has no need to be detained by actual and material writing; thus literal writing can be replaced by the metaphorical "writing of appearances." As a result, reading, which at first seemed to have been fortified by its doubling, loses its consistency as a cognitive activity. Since one no longer reads "for the letter," attention to textual specificity can give way to euphoric illumination.

This view holds even and especially when the effects of the very letter whose importance is being denied make themselves felt. In the case just quoted, a strange grammatical oddity provides the most telling symptom of the spiritualization of writing for which the notion of the inner eye aims, namely the fact that this inner eye is usually imagined in the singular. Why would the mind's eye be designed to see *less* than the body's eyes? What might account for this flattening of the monoscopic "inner" visual field? It would seem that the immediacy of sensation suggested by the notion of "inner vision" requires an absence of depth, of foreground and background. To inner vision everything is brightly lit and accessible without obstruction as though on one plane, much the way we find objects and actions represented in Homer.[37] Things are uniformly present to it, without the hindrance of history or mediation or ideological complication, and certainly without the interference of any other sense. Marshall McLuhan has argued that the most consequential effect of the phonetic alphabet—and, still more flagrantly, of printing—lies in substituting for a synesthetic experience of the world an experience filtered through the single and henceforth predominant sense of sight.[38] This narrowing of all of our senses to vision alone is further tapered by the invention of a new and still more specialized (thus narrower) sense, namely inner vision. Paying tribute to its metaphoric link with vision, it is at the time usually called *imag*ination, *Ein-bild-ungskraft.* "The imagination is simply that wonderful sense," Kittler observes, "that can replace all our senses."[39] This game of substitution is more than mere entertainment for the mental faculties: it becomes the condition of epistemological certainty. Just as the sciences make their truth claims by limiting manifold sense data to the single sense of sight (one measure of progress in the sciences is their growing capacity to translate sound, temperature, pressure, velocity, mass, density, time, etc. into visual—i.e., spatial—information by means of gauges, graphs, displays, printouts, and the like), so the poetry and philosophy of the late eighteenth century vouch for the authenticity of inner vision by limiting its range.[40]

Substituting the ghostly "language of the spirit" for the written letter is typical not only of the works of the two titans of the German *Klassik.* It also pervades the writings of idealist philosophy and of early romanticism, a textual world which Schlegel does not merely observe but in which he takes an active part. The so-called "Ältestes Systemprogramm des deutschen Idealismus" (Earliest Program for a System of German Idealism) of 1796 or 1797, variously ascribed to Hegel, Schelling, and Hölderlin (and possibly written by all three), champions the "idea of *beauty*" as "the highest act of reason," contending that the "philosopher must possess as much aesthetic power as the poet."[41] Yet if we were inclined to believe that such aesthetic power entailed attending to the senses, to shapes and sounds, to the materiality of communicative systems, we would be sorely disappointed. For this prized "aesthetic sense," the author continues, is absent in those who are interested in letters and who are thus mere "philosophers of the letter [*Buchstabenphilosophen*]" (2:648/TP 73). Only the "philosophy of the *spirit* is an aesthetic philosophy" (ibid., my emphasis). That such a usage of the term *aesthetic* requires a 180-degree turn in its meaning (in 1750, Baumgarten still understands it in the sense of *aisthetikos,* relating to sense perception) would merely seem to stiffen the determination with which the material manifestation of the spirit is scorned in favor of its ghostly inhabitant. Even Novalis, whose experiments with poetological concepts come closest to Schlegel's, is known to mock the mere "literalists [*Buchstäbler*]"[42] who fail to appreciate his millennial vision in which a "spirit will chase away those ghosts that have in its place appeared in letters [*Buchstaben*] emanating piecemeal from quills and presses, and it will fuse all people like a pair of lovers" (*Schriften* 2:488 / TP 133).[43]

Novalis not only offers us the interesting spectacle of a spirit chasing ghosts, but connects it, albeit obscurely, to the printing press. He alerts us to the fact that the insistence on a transcendent meaning and the debasement of its material manifestation are encouraged by the changes gripping the social functions of reading and writing. Kittler devotes himself to scrutinizing the structure of this encouragement: the apotheosis of the poetic spirit in the "discourse network around 1800," he argues, is comprehensible only in the context of the immense success of the mechanization of texts. The more readily texts are reproduced and the more easily they are read (thanks to rapidly spreading literacy), the more intensely it is believed that an ineffable spirit speaks through them. We find a version of this discourse analysis in the very discourse network that is here being analyzed. In his *Geschichte der poetischen Literatur Deutschlands* (History of Poetic Literature in Germany) of 1857, Joseph von Eichendorff provides a remarkable diagnosis for what he takes to be the continuing decline of poetry:

> The last and not least blow . . . came from the invention of the art of printing in which the letter [*Buchstabe*] took the place of the living word and the lonely reader the place of the personal, gesticulating speaker. The printed book has for the spirit, like the calculator has for memory, something of the qualities of a mummy, something stationary and stiff on which one can comfortably rest at any time, while the living tradition (so long as it is living) is necessarily involved in continued development. Through printing, all of literature has indeed become one book in which everyone can leaf at pleasure, giving rise to a general dilettantism of producers as of consumers.[44]

Both in its vocabulary ("producers," "consumers") and in its description of the effects of printing, Eichendorff provides an account that, were it not for the cultural pessimism and its corollary, cultural elitism, one might not be surprised to find in McLuhan's *Gutenberg Galaxy*. He pinpoints the very features of the mechanization of textual production that McLuhan highlights and that, in his view, cause "disturbances," both social and psychological.[45]

The shrewdness of Kittler's account lies in reading this as more than a defensive maneuver. He recognizes that the fervency with which writers and readers of the emerging print culture render the letter invisible, replacing its worrisome qualities—strict abstraction and inherent meaninglessness—with a plenitude of spiritual meaning, serves in fact to *promote* the production, circulation, and consumption of printed matter. Only when the brittle scholasticism of textual study, according to Kittler still dominant around the middle of the eighteenth century, gives way to what he calls the "hallucinatory sensualities" (150 / 117) of the romantic imagination, can the technical modes of textual processing be implemented on a large scale. Letters become ubiquitous when they are no longer seen as letters: thus, Kittler shows, mothers are instructed to teach their children how to turn letters into pure sounds, and poets show their readers how to let letters metamorphose into pure spirit. The condition, then, under which literacy and printing expand their range lies in the disavowal of their material substrate—disavowal understood in the technical Freudian sense of rejecting and accepting a fact at one and the same time: rejecting it consciously (on the level of knowledge) while simultaneously accepting it unconsciously (on the level of truth).[46]

Grammatical Interest

It is into this context that Schlegel's literal experiments intervene. It would not be right to set up an opposition, for Schlegel himself pays ample tribute to the *Geist* that allegedly pervades, undergirds, and shines through every letter. In his 1808 book *Über die Sprache und Weisheit der Indier* (On the Language and Wisdom of the Indians) he urges his readers not to regard "merely the form, like letter-learned critics," but to look for "the spirit, the inner life."[47] But alongside his many publicly stated tributes to the spirit, we find in his private notebooks (though not only there) a decidedly different conception of the letter that permits chemistry, understood as an explanatory model situated between mechanism and organicism, to allegorize poetry down to its letters as a set of unpredictably combining elements. Such a conception is never explicitly articulated in his work. Indeed, he seems to have trouble articulating the relationship of letter and spirit with precision, resorting often, as we have already observed, to the language of magic. Thus he programmatically declares in one of the "Ideas" published in the *Athenäum*: "People have been talking about an omnipotence of the letter for a long time without really knowing what they are saying. It is time for it to be taken seriously, for the spirit to awaken and to grasp once again the lost magic wand."[48] Despite the intuitive link that we might assume between alchemical transmutation and magic, the transformation of the letter into a magic wand, of *Buchstab* into *Zauberstab* (a pun of which Schlegel is quite enamored [KA 18:265, No. 846; KA 5:20/LF 58]), is best modeled not by alchemy but by the combinatorial logic of chemistry. Indeed, alchemy would make an apt allegory for a poetic conception beholden to "the logic of the signifieds," which amounts to "a fantasy according to which one irreplaceable signified"—for instance, gold—"replaces all replaceable signifiers."[49] By contrast, "the logic of the signifier is a logic of substitution" (ibid.), which is to say precisely the logic demanded by chemical combinations. Again, it would not serve us well to establish and defend an opposition between alchemy and chemistry, between a poetic and hermeneutic theory based on spirits rather than on matter; just as chemistry in the late eighteenth century remains unpurged of its alchemical ancestry, so no account of poetic production, then or now, can entirely dispense with some version of spirit as that which would seem to exceed the automatism or randomness of writing, regardless of how aware of the material conditions of poetry's medium it may be. Despite its vast scientific advances in the last decades of the eighteenth century, chemistry, in not yielding to a mathematical description, continues to harbor an element of magic; magic in turn, despite appearing to move us into the vicinity of a godhead, is in essence, as Schlegel himself notes, combinatorial (KA 18:388, No. 805). But how is a chemical magic of the letter to be imagined?

One way of approaching this question is through Schlegel's notion of grammar. Earlier I quoted from a letter to Novalis in which the young Schlegel confesses to "understand[ing] you better written than while speaking"; "I am a grammatical nature," he writes, explaining his peculiar preference for the written word with an even more peculiar characterization of his nature. Describing one's nature as "grammatical" may seem less odd if we recall that throughout his writing career Schlegel, an exceptionally well-read classical philologist, shows himself to be acutely aware of the etymological tentacles with which words hold fast to their past moorings. In the case of *grammatical* and *grammar* this means that he never loses sight of *gramma,* the letter. Thus the very first item on a list of how "grammar is to be treated in philosophy" (a plan Schlegel never realized) is "the given; letters."[50] In the same vein he claims: "There is no philologist without philology in the most original sense of the word, without grammatical interest."[51] The interest of this Schlegelian philologist is not confined to the classical idea of grammar (as a critical study of the structure and history of texts) nor motivated by the more recent sense of grammar (be it as a universal grammar of language as such or the particular grammar describing the rules of syntax, inflection, phonetics, etc. of a particular language),[52] but is focused above all on the letters. Thus—applying the theory to its own articulation—a philologist devotes his *philia* to the *logos,* his love to words, to the degree that he acknowledges words *as words* (rather than as veils), to the degree that he is interested in letters. A grammatical nature would be strongly disposed to prefer written to spoken communication because, despite persistent confusion since the introduction of alphabetic literacy, the letter is not a phoneme; it belongs to the register not of spoken but of written language. Schlegel's notion of grammar, while maintaining its denotative link to the idea of a formalization of language, always connotes the presence of *grammata,* hence the presence of writing. A theory of language, and a fortiori of poetry, that has recourse to grammar in this sense is not well positioned to spiritualize, sublimate, or otherwise forget the presence of the letters of the alphabet.[53]

The notion of "grammatical interest" can take us a bit further still. If we take Schlegel's cue about "the most original sense of the word" (meaning not the most inventive, but the most ancient, *ursprüng-lichste Bedeutung*), we would note that grammatical interest is by no means the same thing as a mystical embrace of letters. The spiritistic erasure of the letter, so prevalent around 1800, is not replaced in Schlegel's work by a Cabalistic devotion to it; despite the vocabulary of magic, spirits neither sigh nor burn through his letters.[54] Quite the contrary: his letters are, in Lacan's terms, "the essentially localized structure of the signifier,"[55] and his grammatical interest, just as the original sense of *inter-esse* (to be in-between) might lead us to suspect, is trained first and foremost upon what occurs *between* the letters. This becomes more evident when we read a bit further in the fragment just quoted: "There is no philologist without philology in the most original sense of the word, without grammatical interest. Philology is a logical affect, the companion piece to philosophy, enthusiasm for chemical knowledge: for grammar is surely only the philosophical part of the universal art of separating and mixing."[56] Though this compact conceptual package does not entirely yield to intelligibility, the two references to chemistry make it clear that philology, the love of words, and grammar, the science of letters, are to be imagined according to the "universal art of separating and mixing." If grammar is an instance of universal chemistry, then we can begin to understand the many connections Schlegel establishes between *Witz* and grammar and *grammata,* for as we have seen wit (also called "chemical ingeniousness") is the name Schlegel gives to the operations of chemistry within language. "Everything witty is above all grammatical and to that extent philosophical," he writes.[57] Since the letter is the "agency of wit,"[58] the explosions that wit triggers (KA 2:158, No. 90/PF 11; KA 2:159, No. 104/PF 12–13) are ultimately grammatical, literally literal. They scatter and join letters.

If what makes a work poetic is a letter irreducible to an underlying spirit ("The letter of every work is *poetry*," Schlegel remarks, "its spirit philosophy"),[59] then understanding a verbal artwork (indeed, any text) cannot rely on a telepathic link with a spirit cloaked in lifeless marks, but must always contend with the letters of the text, with its writtenness, its artificiality. It has been argued that this represents a "darkening in the relationship of spirit and letter,"[60] for interpretation becomes, for the first time, a problem endemic to textual communication. Schlegel's question of whether "the communication of ideas . . . is even possible,"[61] the question of the comprehensibility or incomprehensibility of verbal communication, imposes itself once the letter achieves the dignity of being recognized as a constructive principle. In more contemporary terms: when the signifier is no longer conceived of as an obstacle to grasping the signified itself, it loses its *Selbstverständlichkeit,* its quality of being (self-)understood, and gains instead in *Unverständlichkeit.* Untethering the verbal artifact from the spirit of the signified no doubt opens the range of readings, increases the possibilities of understanding and, inevitably, misunderstanding, and thus calls for a science of interpretation. In short, the prominent position of the letter stands not only at the center of Schlegel's poetological conceptions, but it is also responsible for one of the most enduring changes that Jena romanticism has wrought in our understanding of literature: it consist not merely of reversing the usual hierarchy of spirit and letter, but rather of exploring the explosive reactions that arise when letters—characters—are mixed in just the right way, reactions that have been known to give rise to interesting substances known as spirits. This, then, is a theory that attempts to invent a new space for the production and reception of words, one that recognizes the organic spirit for the phantom that it is, while realizing that the mechanical letters, as such and by themselves, are as inert and without interest as a lump of lead. What interests us, what we call "literature," is when those inert pieces of lead "come alive," when a particular arrangement of letters endows them with a special mobility—call it *Witz* or chemistry—that arouse our curiosity precisely because they bristle with odd shapes and incomprehensibilities.

The Agency of the Alphabet

We should be more specific about the process of separating and mixing letters before we consider some of its wider implications. For scattering and joining letters, separating and mixing them, is in Schlegel's writings not confined to the status of a metaphorical insight or a poetological goal. It is very much put into practice, a practice that is experimental, innovative, and impressively bizarre. A notebook from 1805, entitled "German Grammar I," resembles nothing more than a laboratory for the alphabet. Among the assorted thoughts about syntax, rhetoric, spelling, typography, etymology, and language, there are idiosyncratic observations about letters, alphabets in various languages, and presumed relationships based on purely literal coincidences. "*Bin* [am] related to *in* [in]. *asse* [plural of ace] and *esse* [stove, chimney] maybe really one word?"[62] Or: "Does *Danken* [to thank] refer to *Dank* [the noun thanks] or to *Ding* [thing]?"[63] Differences in meaning and function, the main criteria by which words are conventionally understood, are supplanted by a "secret brotherhood" based solely on the arrangement of letters. And the model for such arrangements, for the division and connection of letters, is taken explicitly from chemistry. Schlegel contemplates "divid[ing] the *consonants* according to IRON, *water, air.*"[64] Are some consonants, he wonders, "alkaline, the others acidic?"[65] He goes so far as to wonder which scientific taxonomy will serve the letters best: in some notebook entries he proceeds from the assumption that "consonants [correspond to] chemical substances, vowels to light";[66] in others he tests other combinations: "Vowels perhaps not only light but also the binding and melting *water* in language.—But *consonants* express *stone* and *air.* Or consonants = water + stone, vowels = light + air."[67] In short, "consonants can also signify the basic materials of chemistry."[68]

Schlegel takes this idea literally enough to transfer a quintessential achievement of eighteenth-century chemistry—the table of affinities—to philology. His notebooks contain several versions of what he calls "Tables of Affinities of Letters,"[69] and though even the most elaborate (see fig. 1) is rudimentary compared to the tables chemists were producing at the time, it indicates a determination to display the most essential knowledge pertaining to philology in a scientific form. More precisely: in *the* scientific form. For the table—we might say the genre of the table—is, according to Michel Foucault, the "centre of knowledge in the seventeenth and eighteenth centuries."[70] It is the discursive manifestation of "the project, however remote it may be, of an exhaustive ordering of the world" (89/74); unlike the list, which is potentially endless, the table captures the infinite manifestations of the world in a finite form by reducing the world to "simple elements and their progressive combination" (ibid.). This is precisely what chemical tables do (tables of affinities but also the currently used Periodic Table), and it is apparently what Schlegel's table of affinities of letters is meant to accomplish. The relations between the letters in the table reproduced in figure 1 remain inscrutable (as they do in some of the smaller tables, e.g., KA 16:378–80, No. 130–39; KA 16:444–45, No. 252), partly because Schlegel provides almost no instructions for how to read them (they are, after all, meant only as notes to himself). Yet we would be mistaken in believing that the letters have been spread more or less randomly over the page. As a glance at the messy manuscript (see fig. 2) reveals, Schlegel found a lot to correct: in the vertical series ". . . m n p q r . . . ," " "q" is crossed out and replaced, puzzlingly, by "f"; "r s h" gives way to "r z h." The many insertions, additions, and marginal glosses suggest not only how tentative these experiments are, but also that, in Schlegel's mind, the particular position of this or that letter *matters.* Even if it looks like madness to us, we can see that, in his mind, there is method to it. And it is the method we are after, even—especially—if it courts the possibility of madness. We need not worry about why "r z h" is to be preferred to "r s h," for reconstructing the *specific* attractions and repulsions that Schlegel detects between particular letters or in evaluating their plausibility concerns us little. What does interest us is that the combinatorial logic drawn from chemistry is taken by Schlegel to provide the explanatory template for the most basic—the most elementary—ways in which letters join to make syllables, words, phrases, sentences: to make language. And precisely because the rule according to which such attractions and repulsions work is not available (precisely because language does not yield to a purely formal account), Schlegel can do little more than to list countless instances of the affinities of various letters in various positions.[71]

Such a conception entails a very different idea of language than the ones usually ascribed to writers around 1800. Thus it is increasingly difficult to maintain the widely accepted notion of a fundamental congruence between language and nature, a congruence that can take many forms. As Foucault has shown, the scientific discourse of the time relies on the isomorphism of nature and the encyclopedia.[72] The literary and philosophical discourse at the turn of the nineteenth century prefers a different model. Kittler does not tire of reminding us that that discourse relies on the "logic of the signified," i.e., at base on an *identity* of signs with what they designate. On what level of signification is this identity to be found? Certainly not on the level of words, for words are "scorned by Faust, Herder, Hippel, Nathanael"[73] and all the other exemplars of the discourse network around 1800, among whom Kittler accords Schlegel a prominent place. The identity of sign and meaning can also not occur on the level of the letter, for as we have seen, the discourse around 1800 debases the letter at every turn.

Thus, for this discursive formation, the fundamentally authentic linguistic unit must be located somewhere below the threshold of the word and above that of the letter. That is the point at which language intersects with, indeed is anchored by, that sign which is nothing but a signified. It is also the point at which Schlegel, insofar as he promotes the logic of chemistry, *departs* from the path of the signified—hence from the way in which the discourse network around 1800 establishes meaning and evaluates texts. It is an absolutely decisive point, for on Kittler's account "the threshold that determines the possible extent and usefulness of analyses differentiates discourse networks from one another" (ibid.); in other words, it matters deeply where in the chain of composition of linguistic phenomena an epis-

Verwandtschaftstafeln der Buchstaben

b	b	p	r	l
d	d	t	z	s
w	n	m	h	g
g	w	f		
h	w und f vielleicht auch nur Hauche wie h und ch. —			
k	*b d l* scheint zusammenzugehören.			
l				

```
b        b   p        r   l
d        d   t        z   s
w        n   m        h   g
g        w   f
h        w und f vielleicht auch nur Hauche wie h und ch. —
k        b d l scheint zusammenzugehören.
l

m        n   s   g       m   r   h
n        f   r   p   t   m   h   z   ch) <oder even weich[e] und harte
p        w   l   b   d   n   g   s   h) vermischt.>
f
r
s
z        cpq — h
t        sch redublirt
```

	i	ei	au			
a	u	ü	e	eu		
ä	o	ö	<*schr* selten>			

```
          i   ö   ü   ä  (u)
          o   e   eu  ei  au
          i   u   u
              u   i
          u   a   o   müssen rein bleiben
          k   r   k
                  h
```

i und *u* <und das sch> haben viel Neigung zu einander und Präponderanz in den nasalen Seedialekten. Vielleicht sind die harten Consonanten erst d[ie] abgeleiteten und d.[ie] *gelinden* sind die ersten.

<ξ ψ χ φ ω η fallen weg aus dem griechischen Alphabet, so wie θ.>

```
                  ⎧ r   h   z
      l und s     ⎪ p   t   m
<              12 ⎨                >
      r und z     ⎪ l   b   d
                  ⎩ g   n   s
```

<Oder f und ch beides Hauche. / f v (w) h ch.> |

Fig. 1: Tables of Affinities of Letters, KA 16:378.

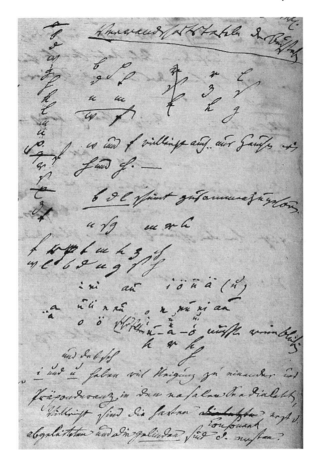

Fig. 2: Tables of Affinities of Letters (Stadtarchiv Trier).

teme finds the semantic point of anchorage, where it believes the "truth" of language to lie. We are still fascinated by this issue: the field of evolutionary cognitive science, the present-day center of the debate, has generated numerous conflicting accounts of the origin of language(s); it has offered, among others, the yelps of pain, the signals among hunters, and the chatter of gossip as the irreducible truths of linguistic genesis and function.[74] In the network around 1800, "each word, down to the least of its particles, had to be a meticulous form of nomination,"[75] i.e., of meaning generation; these molecules of writing are discovered to consist of, as Kittler shows, "the minimal element of significant sounds and sound combinations."[76] Perfectly well-constructed sentences are suddenly broken up by a sighing *ach,* for the sole reason of having meaning breathed into them. Thus, Kittler remarks, "Around 1800, the 'love of the word' or 'philology' applied neither to the word nor to those asignificative elements known as phonemes or letters. Instead it was devoted entirely to the Spirit or signified of language, through whose working [quoting the philosopher Friedrich Niethammer] 'every *word* expresses a form, every usage a grouping, every choice of words a nuance of the picture' and (this is decisive) 'the syllable also becomes meaningful'" (ibid.).

But such a commitment to signifying sounds is hampered considerably (though not rendered entirely impossible, as we shall see) when philology is motivated by "grammatical interest," i.e., by precisely those nonsignifying letters that Kittler takes to be excluded from the discourse network around 1800. If late-eighteenth-century poetic and linguistic theory halts its analysis at the level of the syllable because it regards it as a fundamental morphological—i.e., meaning-bearing—unit, then Schlegel, by experimenting at the level of the letter, opens the door to a conception in which language consists of nothing but the combinations of *non*signifying elements. Language can no longer conform "to the organic model in which elements, which are not by accident called roots, grow first stems and finally whole words," as Kittler would have it (59/45). In the chemical model the smooth, continuous movement of an "augmentation lead[ing] from meaning to meaning" (ibid.), which insures meaningfulness at the top layer of language by finding meaning in the basic building blocks, is interrupted by the irreducibility of the elements of language to meaningful units. Thus organic articulation is replaced with fragmentary combination: with the senselessness of the letter.

When Schlegel calls the letter an "agency [*Organ*] of wit [*Witzes*]" (KA 18:260, No. 797), he is less far than it might seem from Lacan's claim about the letter as an agent in the unconscious. Lacan approaches precisely this point of contact (or blurring) of sense and nonsense, of spirit and letter, when he claims: "We see, then, that metaphor occurs at the precise point at which sense emerges from non-sense, that is, at the frontier which, as Freud discovered, when crossed the other way produces the word that in French is *the* word *par excellence,* the word that is simply the signifier '*esprit.*'"[77] Is *esprit* not (as Lacan himself suggests in a note [177 n22]) the very *Witz* that, in Schlegel's account, is the agency giving rise to words with the suddenness and contingency of the combinatorial method? Indeed, our discussion permits us to go further and to map Lacan's notoriously slippery conceptual troika of the Symbolic, the Imaginary, and the Real onto concepts that may at this point be somewhat easier to grasp for us. The symbolic order (e.g., language, social rules, taboos and laws, etc.) is a region that exists prior to our arrival and is thus external to us; it operates like an independent machine producing completely meaningless statements. When an extension of our intentional self, an offshoot of our curiosity, an imaginary projection of ourselves, extends into that region to communicate, a sort of reaction occurs. In most cases, it is entirely benign and is experienced by us as a successful or at least neutral encounter with external systems. But the fact that it is a reaction with a certain volatility (rather than a tool under our sway) becomes evident in those moments when some unforeseen event occurs and a swerve moves us from our intended meaning: we say *Rate* rather than *Ratte,* or we get entangled in *Unverständlichkeit.* I would understand the Real thus not as a "hard kernel" (the way Slavoj Žižek often does) or a primordial throbbing mass (the way the Imaginary does), but as the form that the disturbance or deviation in the moment of conjunction of symbolic order and imaginary desire takes. (This could be the missing letter *t* in *Rate.*) The Real would be the trace of nonsense in the region of sense and, just as important, the trace of sense in the region of nonsense, a perturbation in the smooth working of the machine that can be blamed neither on the machine nor on its "user."

The consequences of conceiving of language—the material substrate of poetry—as a chemical combination of written marks are far-reaching for aesthetics. Only with difficulty could such a language serve as the medium by which the "genius" of aesthetic theory filters "nature" into artistic production. Once language is reduced to a table of elements, it can no longer be imagined as Herder's "mere channel," and the poet no longer as "the translator . . . of nature into the soul and into the heart of his brothers."[78] If the poet-genius is possessed, as Kant tells us, of "the innate mental predisposition (*ingenium*) *through which* nature gives the rule to art" (KU 307), then a combinatorial language introduces an obstacle in the passage from nature to art. That is because in the case of the poet, a case that is (as we know) exemplary and not one among many, both elements of the equation—nature and art—are so severely altered by the scientific model that they have no choice but to enter into a new relationship. While in the chemical allegory language is still conceived in analogy to nature ("consonants can also signify the basic materials of chemistry"), this nature to which language is being analogized is a nature of a very different sort: chemistry, as we have seen, ultimately only knows the analysis and synthesis—the "separating and mixing"—of what late-eighteenth-century chemistry calls "simple bodies," and is incompatible with the homeostatic organicism of romantic nature that we get in Kant or Rousseau, Wordsworth or Goethe. In the latter view, nature is imagined essentially as an artifact, presented to us, according to Kant, "as if [it] had been given by an understanding (even though not ours) for the benefit of our cognitive faculties" (KU 180); it is an object that, like art, is regarded as if it had a purpose, hence an object that can be judged aesthetically (as either beautiful or sublime).

The chemical conception of nature, however, not only has no use for teleological constructions, it also extends nature's borders in such a way as to remove nature even further from the conventional romantic notion. For as the chemist Martin Heinrich Klaproth emphasized in his lectures at a military academy in Berlin in 1789, the fact that chemistry "penetrates into the innermost regions of bodies, divides them, and investigates their components"[79] represents only one half the equation; the analysis into simple bodies permits in a second step a synthetic "recomposition," yielding products that are "either an imitation of mixtures . . . given by nature, or . . . new products presentable only through art" (ibid.). Once nature's elements become manipulable according to a combinatorial logic, the outcome far exceeds what nature itself has seen fit to produce. Chemistry, setting out, like Faust, to gaze at "the innermost regions" of the natural world, almost immediately finds itself transgressing the line between nature and artifice. If the combinations of its elements are to serve as an allegory for how letters form words—for how poetic production works—then we cannot simply assume a Herderian process of translation from nature into art, for what words emulate or allegorize may itself already be art. Practical chemists like Klaproth see in the region beyond nature—in "art"—only interesting substances that nature has neglected to make, like "phosphorus, brass, glass, porcelain, etc." (ibid.). But we know from writers around 1800 (even from those with little interest in the gothic) that far darker creations of art are possible, that at any moment "the glimmer of error and of madness, or of obtuseness and of stupidity [may] shine through" the letters.[80]

In and Out of the "Great Lalula"

We need to consider in greater detail the conceptual shift involved in moving from an organic to a chemical theory of language. One crucial feature of such a shift is the relationship that linguistic units are thought to maintain with sound. While in the phonocentric model around 1800 the anchor of meaning is ultimately to be found in the sound that every grouping of letters is imagined to represent (and letters are inevitably thought to fall short of accomplishing this task),[81] the chemical model with which Schlegel plays employs material that remains below the threshold of sound: as we observed, it is the consonants, those letters that, as their name suggests, can be sounded only when accompanied by sound (i.e., a vowel), that make up Schlegel's alphabetic elements, his *Grundstoffe* (KA 17:27, No. 138). And even when combined, the compounds can elude the reach of sounding, hence, of intrinsic meaning. Thus one experiment in combinations produces

schw schl schr schn schm
tr tz th tl θλ tm tn
sr st sn sm sl
sb sd sh
kr kl ks kg χς kw km kn
ps pl pr ph pf πν mpf mp
br bl bz bs βς
nt nd nk ng ns nz nf
dr dl dg
st sz sp spr spl
gr gl gn
fr fl ft
lt lf lb lt ls ld
rk rb rd rn rm rz rt
zw
(KA 16:379, No. 130)

Contrast this with a primer published in 1807 by Heinrich Stephani, an influential Bavarian school official, in which children, guided by their home-schooling mothers (as the subtitle of the book insists), are urged to repeat these sounds:

ju jo jö jä je jü ji jau
mu mo ma mö mä me mu mi
mei mai mau mäu Ma-Ma[82]

At the end of three lines, Stephani has managed to arrive at "Ma-Ma," the source not only of the children but also of the sounds that they are to imitate, and with a few more permutations he produces "Pa-pa" and "Bu-be" (boy); as Kittler notes, "after three run-throughs of sounds and sound combinations, the phonetic method led to the signification and benediction of the nuclear family,"[83] which for purely linguistic reasons seems not to be able to accommodate daughters.

That Schlegel's experiment brings forth not "Ma-Ma," the *Ur*-knot tying together signifier and signified, but rather "zw" is simply one of the effects of taking the alphabet seriously. The alphabet cuts, literally speaking, through the syllable, carrier of an allegedly grounding meaning, and produces meaningless components. As linguists and anthropologists of writing have pointed out, the alphabet demands a far greater degree of abstraction than does any other writing system, whether pictographic, logographic, or syllabic;[84] it necessitates, in one linguist's aptly chemical terms, "the decomposition of syllables into signs for consonants and vowels."[85] This decomposition results in elements that maintain a *dis*continuous relationship with meaning. There are historical as well as theoretical reasons for this. Historically, the development of the alphabet entails a loss or a forgetting of meaning. In the Old Phoenician script, most letter-names have a meaning (*aleph*—ox or ox head, *beth*—house, *gimmel*—camel, etc.). But when (by about 800 B.C.E. at the latest) the Greeks borrow that script to make the first alphabet that indicates *both* consonants and vowels in a series of successive signs, this link to a primordial state, a testimony to the emergence of letters from meaningful signs, is interrupted: to the Greeks, the words *alpha, beta, gamma,* etc. have a purely acrophonic function; they name the letter, and only the letter, with which they begin.[86] (In our—which is to say, the Latin—alphabet, itself an adaptation of the Greek, the letter names do not signify anything but the letters.)

The more consequential dissociation from meaning occurs in the theoretical abstraction required to arrive at alphabetic letters: as anyone who has "sounded out" words will know, alphabetic writing, in its ideal form, demands that all aspects of a word's significance be set aside for the sake of its phonetic expression. To achieve this isolation, the word is broken into sound fragments small enough that no meaning may be associated with them. Hence "Mama" does not divide into "Ma-Ma," each of which could (and sometimes does) stand for the whole meaningful word, but into "M-A-M-A," an unpronounceable staccato of sound fragments that has little in common with human language. But this unpronounceability and meaninglessness is precisely the chief virtue of alphabetic writing, for it permits two dozen signs, in different arrangements, to represent an infinite number of ideas. Marshall McLuhan was not the first to have recognized this feature, though he may well have expressed it in the most conceptually trenchant terms: "The unique character of our alphabet," he writes, lies in the fact "that it dissociates or abstracts, not only sight and sound, but separates all meaning from the sound of the letters, save so far as the meaningless letters relate to the meaningless sounds."[87] This separation or abstraction (for abs-traction is finally nothing but a mental act of separation) involved in the structure of alphabetic recording technology opens, according to Foucault, the path for the application of abstraction to that which is being recorded, namely ideas. "Whereas symbolic writing . . . obeys the confused law of similitudes, and causes language to slip out of the forms of reflective thought, alphabetic writing, by abandoning the attempt to draw the representation, transposes into its analysis of sounds the rules that are valid for reason itself. So that it does not matter that letters do not represent ideas, since they can be combined together in the same way as ideas, and ideas can be linked together and disjoined just like the letters of the alphabet."[88] While other forms of writing cause us to slide out of the path of philosophical thought (*glisser* is Foucault's word), alphabetic writing, the argument goes, not only reflects the structure of thinking, but in a feedback loop, also promotes it. Which is why in his view "with alphabetic writing . . . the history of men is entirely changed" (ibid.).

Once sounds are reduced to basic elements, they can be arranged in a grid that displays not only these nonsignifying graphic units but also the logic of the operations by means of which the units are assembled into sequences. Such a grid represents all elements and, at once, all *relations* between elements; it reveals how known and meaningful words (*Mama*) are composed, but it also makes possible entirely meaningless permutations ("zw"). There are infinitely many such new possibilities, since the rules of letter combination are recursive: *m* may be joined with *a* to form *ma,* which can be joined to itself to form *mama,* but also to countless other letters and letter combinations: *maa, mab, mac, maab,* etc. Whether such permutations are actually produced is beside the point; what is crucial is that the very *possibility* of their emergence is encoded in the system itself. This gives an entirely new meaning to Schlegel's dictum that "*unlimited range* is the one great advantage of poetry,"[89] for the very procedure that brings forth the limitlessness also allows for completely new relationships (or "secret societies") among words. As far as the combinatorial system is concerned, *Danken* may indeed be linked as closely to *Ding* as to *Dank.* Such a system crosses the organic filiations of meaning—root, stem, word—and establishes instead combinatorial connections.

But such a practice—and theory of practice—would seem to land us in what Kittler, borrowing the title of a nonsense poem by Christian Morgenstern to which I shall turn in a moment, terms "the great Lalula,"[90] the region around 1900 in which the random selection, combination, and permutation of letters generates nonsense and, entirely accidentally, a small subset of sense. Indeed, at one point Schlegel seems to enter that region when he attempts to calculate the number of words a constrained version of a combinatorial system might yield. In a notebook on poetry, started in July of 1801 in Paris, he considers the following experiment:

> 12 consonants and 5 vowels / in-between all possible permutations—how many could that be?
> 1 V 1 C = 60 and 60
> 1 V 2 C = 720 [91]

Having calculated that using these three-letter syllables (consisting of a vowel and two consonants), 518,400 words of two syllables, 373,248,000 words of three syllables, and 268,735,560,000 words of four syllables are possible, he concludes dryly: "Among these words there are certainly a lot of meaningless ones."[92] But despite the seeming introduction of mathematics as a generating principle for the poetic word, a great distance divides this experiment from the great Lalula. We could only believe ourselves to have arrived there by overlooking a number of oddities in Schlegel's writings, oddities that are symptomatically present even in this combinatorial experiment. If this is to serve as an example of how a mathematical principle is employed to gauge, without regard for the category of meaning, the possibilities inherent in the technology of the alphabet for the benefit of literature, then it is an awkward example, not least because the mathematics in it is flawed. The number of all possible combinations of the three elements, $5 \times 12 \times 12 = 720$, is correct. But then Schlegel overlooks a crucial feature of the system, namely its permutations, for the vowel can stand in the first, the second, or the third position of the syllable; thus the number of three-letter syllables involves a three-fold increase over Schlegel's initial calculation: $720 \times 3 = 2,160$.

How to account for this oversight, especially when it occurs immediately after a calculation in which Schlegel *does* include the permutability of combinations (with one vowel and one consonant, i.e., $5 \times 12 = 60$, he expressly considers the option of switching the order, which doubles the number of possible two-letter syllables: "60 and 60," he notes)? One explanation (which we might call the Kittlerian version, even though to my knowledge Kittler himself has not commented on this interesting miscalculation) would be that in a single vowel-consonant combination even a reversal of order results in perfectly soundable—which is to say, potentially meaningful—syllables (*ab, ba; ac, ca; ad, da;* etc.). No such guarantee can be given, however, for combinations of a vowel and two consonants: the potentially meaningful combination *nip* would, permutated, yield the interesting *pin,* but also the less promising *inp, ipn, npi,* and *pni.* Thus it seems that the initial constraint, namely the requirement of the presence of a vowel (for why not simply $26^3 = 17,576$ or at least 17 [5 vowels + 12 consonants]$^3 = 4,913$?), does not suffice to insure the smooth pronounceability of all syllables. The system must be further constrained by means of a silent prohibition against the possibility of permutation and the assumption that the vowel will always stand where it will facilitate effortless sounding (in our example, in the middle).

This reading is certainly plausible, particularly when we add the fact that Schlegel endows his two-letter syllables with almost cabalistic power, calling them "the original concepts."[93] Yet such a reading is obliged to overlook the presence of a language, here and elsewhere, that is neither mathematical nor indebted to the organicism of full meaning in sound. Schlegel wonders whether "the 720 should signify the *telluric* elements," i.e., those elements belonging to or extracted from the earth.[94] Why this change into the chemical register? Why label his letter grids "Tables of Affinities of Letters"? Why speak of consonants as "the basic materials of chemistry," as *chemische Grund-stoffe*? The bond between letters and elements appears to enjoy its own version of a powerful affinity, for it reappears in the most un-likely context: Eric Havelock, for example, a firm believer in the meaninglessness of alphabetic letters and the cultural significance that results from such meaninglessness, calls the alphabet "an atomic table of elements," a term that is, as we shall see, not entirely metaphoric.[95] The reason for the chemical metaphor, when a magical / organic (Schlegel) or mechanistic metaphor (Havelock) would have been more apt, can be found in a feature of the chemical that is by now familiar to us: chemistry names the degree to which a formal account is contaminated by nonformal (material, signifying) elements, and vice versa.

We saw earlier how, because of the high degree of abstraction re-quired to produce them, the letters of the alphabet in and of them-selves fail at carrying meanings (or the organic seeds of meaning). But that does not automatically make letters the raw, senseless material of a formal system. For letters are denuded of all meaning only in an idealized form of the alphabet; in every real instance of it they do far more than merely hew to their role of indicating one, and only one, sound. I mentioned earlier that in their transfer from Phoenician into Greek hands, i.e., during the transition from a script indicating only consonants to one with signs for consonants *and* vowels, the letter names (*aleph, beth,* etc.) lose their meanings (ox, house, etc.). But let-ters have not, for that reason, lost *all* meaning. In a strange way their utter analytic meaninglessness and the uncertainty of their history (there is no unbroken chain of links relating the letters of different scripts to a point of origin) have made the letters into magnets for elaborate symbolic meanings. Thus their shape, in the analytic ac-count a purely arbitrary feature determined only by a desire for easy coding and decoding, has been both explained by and used as an ex-planation for mysterious phenomena. According to an ancient Greek account, the god Hermes was inspired by the shapes of flocks of cranes in flight when he drew up the letters.[96] More recently, non-mythic explanations of the letters have tried to establish a highly mediated link with a pictographic past in which their shapes are, or are thought to be, *mimetic*—which is to say, meaningful. It has been suggested that the letters *M* and *N*, for example, "were once hieroglyphic representations of sea waves," and "*Z* was at one time understood to express the descending zigzags of the lightning flash."[97] The point is not that such a view may be wide of the mark (for it necessarily relies on a speculative reading of a very fragmentary paleographic record), but rather that, as Johanna Drucker puts it in her cultural history of the alphabet, "throughout history, the letters of the alphabet have occasioned imaginative speculation about the possible hidden value of their visual form."[98] Such speculation can take mythical, hermetic, cabalistic, or oracular form; it can take the shape of more or less fanciful histories; or it can express itself in an aesthetically motivated attention to the shape of the letters. Calligraphy, which Schlegel practiced frequently in different scripts (Latin, Devanagari, Arabic),[99] may not assume a letter replete with meaning (so replete that it can serve as an explanation for the secrets of the universe), but it is nevertheless fueled by a visual surplus far exceeding the function of the letter as a device for the storage and transportation of sounds.

We do not have to rely on mythical, mystical, or aesthetic accounts in recognizing an excess within the senselessness of the letter. A glance at any written document will suffice. The letters on this page are very far from complying with the ideal of rendering as perfectly as possible the phonetic shape of words with written marks. The majority of words in written English contain letters that contribute nothing to—and thus detract from—their effortless phonetic reproduction (rather than reproduxion or reprodukshen). The fact that many efforts at introducing a "true" phonetic spelling have failed is attributable not merely to inertia or to elitism, but also to the desire of writers to preserve a feature of letters that exceeds phoneticism and hence pure meaninglessness. *Reproduction* is preferred precisely because the letter *c* contains the extra-phonetic information linking the word to *reproduce* and *produce* (where the letter is associated with a completely different phoneme), and ultimately with the Latin *producere* (where the connection to the hard *c* is again mediated entirely through the letter, rather than the phoneme).[100] Even strictly alphabetic writing produces an excess above and beyond the sounds that its letters record.

This is not to suggest that Schlegel's unsystematic reflections on the chemistry of letters take such ideas as the stubbornness of non-phonetic spelling or the hermetic or calligraphic features of writing fully into account. It *is*, however, to say that they register in a general way what historical and linguistic accounts of the alphabet demonstrate, namely that sound is always implicated in writing, and writing in sound. Phonetic qualities are indispensable to alphabetic writing (the three-letter syllables are all apparently *pronounceable*) even when it appears to have abandoned the realm of recognizable sense. Yet the graphic is not merely subservient to that requirement, for graphic signs turn out to have their own logic: with mechanical inevitability the graphic system produces a multitude of words among which "there are certainly a lot of meaningless ones." As this assertion makes clear, Schlegel has by no means left the province of meaning: the automatism of sign generation is of interest to him—and I would add, to us—only when meaning somehow touches, enters, or otherwise contaminates the great Lalula.[101] This contamination of nonsense by sense, of the mechanical by the organic, occurs, as we have seen, in Schlegel's alphabetic experiments in which the letters, supposedly purely abstract, are always stained with some semantic content. Thus: "L, R, M, N / L and N just childish—R and M very fitting for greatness. . . . *K* depth, *T* strength, courage, *W* enthusiasm, swiftness, storm, *Sch* lust, the highest."[102] Crucially, this semantic content does not appear to be motivated by a "deep" connection through the sound or shape of the letters: *K* is paired not with *Kraft* and *T* not with *Tiefe*, but precisely the other way around. But just because the meaning sticking to the form seems utterly arbitrary, it blocks any possibility of a thorough formalization of the system. The contamination of form (letters, syntax) by content (semantics) is thus a sort of primordial trauma, not to be negotiated away by means of rational linguistic analysis.[103]

But is even Morgenstern's "Great Lalula" in Kittler's great Lalula? It is, according to Kittler, an example of "the most radical consequence that can be drawn from a discourse network," namely "to write writing,"[104] which in the discourse network around 1900 means playing "a game of dice" involving letters and punctuation marks "to which writers since Mallarmé have ceded all initiative" (267 / 213). Here is Morgenstern's intriguing poem, untranslated:

> Das große Lalula
>
> Kroklokwafzi? Sememi!
> Seiokronto—prafriplo:
> Bifzi, bafzi; hulalemi:
> quast basti bo . . .
> Lalu lalu lalu lalu la!
>
> Hontraruru miromente
> zasku zes rü rü?
> Entepente, leiolente
> klekwapufzi lü?
> Lalu lalu lalu lalu la!
>
> Simarar kos malzipempu
> silzuzankunkrei (;)!
> Marjomar dos: Quempu Lempu
> Siri Suri Sei [ ]!
> Lalu lalu lalu lalu la![105]

The first thing we notice about what Kittler approvingly calls "systematic nonsense" (267 / 212) is that, except for the diacritical and punctuation marks, it could well have been generated by Schlegel's experiment with the twelve consonants and five vowels. The distance between any two vowels is, with one exception ("silzuzankunkrei"), never greater than two consonants, which means that the text consists of all those two- and three-letter syllables spewed by Schlegel's machine. Like Lewis Carroll's "Jabberwocky," the poem is, excepting perhaps punctuation marks such as "(;)" and "[ ]," completely pronounceable. "No voice," writes Kittler, "can speak parentheses that enclose a semicolon . . . or even—to demonstrate once and for all what media are—brackets that surround an empty space" (ibid.). Perhaps, though it is not entirely clear what makes "[ ]" less conducive to performance than "!" or ". . ." are.

In any case, Morgenstern's graphics would not, on a first view, seem more distant from voiced enunciation than all the mixtures of German abbreviation, Greek letters, and mathematical symbols that have appeared in the endnotes here and that typographically reproduce the way many of Schlegel's handwritten notebook entries looked before they were expanded by scholars and editors. Thus the "impossible ideal of π [poetry]" is represented thus:

$$\text{Das unmögliche Ideal der } \pi = \sqrt[1/\infty]{\frac{\overset{0}{R}}{0}}^{(1/\infty)} + \sqrt[1/\infty]{\frac{\pi\varphi}{0}}^{(1/\infty)} + \sqrt[1/\infty]{\frac{\pi\pi}{0}}^{(1/\infty)}$$

(KA 16:148, No. 736)

One can try to decode this (the valiant editors of the critical edition offer this: "infinitely reduced absolute novel raised to the power of infinity + infinitely reduced absolute prophecy raised to the power of infinity + infinitely reduced absolute poetic poetry raised to the power of infinity"), but this "decoding" would, if anything, seem to make even less sense than the coded message. Perhaps we should simply regard it (for we can hardly pronounce it) as a graphic performance of that "impossible ideal" of π. Another example: how do we read the sentence (an anacolouthon really, like most sentences in his notebooks) in which Schlegel muses that "perhaps the ⌒⌒ of

Luc. *nature* and *love,* only that here nature is entirely subordinated."[106] Even if we grant Kittler's claim that "systematic nonsense, which demands inhuman [*non*human?] storage capacities, exists only in writing,"[107] we do not have to conclude that data stored in this way constitute *only* nonsense. In both Morgenstern and Schlegel the (chemical) mixture of sense and nonsense, and the reader's doubt that attends such mixtures, provides both a better description of their writing and a better account of our interest in it. Kittler's claim that "Morgenstern's syllables owe their existence not to a combinatorial method but, at first sight at least, to lovely chance" (ibid.) thus seems, at the very least, debatable. That in an important sense both combinatorics and chance may be involved is indicated by the motto Morgenstern chooses for his book of poetry: "Let the molecules race / whatever they dice together" (Laß die Moleküle rasen, / was sie auch zusammenknobeln). Kittler prefers to register only the throw of dice (267 / 213). The molecules, however, may well have their own ideas, their own affinities, and hence a nonaccidental method of creating combinations.

Foucault has claimed that "since Mallarmé, literature . . . has drawn closer and closer to the very being of language,"[108] leaving us to wonder what this "very being" might consist of. It does seem clear that, even if this being cannot be directly named, in Foucault's view it exceeds the pure materiality of two dozen letters recombined, that it in fact approaches a notion quite familiar to us from Schlegel. A bit further in *The Order of Things*, when discussing "literary" language in relation to "Mallarmé, Roussel, Leiris, or Ponge," Foucault writes in metaphors that hold a special charge for us:

> The idea that, when we destroy words, what is left is neither mere noise nor arbitrary, pure elements, but other words, which, when pulverized in turn, will set free other words—this idea is at once the negative of all modern science of languages and the myth in which we now transcribe the most obscure and the most real powers of language. . . . But it is because it has never ceased to speak within itself, because it is penetrated as far as we can reach within it by inexhaustible values, that we can speak within it in that endless murmur in which literature is born. (119 / 103)

This highly suggestive passage seems to me to retrace the trajectory that I have been trying to sketch with the help of the chemical metaphors. Even in the discourse network around 1900 (or for that matter 1950 or 2000), the radical analysis performed by literature does not yield *purely* senseless elements (noise or randomness) but always more words that engage in a constant, uncontrollable murmur, what Schlegel prefers to call the secret societies among words that permit them to understand each other better than do those who use them. Even when a table of letters has been established (a result of "penetrat[ing] as far as we can reach"), it cannot *as literature* eliminate that murmur. The murmur of language, the leftover that remains in excess of the analytic "pulverization" of language, is in fact what lends special appeal to literature. Far from canceling sense, radical abstraction is *productive* of what Foucault calls "inexhaustible values," which is why literature demands interpretation, why literature is, in his words, "the privileged object of criticism" (95/81). Writers since Mallarmé may have ceded initiative to their material, but because of a murmur in the material (a murmur such as *ver-*, for example), they inexorably generate meaning. What makes the imperative "Stop making sense!" interesting is that no writer or reader, no speaker or listener can possibly comply with it.

Our critical moment has come to call this murmur causing a deviation in meaning the unconscious, but if we understand it structurally (rather than psychologically) it can equally well be called the secret societies between words or the table of affinities of letters. In all of these instantiations, nonhuman (i.e., technological) media, such as writing, produce certain senseless effects that, when filtered through human faculties (intention, memory, desire), carve meaning out of meaningless noise and, at once, bring forth regions of incoherence within a context of meaning. Because of this meaningful—or better: meaning-giving—context, such regions of incoherence cannot appear as pure nonsense (even if "ontologically" they may well be, for example by having been produced by a machine), but are rather overdetermined for every observing consciousness. No throw of dice, not even Mallarmé's, is ever just a throw of dice, at least not when it has been performed by a communicating consciousness.

Even if we grant—*particularly* if we grant—that the direction and severity of the deviation that utterances and other communicative acts undergo cannot be predicted, that there is an element of randomness in communication, it remains the case that such a deviation cannot but be interpreted as a sign of a malfunction—a symptom—

in a *system* of meaning (be it a consciousness, a social unit, or a divine order). In this context, Lacan's strange demand that "a distinction must be drawn between reading coffee grounds and reading hiero-glyphics"[109] gains some plausibility: the stains in the coffee grounds remain untouched by the displacements and condensations (*Verschiebung, Ver-dichtung*) that occur at the intersection of an external symbolic system and a consciousness experienced as internal—that occur, in other words, in a real language, whether lost or not. Accounts relying on a purely external understanding of communicative media may correctly describe some features of human communication, but they will always miss the way the senseless externality of the medium is internalized, the zone between the outside and the inside, which does not fully belong to either. The deviation from the intended path (e.g., parapraxes or other verbal failures) cannot, from the point of view of a consciousness, appear as entirely senseless, but will always be taken as the result of another (hidden, unconscious, divine, etc.) intention.

It is this bond between meaning and meaninglessness, between coherence and incoherence, between an all-pervading spirit of sense and the automatism of nonsense that Schlegel's chemical metaphors attempt to capture. We have seen how moving between and in and out of such categories gives rise to puzzling configurations, to what Schlegel calls "the purest and most splendid incomprehensibility."[110] He develops here a form of writing, both self-aware and self-enclosed while being open-ended, that we have come to call literature, but whose advent has usually been located in the late nineteenth century. "The nineteenth century," Foucault remarks in a passage in *The Order of Things* that we have already encountered, "was to . . . leave behind it, in confrontation, a knowledge closed in upon itself and a pure language that had become, in nature and function, enigmatic—something that has been called, since that time, *Literature*."[111] I am less concerned about engaging in a priority dispute than with the fact that Foucault's notion of "literature" describes with great accuracy what we have found in Schlegel: a self-consciously enigmatic, paradoxical, and playful (which is to say, difficult) form of writing. This is a form of verbal production that does no one's bidding but its own, the mark of its formal success lying precisely in its readiness for hermeneutic failure.

The Elements of Chemistry

We can turn the screw a bit tighter still. Thus far in my argument, the allegorical relationship between chemistry and language has remained one-way; it has been chemistry that has provided the fitful and discontinuous narrative for the workings of Schlegel's conception of language (and a fortiori for that of the romantic, and indeed modern, artwork). But here, at the level of the letter, we may be in a position to open a return path that would further strengthen the allegorical bond between the two systems. For Schlegel's idea about letters signifying "the basic materials of chemistry" points to the fact that the allegory between chemistry and letters can go both ways: not only does chemistry tell the story of the combinatorial operations of language, but the letters themselves can serve as an allegory for the basic components—the elements—of the material words. By this I do not mean the convention, still current today, by which letters inertly *stand in* for chemical elements (a notation that, at any rate, establishes itself only in the first half of the nineteenth century, hence after writings that are our focus here),[112] but rather the practice by which the behavior of chemical elements *becomes evident* through the letter. The alphabet becomes the epistemological condition for discovering (or proposing) the combinatorial logic in chemistry.

An important part of the "revolution" in late-eighteenth-century chemistry lies in the introduction of a revised nomenclature. (Thus the large number of chemical dictionaries published in French, English, and German at the time, which present the known world not according to a myth of creation or the ontological order of a Great Chain of Being but rather according to the caprice of alphabetical order.) Indeed, in many important ways the new nomenclature that Lavoisier, Guyton de Morveau, Berthollet, Fourcroy, and other chemists devise in their *Méthode de nomenclature chimique* (Method of Chemical Nomenclature) of 1787 *is* itself the chemical revolution.[113] That the chemical revolution is an event of language is not merely the interpretation one might expect of a literary critic; it is in effect the one provided by Lavoisier himself. In the preface to his *Elements of Chemistry,* he notes: "While I thought myself employed only in forming a Nomenclature, and while I proposed to myself nothing more than to improve the chemical language, my work transformed itself by degrees, without my being able to prevent it, into a treatise upon the Elements of Chemistry."[114] Since the chemical revolution follows, inevitably and without Lavoisier being able to prevent it, from a change in linguistic practice, one indicator of the new theory's success becomes the degree to which the new nomenclature is adopted. This it does with astonishing swiftness.[115] So rapid is the spread of the new language that "fifty years later . . . pre-Lavoisier works on chemistry had become unreadable and were discarded into the dustbin of distant prehistory."[116]

The new chemical terminology, then, does not merely reflect the new understanding of reality, but is its condition of possibility. Thus instead of a slew of traditional terms for various substances containing sulfur, the *Method of Chemical Nomenclature* proposes a systematic terminology: the combination of sulfur and oxygen yields, depending on the quantity of the latter, either sulf*ur*ous or sulf*ur*ic acids, which when further combined form sulf*i*tes or sulf*a*tes.[117] But what this nomenclature makes possible is to permit an understanding not merely of the change in paradigm initiated by Lavoisier, but unwittingly also of future advances. The language, in other words, encodes theories of chemistry entirely unknown to Lavoisier and his collaborators, in particular the atomic theory of combination; for this reason it has been modified but not overthrown by another language (which is why Lavoisier is still readable and has not landed in the dustbin of chemical prehistory). This encoding of future theoretical advances, moreover, takes place precisely on the level of the *letter.* Does the switch from sulf*i*te to sulf*a*te not perform the game of atomic recombination long *before* chemists manage to conceptualize it? Does the minute change between the terms *sulfurous* and *sulfuric* not anticipate a theoretical model that, years after Lavoisier, will in fact express the difference between the two acids in terms of one oxygen atom, or one additional letter O (H_2SO_3 and H_2SO_4)? The substitution of *letters* allows us to see what effect a substitution of *atoms* can have, even before an atomic theory of matter is available.

The work of the Swedish chemist Torbern Bergman makes clear how the use of letters (as distinct from the nonalphabetic graphical symbols of alchemy) permits new insights about matter itself. Explaining simple elective affinities in his 1775 *Attractionibus electivis,* Bergman writes: "Let there be material A, which other heterogeneous substances a, b, c, etc. attack: if, in addition to A, c is added until saturation is reached (τϖc), (which we indicate by Ac in the following), and b being added to form the same union with ejection of c (τγc), A is said to be more strongly attracted to b than c."[118] The better-known, and better-written, version of this story is told some thirty-five years later in the fourth chapter of the first part of Goethe's *Elective Affinities,* where Eduard asks the Captain to explain the chemical principle to Charlotte:

> "If you don't think it looks pedantic," replied the Captain, "I'll use signs [*Zeichensprache*] for the sake of brevity. Think of an A, tightly connected to a B, unable to be sundered from it by force or any other means; and then think of a C, related in the same way to a D. Now bring the two pairs together: A will fling itself at D and C at B in such a way that it will be impossible to say who left the one or bonded with the other first."[119]

Of course chemistry (and its forerunners) always did use the language of signs, but alphabetic letters never figured in it systematically.[120] The Captain's conflation of the two is understandable, for to a literate mind there is really no more evident or elementary a *Zeichensprache* than that of letters. Like most hands-on teachers, the Captain is mistaken when he promises that demonstrating the experiments will make them "clearer and easier to grasp" (275/116). The opposite is the case: only when the chemical elements have been reduced to a letter, when their rich complexity has been removed, do they become irresistible storytellers, regardless of whether the story of "elective affinity" plays itself out between elements or people. The chemist depends on the allegorizing power of letters as much as does the novelist or aesthetic theorist.

The attraction of the alphabetic allegory lies in its power of abstraction, in removing from substances precisely those qualities that interest alchemists, pharmacists, and practitioners of the art of chemistry, in order to allow a clear view of the underlying principles governing them. It is the first step toward describing chemical reactions mathematically. But it is also more than that. At this point of intersection, where letters encode the behavior of elements ("Let there be material A . . .") and elements encode the behavior of letters (consonants as iron, water, and air), where writing becomes a kind of chemistry and chemistry a kind of writing, we find in Schlegel a peculiar instance of Kittler's "notation systems."[121] Both systems—chemistry and writing—process data, but both also fail to fulfill one of the central requirements of computing: they are not media-independent.[122] Rather, they rely for their functioning (and, hence, for their *mal*functioning) on their material substrates. Schlegel not only insists on the centrality of the letter in art and science but also repeatedly identifies it with the "basic materials of chemistry," the *Grundstoffe;* hence the materiality of letters—their shapes, sounds, associations, and manners of combination—is embedded in his conception of the way they generate meanings. Letters are not elements of a neutral symbolic system, but follow—just as do the basic materials of eighteenth-century chemistry—elective attractions that remain opaque to us but which we must understand as belonging to their material composition.

I would like to make one final point about the mingling of letters and particles of matter. Saying that elements *are* in crucial respects letters is merely to refer to ancient history (both Democritus and Lucretius make that claim) and to repeat what dictionaries report. Both the *Oxford English Dictionary* and *Grimm* identify *element* as a translation of the Greek *stoicheion,* meaning unit of a series, constituent part of a whole, but above all letter of the alphabet. What is more, like *alphabet* and *abecedarium, element* not only *refers* to the letters of the alphabet, it *consists* of them in a way that few other words do. Though its etymology is uncertain, it has been argued that the Latin *elementum* goes back to the alphabetic sequence L-M-N, used in schools to refer to the second half of the alphabet.[123] Element, then, is spelled by letters and, at the same time, spells them out. While letters are usually marshaled to imitate a (purportedly) preexisting sound, here the sounds imitate the letters. In a wonderful case of words understanding each other better than their users, the word for the fundamental part of an ensemble explicitly comes *after* the very letters that are presumably invented to describe both part and ensemble. Besides being a structural property of the word, this belatedness is also underlined by the word's referent. For as Gregory Nagy points out, the *element* begins, as it were, in the middle, with L-M-N rather than, ob ovo, with A-B-C.[124]

For all these reasons, *element* is a fittingly allegorical name for the chemical elements. As we discussed earlier, these are primary substances that are, however, *made* rather than found (made by an ever more sophisticated apparatus, including the conceptually innovative apparatus of using letters in place of elements). Chemistry, like the word *element*, begins, as Schlegel writes about philosophy, "in the middle."[125] Unlike the *Grundsatz,* the singular foundational sentence that the idealist philosophy of the time attempts to formulate, Schlegel's letters, and hence letter combinations, are no more and no less than the (tellingly plural) *Grundstoffe,* the irreducible parts of matter whose irreducibility turns out to depend on a combination of written marks.

6 ■ The Politics of
Permanent Parabasis

Communication as Politics

One of the questions that I posed at the outset of this study was: what effects does Schlegel's idea and practice of the work of art, conceived in its fragmentary form, have on philosophical aesthetics, a conceptual field deeply engaged with the problem of the mediation of fragment and totality? I have argued that the effects are to be found not in an *object* resulting from a (successful or failed) synthesis, but, if anywhere, in what Roland Barthes has called the "production without product,"[1] which consists of nothing but the process of succeeding or failing to produce this synthetic totality. And I have suggested that the most powerful way in which we encounter such a process in Schlegel's work is through his sustained description *and* performance of writing as a series of materially charged combinations and separations. In seeing how frequently he invokes chemistry and how widely and deeply its allegorical reach extends, we have been able to get a measure of the extent to which Schlegel's writing transforms ideas central to aesthetics. We have observed how this conception of writing—and that of the artwork derived from the conception of writing—impedes attempts at closing off its meaning, and hence refrains from either acquiescing in the organic notion of the work of art that romanticism is said to promote, or from advancing an allegedly modernist notion of the random production of writings bereft of sense. Instead, it experiments with sense (which is to say, courts nonsense) and attempts to find ways of constraining combinatorial nonsense (which is to say, courts sense). These experiments, I have tried to show, are notable not merely for what they set out to achieve but, more important, for what they are prepared to give up, namely the sovereignty of the author. Their greatest innovation lies in theoretically registering and practically dramatizing the deviations inherent in a course laid out by the best or worst intentions, deviations that are embedded in the very material of verbal communication itself.

If the account I have offered thus far has been plausible, then a question that has remained in the background can now be allowed to emerge: does this chemical model of writing and of language (insofar as language is conceived along a chemically combinatorial model) not imply a social theory? Or does it not at the very least have consequences for social theory? The young Schlegel's disregard for philosophical decorum, his syncretic ability to mix and match anything that interests him, his willingness to invite paradox, contradiction, incoherence—all this would seem to predispose, if not himself, than at least his writings to a strong version of antiauthoritarianism. By holding up that side of his work that espouses difference against identity, dialogism against monologism, nonidentity against identity, have we not implicitly claimed him for emancipatory politics? Indeed, even if Schlegel himself is reluctant to make those claims (and he often is), we could, with the assistance of semiological critique, help his writings accomplish the leap from experimentation with the signifier to what Barthes's *S/Z* has called "a liberatory theory of the signifier,"[2] the leap, that is, from linguistic self-enclosure to political intervention.

It has been one of the axioms of poststructuralist writing that setting free the signifier is also and perhaps primarily a political act. Since we can imagine a reading that would gather Schlegel's experiments with fragmentation, multiplicity, deferral, and ungroundedness into an early version of poststructuralism[3] (though such a reading might find it difficult to account for the prominent presence of ideas of systematicity, organicism, and coherence that earlier critics had tended to emphasize), it would almost follow by itself that his early work adds up to a "gay science of poetry," brimming with liberating political energy. In a suggestive book of this title, Jochen Hörisch makes just this claim. He argues that, despite its "self-misunderstandings," "early romantic aesthetic absolutism is the model of political reason."[4] And it performs this role, he reasons, because "poetry"—in its Jena conception—"counterfactually anticipates the meta-discourse free of domination, which is the sole condition under which communication about matters of fact [*Sachverhalte*] can succeed" (142). Poetry, then, is conceived as a utopian counter-model to the negativity of social reality: it is not difficult to hear the murmurs of T. W. Adorno's aesthetic theory in the background.

Such a judgment would find corroboration in the young Schlegel's sympathetic view of the French Revolution, his engagement for the emancipation of women, and his violation of erotic taboos (for example in *Lucinde*), which have led some readers to celebrate his kind of romanticism as "a continuation of the bourgeois revolution in the field of ideology."[5] That Schlegel at this point supports the French Revolution is well-documented:[6] when reflecting on letters from Caroline Böhmer, a fierce supporter of both the Revolution and the short-lived Mainz Republic (who would marry, first, August Wilhelm Schlegel and later Schelling), the twenty-one-year-old Friedrich Schlegel confesses to being "drunk" with "this enthusiasm for a great public matter."[7] A few years later, in 1796, he writes his conservative and deeply anti-republican brother: "I don't want to deny that republicanism is still a bit closer to my heart than divine criticism and the most divine poetry."[8] That, as we by now know, is saying a lot.

Schlegel's most sustained reflection on (and defense of) republicanism occurs in his 1796 "Versuch über den Begriff des Republikanismus" (Essay on the Concept of Republicanism), a text that announces itself as a review of Kant's political treatise "Zum ewigen Frieden" (Eternal Peace), published a year earlier, but which has in fact far greater ambitions. Readers of the essay have tended to highlight a glaring and important point at which Schlegel distances himself from Kant.[9] The latter embraces republicanism (defined as "the constitutional principle according to which executive power . . . is separated from legislative power")[10] but repudiates democracy: it is, Kant writes, "a *despotism* in the specific meaning of the word, because it establishes an executive power where all decide about and, if need be, against one (who thus does not agree), so that All are nevertheless not All—which is a contradiction of the general will with itself and with freedom" (ibid.). This cleavage between republicanism and democracy, which gives Kant leave to endorse monarchy in general and Frederick the Great in particular, is directly contradicted by Schlegel. He starts from different premises: given that the general will "exists only in the world of pure thoughts," given further that the "particular and the general are separated by an infinite chasm, which can only be crossed by means of a somersault," all that remains for practical politics is to establish "an empirical will as the *surrogate* of the a priori and absolutely general will by means of a *fiction*."[11] For the purposes of such a fiction, democracy seems the best approximation to the republican ideal: "The *will of the majority* should be effective as the surrogate of the general will. *Republicanism is thus necessarily democratic,* and [Kant's] unproved paradox . . . that democratism must necessarily be despotic cannot be right."[12]

This is without a doubt an important engagement, for it not only makes plain Schlegel's sympathies with the ideals of the French Revolution, an act not without its perils, but also establishes the far more serious theoretical connection between the idea of republicanism and a democratic form of government that should, as much as possible, approach radical democracy (where the fictional coincidence with the general will would be greatest). Yet for the purposes of our present argument it seems to me that a different point of divergence between the twenty-four-year-old upstart and the Sage of Königsberg is of greater importance still. It concerns the principles—the founding fiction—of social organization as such. Kant's declaration that the "civil constitution in each state shall be republican" (349 / 437), i.e., that the republican is the *sole* legitimate form of constitution, is derived from the formalist premise of "the idea of an original contract upon which all rightful legislation of the state must be based" (350/437). Schlegel bases his political theory on a very different bedrock: he proceeds from the anthropological premise that "besides the capacities that each purely isolated individual as such possesses, man in his relations to other individuals of his species is also endowed with the *capacity for communication* (for the activities of all other capacities)."[13] This capacity for communication—for *Mit-teilung,* for imparting oneself, for giving up and sharing with others part of oneself—becomes for Schlegel "the foundation and object of *politics.*"[14] The significance of this theoretical claim is, for us, that the founding principle of politics as such—communication—is merely the general form of the activity that has been holding our interest throughout this study, namely aesthetic communication. If what gives rise to poetry is also what gives rise to politics, then the two can hardly be divorced. If, furthermore, this common source consists in imparting or parting oneself, then the poetological project of fragmentation would seem to give expression to that original impulse with great precision.

Schlegel's philosophical and anthropological arguments for republicanism and radical democracy have often been made light of as an ardent enthusiasm for the revolution in France, a romantic infatuation not only with freedom and equality but also, and quite possibly primarily, with Caroline Böhmer, an activist for those causes.[15] They have, in a more serious vein, been relativized as claims not primarily about Germany but about ancient Greece.[16] Though such a claim diverts our attention from Schlegel's present to a past that for all intents and purposes is imagined according to the logic of myth, the reference to the Ancients calls to our mind passages that are valuable for the deep connection they establish between art and politics, specifically republican and hence (for Schlegel) democratic politics. In notes entitled "Charakteristik der griechischen Tragiker" (Characteristic of Greek Tragedians), written at around the same time as the essay on republicanism, in 1795, Schlegel attempts to determine the relationship between Greek politics and Greek tragedy. One important element of what he calls the "republicanism of tragedy"[17] is the fact that the chorus constitutes the "representation of the people."[18] But crossing the barrier of the proscenium and placing the people on both its sides—as members of the audience, as members of the chorus—can become problematic in unfavorable political conditions:

> The boundaries of the dramatic sphere are determined by the strongest will of the mass of the audience, which necessarily dominates and guides dramatic representation. When for example higher estates or the will of the few rules, then they will establish as law their *conventional* and accidental concepts; their pettiness becomes the boundary of art. Limits of this kind would then be decency etc. These limits disturb the freedom of art. But if the will were really public and if there were only the law that the representations should be *civil,* republican, public: that really imposes no limits on the poet.[19]

The connection, then, between politics and poetry is not only primordial (in their common source of communication) but immediate and empirical. Oligarchic forms of government constrain aesthetic communication because they constrain communication as such, while democratic ones impose no constraint, for all they require of the poet is to communicate publicly.

Unpacking the political implications of Schlegel's aesthetic theory (if we may, for brevity's sake, call it that), far from being illegitimate, becomes an urgent task. He makes the connection explicit not only in Greek tragedy but in self-reflexive reference to his own work. Thus he imagines fragments as members of a *social* system: "Some witty ideas"—and fragments certainly fall into this category—"are like the surprising meeting of two friendly thoughts after a long separation."[20] Even if fragments are little more than "a motley heap of ideas," they are bound—*verbunden*—by "that free and equal fellowship in which the citizens of the perfect state . . . will at some point find themselves."[21] Not only does Schlegel acknowledge that his poetic theory can extend into an allegory of social relations, that "*experimentation* is very much in the spirit of revolutionary practice,"[22] but he seems to suggest that the ensemble of chemical fragments lends itself to *progressive* social relations. "Poetry is republican speech," he writes in the *Lyceum,* "a speech that is its own law and its own end, in which all parts are free citizens and have an equal say [or vote]."[23] That a society of free and equal elements, bound only by elective attractions, looks very different from the one Schlegel inhabits, must have been evident to his readers; yet in case some of them missed the utopian charge of this model, he reminds them of the oft-invoked connection between Lavoisier's advances and the storming of the Bastille: "The age is a chemical age. Revolutions are universal movements, not organic but chemical."[24]

All the evidence seems to be in place for making the Barthesian leap from semiotics to politics: his poetico-theoretical practice certainly promotes the "liberation of the signifier"; Schlegel himself advocates the liberation that republicanism offers against despotic monarchism (though later he would become a loyal, if ineffective, official in Metternich's Restoration government); and he explicitly sanctions a connection between poetic practice and a democratic politics. One could hardly need more to establish a strong link between avant-garde poetics and avant-garde politics.

Yet it seems to me that the argument is flawed. Not that straddling the poetic and the political is not legitimate: it undoubtedly is. The question is what *kind* of social life can be said to emerge from the table of affinity of letters. The project embedded there is, in a strict sense, revolutionary and it does promote a "meta-discourse free of domination,"[25] yet what might be entailed by such models is far more disturbing than their critical endorsement seems to suggest. It is true that the chemical model represents, as a critic has recently stated, "an aspiration not only for a new kind of art but for a new kind of society," but this is not therefore a society in which "friendship and the sharing of intellectual ideas" are practiced.[26] Just as Schlegel's many organicist and stereotypically "romantic" statements about poetry are relativized, if not contravened, by the possibility of "error and of madness, or of obtuseness and of stupidity"[27] implied by his combinatorial poetics, his right-thinking political sentiments are belied by the ambiguous political values tacit in his aesthetic theory. Despite the evidence I offered for a *continuity* between radical politics and radical poetics, in fact the *conflict* between a political position and a literary practice is, in this case, far more plausible. For if the verbal artwork is indeed undergoing in Schlegel's hands a development into the direction of greater autonomy, and if this development is caused by, *inter alia*, a recursive loop of self-reference and self-reflection, then the price exacted by the increased autonomy of the literary text lies in the inevitably arising areas of hermeneutic bewilderment that just as inevitably undermine an unequivocal moral reading. In this sense, there *cannot* be a neat relation between "literature" (in Foucault's sense of a discourse that draws "closer and closer to the very being of language")[28] and political—and hence necessarily moral—models of social organization. To the degree that the verbal artwork displays its self-confidence and stability by flaunting paradoxes and indeterminacies, it becomes an unfit carrier of political messages. One of the ways of making this general observation much more concrete with regard to Schlegel is by looking more closely at the uses to which the chemical allegory is put in his writings.

Illness as Metaphor for Writing

If we believe that the argumentative invocation of the organic entails, in Klaus Scherpe's words, a "cancellation of analytic thinking,"[29] then we may also be inclined to believe that Schlegel's critique, or at least deferral, of the organic in favor of the chemical might promote reason, enlightenment, progress. That is not always the case. The passages I have chosen from Schlegel, when taken together, provide a more or less coherent allegorical picture of the workings of chemistry (even if that picture depicts a scene that *itself* lacks coherence). But Schlegel's recourse to chemistry is, in fact, far more bizarre than I have made it seem. At times, his chemical metaphors seem to run amok. "My practice (oxygens, nitrogen = theory) ends in consumption, like breathing in oxygen,"[30] he writes. Schelling's philosophy, which is commended for "a certain chemical obsession,"[31] is diagnosed as being "over-oxidized."[32] One notebook entry asserts: "Chemistry must have three principles. Philosophy and poetry = nitrogen?

Oxygen ethical atmosphere. Contemporary philosophy [is] probably pure living air."[33] That these cannot be the three principles of Lavoisier's or even Stahl's chemistry but can only be imagined to apply to the strange chemical writing experiments is a plausible supposition, but still only a supposition. Chemical metaphors are permitted to expand so recklessly and uncontrollably (nothing else is meant by dissemination) that it infects the conception of what is human: "humanity itself as a process is the highest power of oxidization for this epoch of the earth."[34] When Schlegel applies chemistry to erotic life, the results are predictably more violent than what we find in the *Elective Affinities* or in our own vague notion of "chemistry" between people: "Every burning [is] only a repetition of the oldest love story. Oxygen hurls itself on hydrogen, which escapes. No other lover flies into such passion, no woman is so light and brittle."[35]

Nitrogen = theory, over-oxidized philosophy, humanity as a process: none of this even appears to allow for the possibility of comprehension. But is this undisciplined deployment of the metaphor of chemistry not built into the logic of chemical experimentation itself? Does the genre of the experiment, be it in writing or in material reality, not entail that one is prepared to end up not only with glorious novelties but also with bizarre, unstable, oddly shaped contraptions?

Chemistry's capacity to generate failure is of such importance to Schlegel's conception of it that at times he reduces the process of mixing and separating to its sheer destructiveness. "The chemical process is to be regarded as an evil principle and as an *illness*," he notes.[36] "If chemistry in general is the evil principle in nature," he speculates at around the same time, "then *water* is the first great sin on the earth's surface."[37] This eccentric cosmology is not, as it might seem, the result of an obsession with purity, where *any* combination or mixture embodies impurity, even one yielding the limpid substance usually regarded as the quintessence of purity. In Schlegel's bizarre view, illness is constitutive of the entire system, for "perhaps the elements are illnesses";[38] pathology, it seems, is not the product of a process gone awry, but a feature of the process itself, down to its most basic elements.

We can extend Schlegel's idiosyncratic logic a bit further: if illness is a metaphoric feature of chemistry, and chemistry a metaphor for poetic production, then illness should extend its metaphoric reach to writing, to poetry, to art as such. Schlegel himself follows this logic to its strange conclusion: "Perhaps every *artistic skill* is an *illness of the spirit* with which one has to be artificially inoculated."[39] The illness— "*Krankheit des Geistes*"—produced by this artificial inoculation is a grammatical inversion, a recombination, of the better known *Geisteskrankheit,* the madness that shines through in moments of great poetic profundity. "Whence," Schlegel concludes, as though it were perfectly obvious, "the epidemic quality of art."[40]

The conclusion I would like to draw from this is that we are not obliged to read the organic only as the telos, the future promise, of the chemical, with which Schlegel at times identifies it: the fragment, for example, that declares his own age to be a chemical one, goes on: "By analogy to what I said before an organic age would follow the chemical age."[41] The telling subjunctive mood in which he puts the arrival of the promise reflects the thorough contamination of the organic by the chemical process that we observed in the passages above. The imagined sanctity of life turns out not to be safe from the mindlessly epidemic self-replication of chemical combinations. Such infection of the organic by the chemical is by no means the phantom of a febrile young mind alone. What Schlegel expresses in exaggerated form reflects the fierce and enormously influential debate in the second half of the eighteenth century over the question of how, precisely, life is to be understood.[42] By the later eighteenth century, the biomechanical model, powerfully operative since Descartes, seems less and less adequate at explaining complexities observable with sophisticated surgical tools, while the metaphysical notions of "soul" or "life force" proposed by vitalism seem untenably vague. Thus some romantic scientists such as Caspar Friedrich Wolff and Johann Friedrich Blumenbach attempt "to chart a course between the Scylla of reductionist mechanics and the Charybdis of vitalism."[43] Even those upholding the strict categorical difference between the organic and the inorganic, such as Schelling, explain the life process by recourse to such chemical concepts as mixture and solution. By the late eighteenth century, even accounts devoted to the singularity of the organism need to work with chemical models; chemistry is lodged, as it were, in the heart of organicism.[44]

A deconstruction of the organic/chemical distinction still maintains the concepts as distinct entities, even while pointing out that their deployment (for example in the distinction of the healthy and the ill, usually mapped onto beauty/ugliness) deeply implicates one in the other. But the chemical model permits the complete abolition of the distinction. We can think of the organic as a species of the chemical and of health and illness as various chemical states as they are observed by another chemical state (usually called life). Schlegel himself would seem to encourage a redrawing of the imaginary line separating health from illness. "It should be possible," he notes, "to die of good health."[45] That is, apparently, because it should also be possible to be born from death: "The seeds of the future organization are first poison and also the waste products of putrefaction";[46] "there is only one organic matter—POISON."[47] If the organic is not opposed to the chemical but merely one version of it, if the "evil principle" and "illness" of chemistry goes to the very core of the organic, we need not try to explain away Schlegel's organicist statements as embarrassing remnants of a view supposedly long since overcome. Instead, the organic formations can be seen as particular cases of the combinatorial system, outcomes that under some circumstances will be regarded as exceptionally coherent. But in principle, they belong to the same system of utterance formation that also brings forth pathology, incomprehensibility, the pharmakon. The most coherently organic works, then, share a principle of generation that also brings forth the "Great Lalula."

Permanent Insurrection

We can make clearer still the awkward fit between Schlegel's poetics and his invocation of the Rousseauist notion of "free and equal fellowship" by looking more closely at those points at which the allegory of chemistry appears to operate in both aesthetic and political discourses. After all, a statement like "revolutions are universal, not organic but chemical movements," while not exactly a battle cry, appears to align the chemical process, with which poetry is so deeply infused, with a progressive political agenda. The triple analogy among poetry, chemistry, and revolutionary politics is performed in compact manner in an early essay Schlegel writes about Lessing: "Lessing finally was one of those *revolutionary* spirits who, . . . like a sharp separating agent, everywhere spread the most intense fermentations and the most violent tremors."[48] I propose making the link between the three more evident through the concept of writing. As we shall see, the path from poetry to politics (i.e., the path that permits conceiving of art as a social utopia) is seriously disrupted at a way station that is often ignored, where we must consider the conception of the individual consciousness that is implicated in both poetry and politics.

The hinge linking poetic production to political action is the idea of interruption. We have seen that the abrupt break is a defining feature of the fragments. Every writing that is not a work (i.e., organically self-enclosed), Schlegel writes, "cannot close, it can only cut off or stop; it thus necessarily ends in an annihilating or ironizing manner."[49] Interruption marks not merely the end of the fragment collections but also the end of each and every fragment; the collection consists, in this sense, as much of the white spaces separating the fragments as of the fragments themselves. What is more, the interruptions are not confined to the space between fragments, but are lodged within every fragment, just as much as the chemical poison inhabits every organic formation. As Paul de Man has shown, interruption *defines* Schlegelian irony; it occurs in those moments, de Man maintains, when there has been an interruption in the narrative line, specifically an interruption of the kind that on stage is called an aside, and in the language of rhetoric, a parabasis.[50] It is not hard to see how this creates an ironic text, even according to the most banal understandings of irony, for by means of parabasis the character, or the textual voice, intervenes into a narrative from another narrative position with the result that doubt is cast on the reliability of the first. But Schlegel goes further, defining irony as "*permanent* parabasis" (my emphasis),[51] as an interruption of *all* points in the narrative. De Man is correct in pointing out that this "is saying something violently paradoxical" (179), for an interruption can only be recognizable as such against a noninterrupted, continuous background.

Schlegel provides us—or, more precisely: the four members of his audience at his lectures on "the history of European literature"—with his own derivation of the trope of parabasis:

> The only difference [between Greek comedy and tragedy] consists in parabasis, a speech that in the midst of the play was held by the chorus in the name of the poet to the people. Yes, it was a complete interruption and dissolution of the play, during which (just as in the play itself) the greatest licentiousness reigned and the chorus, which had stepped out to the outer limits of the proscenium, said the grossest vulgarities to the people. The name is derived from this stepping out (*ekbasis*).[52]

I should mention in passing, merely to support my earlier contention that fragmentation and systematicity are not mutually exclusive, that Schlegel does not consider this "complete interruption and dissolution" of the performance to have harmed the unity of the comedy. It lies in the very form of comedy, as "*pure comedy*," to "dissolve in itself all ends and all intention"; in comedy "nonform itself is . . . the highest art."[53]

More crucial for the present argument is that Schlegel clearly registers the effect that this form of comedy has on the public. For this kind of joking [*Witz*], Schlegel solemnly tells his listeners, "an audience is necessary in which everyone is mature and does not abuse freedom."[54] For "if there is to be a poem of wit"—we hardly need to translate: if there is to be romantic poetry—"then wit must be boundlessly free. This freedom is to be permitted when it is meant for a small audience which has the right to take part in such freedom. Under no circumstances is this for the mixed crowd which is entirely unworthy of this freedom, where the most unpleasant, the most pernicious consequences could be feared."[55] Athens, where the highest form of comedy was available, is an example of such abuse. "The magistrate was really forced," Schlegel notes, "to ban both the personal satire and the chorus with parabasis. But this coincides with the decline of republicanism and democracy."[56] The point is not whether at the time and place that he utters these sentences—Paris, 1803–4—Schlegel supports or condemns republicanism (more likely the latter, certainly in public). What is crucial is that this line of reasoning reproduces the *logic* of the arguments from 1795 about the dependence of poetry for its freedom on democracy quoted earlier. While its *evaluation* may have changed, the basic point remains that a tight, indeed causal, link is assumed between political freedom (promoted by republicanism and democracy) and the boundless freedom required for the operations of parabasis and *Witz*, required, in short, for unrestrained irony.

To understand its exact political consequences, we need to look more closely at the trope of parabasis. If we describe its mode of operation in the language of the chemical allegory, we can avoid the temptation to think of the textual irony in mental terms, which would immediately provide us with a second, "higher" consciousness "staging" the irony (even if a permanent irony) for our benefit. Permanent parabasis is, so to speak, the inverse of the process of combinatorial coupling that we have been describing, for a *re*combination is only thinkable if we assume a momentary state of pure potential in which all valences are open and anything can happen. This chaotic state, in which substances are thrown into disarray (recall, in the *Elective Affinities,* the Captain's talk of *A* "flinging" itself at *D*), needs to occur before each new combination. Interruption is not an intrusion from outside (not a second voice), but rather a defining feature of the progression of the process itself. Interrupted, the process goes on.

In such a state, distinguishing process from interruption is no trivial task. We could say that the chemical process consists of a long series of fluctuating states interrupted by the occasional stable compound. As in Wittgenstein's and Escher's famous drawings of Gestalt switches, we can flip the interruptions from the foreground into the background. In this precise sense, they are permanent, a series of uninterrupted interruptions. Thus we need not oppose writing and the system-work (as does the fragment about the "annihilating and ironizing manner" in which some writings end) if we understand the system to be a work insofar as it is a work-in-progress. The system then can be maintained only under the condition of its radical inconstancy; it can be produced, but its half-life approaches zero. This is, perhaps, why another deeply cryptic fragment places parabasis at the very center of systems: "In every systematic work there must be a *prologue,* an *epilogue,* and a *centrologue* (or a *parabasis*)."[57]

When Schlegel writes that the poetry of *Witz* is "meant for a small audience" worthy of such boundless freedom, we are likely to frown upon such elitism or at least nod with condescension. Such gestures certainly have the advantage of permitting us to congratulate ourselves on our great courage in standing on the side of republicanism and democracy and against the limitations of freedom. It may, however, have the disadvantage of obscuring our view of the most radical, as well as the most ethically and politically troubling, aspects of Schlegel's conceptions, poetic *and* political. For his is not a theory in which one can put one's feet up; it is uncomfortable at *all* points. He does not confine permanent interruption to *Witz* or parabasis or irony, not in other words to written communication in philosophy and literature, but extends them to the life process itself. "Life is possible only by means of a continuous, constantly repeated disturbance," he declares.[58] And if life itself comes into being (if one can even use such an ontological formula here) by means of the permanent parabasis of disturbance—if it, in fact, consists of *nothing but* the repetition of the disturbance—then we have every reason to assume that mental life cannot exempt itself from this staccato of continuous interruption. Accordingly, another notebook entry reads: "On the inside of a human being who has achieved a certain height and universality of education there is a continuous chain of the most tremendous revolutions."[59]

What must be troubling to classical humanism is that the continuous chain of discontinuities is imagined to occur *after* the process of education—*Bildung*—has "achieved a certain height." *Bildung* here does not consist of a developmental narrative resulting in a subject so well-rounded that it can only be conceived along the reposeful lines of a classical Greek statue; on the contrary: in this account, *Bildung* produces the very shaken subject that its standard account (as provided most influentially by Herder) is meant to thwart. Schlegel puts this insight about the constitutive fragmentation of the self in language that anticipates the Freudian theory of the soul a hundred years later: "*we are only a piece of ourselves,*" and connects this fragmentation to the activity—better yet: to the process—that I have been describing and redescribing throughout this study. "That activity," he continues, "through which consciousness reveals itself most acutely as a fragment is *wit;* its essence consists in rivenness and in turn arises from the rivenness and derivativeness of consciousness."[60] He then defines wit, as we might expect, by means of the very combinatorial wit of letter substitution: *Witz* is a *Blitz,* a bolt of lightning, that comes neither entirely from outside consciousness nor from inside, brought forth and guided by consciousness. Wit is "a bolt of lightning from the unconscious world, which for us always exists alongside the conscious world, and it thus accurately represents the fragmentary state of our consciousness. It is a combination and mixture of the conscious and the unconscious."[61] It will immediately be pointed out by the history police that around 1800 "unconscious" does not mean the same thing as it does around 1900. No doubt, but the general meaning of the word is not at issue here; I am rather concerned with a specific occurrence within a very particular conceptual network: wit, chemistry, parabasis, interruption, fragmentation. And in this context the structural—and now lexical—parallels with the psychoanalytic notion of the unconscious are not only striking but also very useful in gauging the range and direction the concept can take in Schlegel's writing. As the agency that brings to consciousness what Schlegel has been designating with the metaphors of chemistry—the half-willed, half-accidental process of combining and mixing elements that turn out to follow affinities of their own—*Witz* lies precisely between knowledge and its lack, between sense and nonsense, between intention and chance. "Without all intention and consciousness something is found"—Schlegel writes, aptly in the passive voice, about wit—"that has no connection with what came before it; on the contrary: it always stands, as it were, in stark contradiction to it."[62] "Chemical philosophy" and "chemical poetry" have, according to the infectious logic of chemistry, expanded their range into a chemical consciousness in which "combinations and mixtures," while not within the reach of consciousness, nonetheless illuminate its workings in ways before unknown.

The expansion of the permanent interruption of chemical wit into consciousness holds the key to why Schlegel was never able to turn his thousands of fragmentary notebook entries into the coherent autobiographical bildungsroman that, in allusion to Goethe's *Wilhelm Meister's Apprenticeship,* he planned to call "Philosophical Apprenticeship." What genre, after all, could have been better suited at demonstrating—i.e., representing *and* presenting—the "continuous chain of the most tremendous revolutions," not to mention the "combination and mixture of the conscious and the unconscious," than the non-genre of the fragments? In this sense, there is a logic to Schlegel's failure: the convoluted mess of the philosophical and literary notebooks is not an experimental stage toward the preparation of an orderly—and organic—work, but is itself already the Schlegelian version of the auto-bio-graphy, a writing that writes its own interruptions into life. There is interesting textual evidence to support this idea: far from being documents of the immediacy of thinking, at least five of the twelve notebooks comprising the "Philosophical Apprenticeship" appear to have been copied by Schlegel;[63] it seems puzzling that a text supposed to be raw material for a future project should have been copied *in its rawness,* unless that form contained its own moment of truth.

The idea that the life of a subject is nothing but a series of uninterrupted interruptions is repeated in the last of the *Athenäum* fragments, but instead of applying it to the *Bildung* of one individual, it is made to encompass the totality of consciousness, human and divine: "The life of the universal spirit is an uninterrupted chain of inner revolutions; all individuals, the original and eternal ones, live in the spirit. It is a genuine polytheist and harbors within itself all of Mount Olympus."[64] Instead of the organic link between microcosm and macrocosm, the model employed here to unite the two relies on systemic interruption. The divine order of "Mount Olympus" is itself comprised by the "universal spirit," as are "all individuals"; yet far from offering the comfort of a capacious, eternal, and omnipotent deity, this spirit consists of nothing but parabases. It surely ranks as one of the strangest theologies to have been dreamed up.

The social model entailed by this radically nonteleological, materialist model of system formation is equally strange and perhaps more troubling still. If we are willing to accept that fragments and individuals in society are to be imagined analogously—the meeting of two friendly thoughts after a long separation—then we must admit that we have subscribed to a disturbing model of social interaction. For such a meeting, as Schlegel takes pains to point out, must always be interruptable: "Even a friendly conversation that cannot freely break off *at any moment, with absolute arbitrariness,* has something illiberal" (my emphasis).[65] This is Lacan's short session *avant la lettre,* with two radicalizing features: first, it is not confined to the structured context of an analytic situation but comprises *all* social interactions; and second, it extends the privilege of arbitrary interruption reserved for the analyst to *all* members of a communicative situation. We should be more precise: it is not, in fact, the speakers but the conversation itself that is the subject of the quoted sentence and that, lest it be constrained, must take the liberty of performing the interruption.

Interruption—irony, parabasis—is not the result of an agent intervening in a discourse but of the discourse, the speech act, the chemical process intervening into itself. Given this context, the seemingly anodyne opening sentence of the "Conversation on Poetry"—"Poetry befriends and binds with indissoluble bonds the hearts of all those who love it"[66]—gains a certain disquieting edge, for we now know what sort of bonding (*binden, Banden*) poetry performs. If we regard the social model implied in the fragments to be utopian in that it offers the hope for a "metadiscourse free of domination," then we must also realize that the very lack of domination, insofar as it is an absolute lack, entails the possibility of a *permanent* revolution, a ceaseless transformation of the very conditions of interaction, the chance that a social bond will be severed at *any* moment. This condition is not far from a general social psychosis.[67]

On the explicit level, Schlegel's essay on republicanism excludes precisely such a possibility. The political act of insurrection, he reasons, is justified when "its end is the organization of republicanism," yet "*permanent insurrection*" would be "inauthentic," "for authentic and politically possible [insurrection] is necessarily transitory."[68] But on the implicit level, the essay registers this possibility of a permanent interruption by attempting to prevent the very possibility of its arising. It will be recalled from the brief discussion of the essay at the outset of this chapter that, in Schlegel's account, a somersault (*Salto mortale*) is necessary to traverse the chasm between the theoretical and unrealizable *idea* of a general will and its empirical *surrogate* in politics. The particular shape that this somersault takes is that of a "fiction," the fiction for example that one individual or a certain cabal or the majority of voters embodies the empirical surrogate of the ideal general will. It seems plausible to bring this notion of fiction into relation with poetry and poetological theory, yet that would seem to me to overlook an important distinction. This fiction "is not only legitimate, but also practically necessary"[69] precisely because it allows us to avert our gaze from the chasm between the ideal and the surrogate will. It is a shield, a construction that blocks a certain form of knowledge in order to enable action—in short, it is what Slavoj Žižek has termed an ideological fantasy.[70] Why such a fantasy, as Žižek has argued, cannot simply be subtracted from our perception of the world to open our view to "the way things really are" becomes abundantly evident in Schlegel: social life would not be different without the fantasy construction; it simply would not be.

Yet poetry, imagined in the freedom that Schlegel demands for it, does not operate in the register of fantasy, or at least not there alone; at its most unrestrained, it exceeds fiction and names, or perhaps, performs the truth, the truth of language and of linguistic communication and, since these are taken to be analogical, the truth of politics. This is what I take Foucault's enigmatic phrase about literature "draw[ing] closer and closer to the very being of language" to suggest:

not a mystical, cabalistic union with the Word or the Letter, but a precise seismographic record of "the most violent tremors" set off by the separating agents of poetic writing. By devoting itself to the logic of its material, poetry—in Foucault's vocabulary, "literature"—manages at some points *not* to avert its eyes when it comes face to face with the chasm. Thus the idea that a society modeled on Schlegel's poetological insights would resemble a psychotic state can also be put differently: the psychotic state is not opposed to the notion of a free and democratic society, but is one of its possible instances. It is embedded in the logic of any political order (whether despotic or democratic) just as the possibility of interruption at any moment is a necessary feature of every conversation. Certain rules of conduct permit us to avert our eyes from this possibility most of the time, but, as Schlegel writes, "these rules of propriety and politeness are valid for life, never for art."[71] In those moments, art affords us not a positive utopia of what social relations might ideally look like, but a glance at the real and horrifying possibility that social bonds might, at any moment, dissolve.

Afterword: The Chemical Critique of Idealism

The main concern of this study has been to gauge how Schlegel's writings, considered thematically and formally, transform the concept of the verbal artwork by recourse to metaphors, concepts, and images taken from chemistry. While *our* interest has been focused on the poetological consequences, Schlegel's is trained at least as much on philosophy as it is on poetry. As we have seen, philosophy too is imagined in chemical terms: philosophy, he writes, is "a sort of transcendental chemistry,"[1] "the science of all sciences that forever mix and again divide themselves, a logical chemistry."[2] Philosophy in this conception not only *acts* according to a chemical model, but is also *acted upon* by the logic of chemistry. It is one of the commonplaces of romantic scholarship that romantic authors cease to conceive of philosophy and poetry as separate activities and merge them into one undifferentiated cognitive, sensory, and creative capacity. What is less commonly pointed out is that, in Schlegel, the metaphorical terms of this merger have a distinctly chemical flavor: "poetry and philosophy," we recall, "will *permeate* each other ever more deeply" (my emphasis); they will "now mix, now fuse."[3] A promising question would thus be: what effects does the chemical model have on the sort of philosophy that nourished Jena romanticism, above all on idealism? The following pages are meant to sketch the outlines of an answer.

First we need to ask whether idealism, and indeed modern philosophy, has not always been chemical. If the metaphorical evocation of chemistry is to mean that philosophy operates according to chemistry's principles, does this in any significant way alter our understanding of the point at which poetry and philosophy touch? After all, Schlegel seems to maintain the exceptional position of philosophy as standing *above* other modes of inquiry (it remains "the science of all sciences"). As for his idiosyncratic characterization of philosophy as "a logical chemistry": if we replace the terms *dividing* and *mixing* with *analysis* and *synthesis* (and the fact that chemists of his time themselves do so permits such a substitution), then we seem to be back in very familiar territory. For *analytic* and *synthetic* comprise, as Niklas Luhmann has claimed, the most successful conceptual distinction philosophy has yet introduced.[4] In a rigorous way, the pair's operations are formalized by Descartes's method of doubt, an essentially divisive process (as the word *zwei*—"two"—which lies at the root of the German *Zweifel*—"doubt"—confirms) that leads him to an indubitable—which is to say, indivisible—point of certainty, which in turn allows for a long series of synthetic operations that give rise to the complex world he inhabits.

The philosopher who uses these terms in a manner much closer to Schlegel's work—both temporally and in terms of the anxiety of influence it provokes in Schlegel—is Fichte, for whom analysis and synthesis are the cardinal operations of philosophy, so intertwined that, as he claims in his *Foundations of the Logic of Science* of 1794, "they are distinguished only in reflection."[5] As in Descartes, here too the process of distinction and connection serves to guarantee a method by means of which, Fichte maintains, "our course is firm and certain . . . and we can know in advance, that with due attention we simply cannot stray from our path" (1:115). For Fichte it is obvious (so obvious that he does not bother to state it) that such a path must have a clear beginning and an equally clear end toward which it extends. We arrive at the beginning (and Fichte is aware of the circularity implied in *arriving* at the beginning) when "some fact of empirical consciousness is posited; and one empirical determinant after the other is removed [*abgesondert*] from it, until all that purely remains is what absolutely cannot be dismissed in thought, and from which nothing further can be removed" (1:92). This chemical process of analysis yields the most desired of substances, the ab-solute, that which cannot itself be dissolved into further substances; in the *Logic of Science* this turns out to be the famous sentence "I am I," or in Fichte's alteration of Descartes: *sum, ergo sum.*

From this starting point, which he takes to be an indissoluble rock of certainty, Fichte sets about on the "firm and certain" path on which "opposites must be united [*verbunden*] so long as anything opposed remains, until absolute unity is effected" (1:115).[6] Except for the first thetic statement, by necessity everything that follows takes the form of synthesis and analysis (which Fichte likes to call anti-thesis), indeed—and here we are again reminded of chemistry—of both at the same time: for as Fichte shrewdly points out (1:112–14), the most basic operation of analysis consists in establishing a *difference* between two things (negation), that of synthesis in establishing a *sameness* between two things (affirmation). Yet in order to see a difference in *one* respect, I must first have established sameness in *other* respects; hence analysis requires synthesis. And in order to see a sameness in *one* respect, I must establish differences in *other* respects; hence synthesis requires analysis. Calling all this chemical would not, at first glance, seem to challenge philosophy's self-understanding nor to change significantly its mode of operation.

Yet despite the apparent affinity of a fundamentalist philosophical discourse from Descartes to Fichte and beyond with the language of chemistry, vast differences emerge, and vast consequences follow, when a writing—as is the case with Schlegel's—opens itself to the possibilities of the model it evokes by means of both metaphors and practices (such as experimentation), thus registering that model's full implications. The crucial point of difference is this: while a philosophy in search of foundations imagines the process of taking apart and putting together as a way of fashioning a *coherent* totality shaped by the absolute starting point and the absolute unity toward which the path of thinking is thought to lead, while it relies in other words on analysis and synthesis to lead *predictably* and *necessarily* from *arche* to *telos,* chemistry begins and ends in a messy middle. Instead of the two absolute unities determining the movement of analysis and synthesis in philosophy (absolute beginning and absolute end, which are really one, since the former necessarily entails the latter, as both Fichte and later Hegel demonstrate), eighteenth-century chemistry is occupied with multiplicities. It abandons alchemy's search for the (tellingly named) philosopher's stone, a device we could understand as being designed to transmute all multiplicity into the unitary value of gold, just as it declines to participate in the search for a *prima materia* from which all phenomena would be formed.

The double refusal of a point of inception and of a telic movement derives from the revolutionary changes that chemistry undergoes in the late eighteenth century. We have observed how at the time chemistry is in utter confusion because it finds itself in the midst of a triple transition. First, it is involved in the process of negotiating the Kuhnian paradigm shift from phlogistic to antiphlogistic chemistry, to most chemists a bewildering negotiation. Second, it struggles to establish itself as a science by distinguishing its theoretical and practical procedures from the artisanal (i.e., pharmaceutical, medical, metallurgical, etc.) practices, a difficult separation since chemists use the very skills and insights of their predecessors to disavow them. And third, chemists are at pains to cleanse their field of alchemical traces. This involves an important sociological shift away from concealment (hermetic signs, mysterious practices, secretive practitioners) to a demonstratively open display of the science (transparent nomenclature, publicly performed experiments, published results). What is more important for our present argument, all three transitions, but particularly the last, require a thorough reconceptualization of matter. As we saw, chemists forgo two crucial features of matter: they are uninterested in the most fundamental building blocks of matter, because, being presumably homogeneous, they contribute nothing to a chemical understanding of the world. Our review of eighteenth-century chemistry revealed that chemistry requires heterogeneity *all the way down*. Furthermore, along with the four or five basic elements (depending on whether one is Empedoclean or Paracelsian) chemistry also discards the notion of a metaphysically grounded, intrinsically defined notion of element. The notion of the basic element thus becomes dependent on the observer and his experimental—which is to say, theoretical and technological—skills.

If philosophy is indeed to be imagined as a sort of chemistry, as Schlegel urges us toward, then what are the effects of this chemical theory of matter and the experimental practice it entails on the foundationalism that the most prominent (though by no means sole) strand of German philosophy in the late eighteenth and early nineteenth centuries seeks to establish? If in Fichte's wake, as Schlegel maintains, philosophy has become "an absolutely experimental science" whose "rigorous march can now resemble . . . that of the immortal Lavoisier," if "the method of idealism is *combinatorial experimentation*," how are we to imagine philosophy?[7] We are dealing with more than extravagant images and rhetorical flourishes, for such references to chemistry are embedded in a network of metaphors whose logic seriously hampers philosophy's efforts at self-grounding. Any process that behaves even approximately according to the "absolutely experimental" models available in late-eighteenth-century chemistry will fail to march on Fichte's "firm and secure" road to the Absolute, and will also fail in the certainty of knowing "in advance, that with proper attention we cannot err in our path." For the path of experimentation by definition harbors unpredictable turns and hence remains open; it even *produces* the possibility of an opening where received knowledge had assumed closure. By the same token, it is open to—or produces an opening for—error, stupidity, and nonsense.

While the appearance of incoherence and meaninglessness may come to be seen as a virtue in *poetic* discourse (as we saw in chapter 5), it cannot but have corrosive effects on foundational philosophy. Where the latter requires certainty and stability (certainty in its grounding sentence and in the absolute toward which it strives, stability in the path leading from the one to the other), eighteenth-century chemistry offers a set of operations whose ad hoc rules can change at any moment. If idealist philosophy is above all intent on finding the one founding position—the *Grundsatz*—of all cognition and intuition, then its project would seem to be disturbed by an experimental practice, developed contemporaneously with idealism, that causes the number of basic elements to proliferate. The notion of a homogeneous starting or ending point is simply not available to chemistry; and even the middle ground over which it moves is riddled, as we observed, with elective affinities and strange attractions that do not yield to the control or even comprehension of the scientist.

When it operates chemically, philosophy will necessarily fail to derive from pure, absolute principles. It must, as Schlegel maintains, "begin in the middle."[8] Directly referring to Fichte's philosophy, built as it is on the "first absolutely unconditioned founding position [*Grundsatz*]" (§1 of the *Science of Logic*), Schlegel contends: "If the possibility of a science of foundation"—of *Grundwissenschaft,* as Schlegel calls "true philosophy"[9]—"is admitted, then it can be shown a priori that *it must consist of nothing but theses and antitheses.*"[10] This is another way of saying that "philosophy must begin with infinitely many sentences, with respect to its formation (not with One)."[11] Right from the start—*gleich bei der Entstehung,* as *Athenäum* fragment 24, acknowledging the presence of fragmentation in modernity, puts it—there is not One but Many. In the vocabulary with which I started: not system but fragments. Introducing metaphors of chemistry—especially when they appear not individually and locally, but as a network—effectively unhinges the very conceptual apparatus of a philosophy that they were evoked to represent.

But is this argument not skewed? Would the chemical equivalent of the all-founding *Grundsatz* not be chemical *principles* rather than chemical *elements*? I think not, for reasons that have to do with chemistry's confused state. In the late eighteenth century, there is no strong or coherent metatheoretical justification of the practice of chemistry. Chemistry textbooks do not lay forth principles formulated in mathematical terms, but largely offer instructions for dividing and mixing substances—essentially they list recipes. Chemists have not yet developed a mathematical language that would allow them to manipulate symbols instead of substances; when they do chemistry, they have no choice but to get their hands dirty. "Chemistry [in the eighteenth century] was work," the historians of science Bernadette Bensaude-Vincent and Isabelle Stengers maintain, "in the sense in which 'work' at that time meant the kind of painful and slavish labor that humbled those who practiced it."[12] This prevents late-eighteenth-century chemistry from stating first principles or final purposes that would attain the status of a *law* and that would lie outside the *practice* of chemistry. Thus when considering chemistry as an allegory for philosophy or poetry, I am not concerned (and I do not believe Schlegel is) with abstract principles of scientific investigation *outside* of chemical practice (laws, rules of evidence, etc.). A search for "foundations" in chemistry means, at this point, very much a practical, experimentally driven search for the fundamental building blocks of matter—the elements. And the "analytic and synthetic" procedure points to nothing but the material couplings and uncouplings of matter that chemists effect, observe, and attempt to control. Lacking a theoretically coherent paradigm, chemistry finds its truth in its material practice.

The idea being developed here—that Schlegel's insistent recourse to models of analysis and synthesis available in eighteenth-century chemistry disables the workings of the foundational philosophy of his day—supports and furthers arguments that some scholars of romanticism have been advancing over the last two decades: that, contrary to the idée reçue, Jena romanticism is not a continuation of German idealism by other means, that Schlegel's fragments in fact gather into a shrewd critique of a philosophy building upon a first principle. Philippe Lacoue-Labarthes, Jean-Luc Nancy, Winfried Menninghaus, and Manfred Frank have given what I take to be the most significant versions of this critique.[13]

Lacoue-Labarthes and Nancy read Jena as "form[ing] the exergue of philosophical idealism," shaped by and around idealism, yet also shaping idealism from its margins.[14] While the idea of romanticism working at the margins of idealism, at once inside and outside of it, is highly suggestive, the particular form it takes in the *Literary Absolute* ends up relying on a problematic notion of the work of art that progresses "from the dialogical to the *dialectical*" (66 / 46), thus promising to complete philosophy with the "infinity of the work of art" (69 / 48). As we saw in chapter 2, in their account, this notion of the artwork depends on a fundamentally organicist homology.

Winfried Menninghaus discards the ambiguity between inside and outside in favor of a strict opposition that he sees early romanticism (here consisting basically of Schlegel and Novalis) maintaining vis-à-vis a central philosophical trope of modernity, namely that of a certainty born of self-consciousness—in the technical language of philosophy called self-reflection. In the writings of the early romantics, he argues in his *Unendliche Verdopplung* (Infinite Doubling), self-reflection does not bring forth a self-identity arising from the assurance of an immediate and palpable presence of the self to itself; far from it. Contrary to what Descartes and Fichte hope, early romantic writings show that "the movement of reflection in the first place constitutes . . . both what reflects *and* what is reflected."[15] Self-reflection does not guarantee the validity of the self-conscious ego, and hence the validity of any philosophy built on this ground, because "beyond a reflection in the other, there is no ego, no absolute, nothing identical" (92). As presented in early romantic texts, the alternation or exchange—*Wechsel*—that characterizes the movement of reflection does not serve to certify a graspable identity prior to reflection, Menninghaus argues, but rather establishes identity *in* and *as* reflection— identity as *différance*. Thus the early romantic critique of idealism "anticipates . . . the poststructuralist metacritique and radicalization [of structuralism], as it has been performed above all by Jacques Derrida" (25); in fact, Derrida finally "remains behind" the romantics (131).[16] While in Menninghaus's argument the essential monism at the heart of idealism gives way to a dualism of early romanticism, I have preferred, in relying on the "eternally dividing and mixing forces," to point to the open-ended *multiplicity* in romantic writing and its disseminal effects on philosophy. The logic of chemistry, with its contaminations and weird aberrations, appears to me to be a better vehicle for rendering—in the sense of describing *and* producing—such a model than the logically interesting yet ultimately tidy model of optical mirroring on which the notion of self-reflection relies for metaphorical support.

For his part, Manfred Frank combines a rich account of Schlegel's critique of idealism with a detailed review of the historical context in which it takes place. Here Schlegel does not play the part of the prophet for a philosophy to come but that of a follower (though by no means an epigone) of a critique of foundational philosophy that has gathered considerable force before Schlegel makes his contribution. Thanks to eminent philosophers such as Karl Leonhard Reinhold, the university of Jena becomes a center for the foundationalist philosophy building on Kant's work as early as the first half of the 1790s (i.e., even before the arrival of Fichte in 1794 and of Schelling four years later); scholars have thus assumed that it is from this source that Schlegel draws when he arrives in Jena, twenty-four years old, in August 1796. But Frank, relying on a research project directed by Dieter Henrich on Jena philosophy in the early 1790s, points to a lively network of essays, lectures, letters, and discussions by and among a group of Jena thinkers who collectively mount a serious critique of the foundational philosophical system that is taking shape in front of their very eyes.[17]

Like Henrich and his group, Frank paints a picture of the state of philosophy at that time that is considerably more nuanced than accounts suggesting the hegemony of idealism. It is his argument that, even though Schlegel meets Fichte a mere two days after his, Schlegel's, arrival in Jena (KA 23:328), and even though he most likely attends Fichte's lectures throughout his one-year stint in Jena, Schlegel early on drinks from the cup of skepticism, abruptly turning away from Fichte's foundationalism and subjecting it to a far-reaching critique. Indeed, Frank concludes that Schlegel "has carried out the break with foundational philosophy more energetically" than any of his contemporaries.[18] Putting his critique into an aesthetic register, Schlegel, according to Frank, "veers completely from the constellation that one commonly calls 'idealist philosophy'" (859). But we saw in chapter 2 that Frank, precisely by attending to the aesthetic register in Schlegel's work, in fact prevents such a complete veering away from the path of idealist philosophy. The topos of "infinite approximation" is brought in to rescue the poetic project from a catastrophic ending. Just as in idealism (this time Schelling's and not Fichte's), in Schlegel's work too, as Frank puts it, "philosophy completes itself in and as art,"[19] even though here the completion is performed by infinite approximation. By contrast, the chemical model, I have argued, eschews the possibility of a teleology and thus of an approximation to the absolute. Its critique is not one that can easily be taken back by means of a dialectical flip.

It may well be for this reason that critical and idealist philosophy does not look kindly upon chemistry; it is deeply suspicious of a method of establishing the primary units of matter that operates without a concept given in advance, without a theory that could explain (and predict) the proliferation of elements. (Only in 1869 would such a theory become possible with Mendeleev's invention of the Periodic Table.) Because its results arise from a posteriori experimentation rather than a priori concepts, Kant precludes the possibility that chemistry might arrive at any sort of truth, concluding: "Chemistry can become nothing more than a systematic art or doctrine of experimentation, but never a proper science."[20] Schelling attenuates Kant's radical position somewhat by granting that chemistry, were it capable of expressing itself in mathematical language, would become a "very useful scientific *fiction,* by means of which an otherwise merely experimental art could become science and attain (if only hypothetical, within its borders, but nevertheless) complete clarity."[21] Needless to say this is not meant as a ringing endorsement, of which, however, the busy chemists of the time do not appear to be in great need.

I should note one further way in which a world understood according to the concepts used in late-eighteenth-century chemistry does not lend itself to the sort of philosophical monism that pervades the debates in which Schlegel engages. Chemistry's reluctance to embrace one primary origin or one final destination (and neither is available without the other) is not only a result of its being entrapped in the empirical manifold; it is constitutive of its practice. Quite apart from its empirical *method* (which in the absence of a compelling theoretical model is still the reigning paradigm in the eighteenth century), the very idea of chemistry as the art or science of mixing and separating necessarily (a) presupposes a starting point which is not unitary and homogeneous but rather multiple and heterogeneous, and (b) precludes a drive toward a point at which "opposites must be united so long as anything opposed remains, until absolute unity is effected" (Fichte). Why? Because what Fichte so lucidly recognizes about anti-thesis (i.e., analysis) and synthesis in philosophy, also holds for mixing and separating in chemistry: each requires and presupposes the other. Thus Gren insists that proper chemical mixing occurs only in the combination of "unlike parts into a homogeneous whole." Schelling points out in his *Ideen zu einer Philosophie der Natur* (Ideas Toward a Philosophy of Nature) of 1797 that in order to get any chemical mixing off the ground, "a *heterogeneity* [*Ungleichartigkeit*] of matter" must be assumed.[22] The empirical multiplicity, then, effected by the method of experimentation (which requires at least two procedures: mixture and separation) finds its counterpart in a theoretically mandated "originary" multiplicity required for the matter on which the method acts. By the same token, an ultimate synthesis of all multiplicities is not possible by means of chemistry, for at that point there would be neither elements nor compounds, but only a "homogeneous whole," an undifferentiated mass; chemistry itself would cease to exist. Put in the language of ontology, the matter of chemistry *is* not as long as it is chemical, for it metamorphoses incessantly, and should it ever *be*, it would no longer be the matter of chemistry. (Like Schlegel's characterization of romantic poetry, it is "eternally becoming, never completed.") As long as there is chemistry—the play of eternally mixing and dividing forces—things are subject to a process that turns away the demands of an ontology keen on stability.

But that does not mean that chemistry annihilates philosophy, makes it impossible, cancels it as a linguistic activity. Annihilation is not an effective form of critique, as Schlegel himself recognizes. "The fact that one can annihilate a philosophy—in the process of which a careless person can at times easily annihilate himself as well—or that one can prove that a philosophy annihilates itself is of little consequence," he writes in an *Athenäum* fragment. "If it's really philosophy, then, like the phoenix, it will always rise again from its own ashes."[23] The chemical critique is more effective, for it lodges its own logic—the logic of analysis and synthesis, the logic of sense and nonsense—into the workings of philosophy itself.

Notes

Introduction

Epigraph: Blanchot, *L'écriture du désastre*, 98/59.

1. Derrida, *La Dissémination*, 240/211.

2. I use *poetological* as the adjectival form of *poetics*, since *poetic* is already taken as the adjective belonging to *poetry*.

3. "Vor der Δ [Dreiheit] Anim[alität] Veget[abilität] Min[eralität] (oder οργ [organisch] χεμ [chemisch] μεχ [mechanisch]) . . . ," KA 18:147, No. 287. Schlegel's weird use of pseudomathematical and other graphic elements will be discussed in chapter 5.

4. "Verstand ist mechanischer, Witz ist chemischer, Genie ist organischer Geist," KA 2: 232, No. 366/PF 75.

5. "Ideale die sich für erreichbar halten, sind eben darum nicht Ideale, sondern mathematische Fantome des bloß mechanischen Denkens. Wer Sinn fürs Unendliche hat, und weiß was er damit will, sieht in ihm das Produkt sich ewig scheidender und mischender Kräfte, denkt sich seine Ideale wenigstens chemisch . . . [N]ur der vollendete Geist könnte Ideale organisch denken," KA 2:243, No. 412/PF 83.

6. "progressive Universalpoesie," KA 2:182, No. 116/PF 31.

7. In his suggestive article, Matthew Tanner points in a similar direction: for him, the chemical model seeks "not the product but the production of systems" (Tanner, "Chemistry in Schlegel's *Athenäum* Fragments," 141). His study does not elaborate this insight.

8. Barthes, *S/Z*, 11/5.

9. I borrow this term from Eric Santner's *Friedrich Hölderlin*, 6.

10. Wellek, *Concepts of Criticism*, 128–98; Kittler, *Aufschreibesysteme*, 11–220, esp. 82–88/3–173, 63–69.

11. "geheime Ordensverbindungen," KA 2:364/TP 119.

12. For mathematically inspired terminology, see the very different accounts of Neubauer, *Symbolismus und symbolische Logik*, esp. 75–88 and

126–33; de Man, *Blindness and Insight,* 222, and de Man, *The Rhetoric of Romanticism,* 263–90; as well as Menninghaus, *Unendliche Verdopplung,* esp. 155–69. I discuss these in greater detail in what follows.

13. Novalis, *Schriften,* 2:672/TP 145–46.

14. *Schriften,* 3:50; see also *Schriften,* 3:360, No. 547.

15. La Mettrie, *L'Homme machine,* 186.

16. Kuhn, *The Structure of Scientific Revolutions,* 53–56 and 69–72.

17. Cf. Bensaude-Vincent and Stengers, *A History of Chemistry,* 39, 64–67.

18. Foucault, *Language, Counter-Memory, Practice,* 116.

19. "Der Buchstabe ist d[er] wahre Zauberstab," KA 18:265, No. 846. Also in *Lucinde,* KA 5:20.

20. Harry Levin, preface to Lord, *The Singer of Tales,* xiii.

21. Havelock, *The Literate Revolution in Greece,* 120.

22. Cf. his claim that the irony that hovers over Goethe's *Wilhelm Meister* can only be communicated by someone reading it out loud (KA 2:137–38). A formalized version of this claim is found in his lectures *Die Entwicklung der Philosophie in zwölf Büchern,* held in Cologne in 1804 and 1805: "To be sure, language . . . cannot be a sign language; all sign language is only a weak surrogate of true language that can only be based on sound and tones" (Die Sprache . . . kann freilich keine Zeichensprache sein; alle Zeichensprache ist nur ein schwaches Surrogat der wahren, die nur auf Schall und Tönen beruhen kann [KA 12:347]). But even this seemingly unambiguous endorsement of sound—which in this context entails a promotion of the sense of hearing and a demotion of sight—is complicated and partially taken back through a reference to the ancient topos of the Book of Nature. In the very next sentence, Schlegel writes: "There is also, however, a natural language, which reveals itself in the form of objects. . . . If we know how to intuit it, each object reveals in its natural language a higher meaning. Sight is the sense for this language. . . . Sight in its higher development is thus, as it were, the sense of sense" (Indessen gibt es dennoch auch eine natürliche Sprache, die sich in der Gestalt der Gegenstände offenbart. . . . [J]eder Gegenstand, wenn wir ihn recht anzuschauen wissen, [offenbaret] uns in seiner natürlichen Sprache eine höhere Bedeutung. Das Gesicht ist der Sinn für diese Sprache. . . . Das Gesicht in der höhern Vollendung also ist gleichsam der Sinn für den Sinn [KA 12:347]).

Underlying and structuring the sense of hearing is the sense of sense; as we shall see in chapter 5, the structure of the material that this sense of sense makes available itself relies on writing. The "weak surrogate" is in fact what lends support to "true language." During the same lectures, Schlegel confirms this structure by putting the act of writing into an analogy with the original act of production: "There is, however, one kind of thinking that produces something and that therefore bears great resemblance to the form of the creative faculty that we ascribe [!] to the Ego of nature and to the World-Ego. Namely *writing poetry;* this *creates, as it were, its material and is a playful activity*" (Es gibt zwar eine Art des Denkens, die etwas produziert und daher mit dem schöpferischen Vermögen, das wir dem Ich der Natur und dem Welt-Ich zuschreiben, große Ähnlichkeit der Form hat. Das *Dichten* nähmlich; dies *erschafft gewissermaßen seinen Stoff selbst und ist eine spielende Tätigkeit* [KA 12:371]).

23. Despite its scattered occurrence in his work, Schlegel's usage of the term *Literatur* foreshadows its taxonomy in nineteenth-century historiography and its institutionalized study in the university to this day: *literature* usually comes not by itself (like poetry), but with a linguistic or geographic qualifier. We thus find among his notes German, English, European, Hebrew, Oriental, Hungarian, and Saxon literature (but also odd combinations such as ancient, esoteric, grammatical, critical, or Catholic literature).

24. Kittler, *Aufschreibesysteme,* 150/117. For the dating of literature to 1880 and its connection to competing media, see Kittler, *Grammophon Film Typewriter,* 27.

25. Menninghaus, in his *Lob des Unsinns,* traces the production of nonsense literature back to romanticism, though, as we shall see, he understands the phenomenon, and the poetic conception giving rise to it, differently.

26. "lebendig und entgegenwirkend," KA 2:161, No. 112/PF 14.

27. E.g., Foucault, *Les mots et les choses,* 103/89.

28. I rely here on Niklas Luhmann's terminology developed in his summa, *Die Gesellschaft der Gesellschaft,* and, with reference to the art system, *Die Kunst der Gesellschaft.* Schmidt, *Die Selbstorganisation des Literatursystems im 18. Jahrhundert,* esp. chapters 10 and 12, provides valuable support for Luhmann's thesis.

29. For a reading of "Über die Unverständlichkeit" in terms of sociological systems theory and information theory, see Rasch, "Injecting Noise into the System."

30. "zugleich Poesie und Poesie der Poesie," "Transzendentalpoesie," KA 2:204, No. 238/PF 51.

31. For more on the notion of second-order observation in romanticism, see Luhmann, "A Redescription of 'Romantic Art.'"

One: Of Incomprehensibility

1. See Goethe, *Briefwechsel mit Schiller,* in *Gedenkausgabe,* 20:605, where Goethe admiringly refers to Schlegel's fragments as a "wasps' nest." For the contemporary reactions to the *Athenäum,* see Hans Eichner's introduction, KA 2:xcviii–xcix.

2. The problem of the periodization of late-eighteenth- and early-nineteenth-century writings is debated with great fervor and, in my view, to little end, since establishing taxonomies usually says more about the taxonomizers than about the taxonomized. I use early, or Jena, romanticism (*Frühromantik*) to refer to a group of texts that is by convention placed under that rubric, and do not mean to draw ontological conclusions from this.

3. Lacoue-Labarthe and Nancy, *L'Absolu littéraire,* 17/8.

4. "daß man die reinste und gediegenste Unverständlichkeit gerade aus der Wissenschaft und aus der Kunst erhält, . . . aus der Philosophie und Philologie," KA 2:64/TP 119.

5. "die Frage, ob [die Mitteilung der Ideen] überhaupt möglich sei," KA 2:63/TP 119.

6. "und damit das ganze Geschäft sich nicht in einem gar zu handgreiflichen Zirkel herumdrehen möchte, so hatte ich mir fest vorgenommen, dieses eine Mal wenigstens gewiß verständlich zu sein," KA 2:64/TP 119.

7. "Gelegenheit über die Möglichkeit oder Unmöglichkeit dieser Sache mancherlei Versuche anzustellen," KA 2:63/TP 119.

8. "daß die Worte sich selbst oft besser verstehen, als diejenigen von denen sie gebraucht werden," KA 2:64/TP 119.

9. Adelung's dictionary notes that *ver-* is a "particle" "which used to be common by itself," without, however, providing evidence (*Grammatisch-kritisches Wörterbuch,* 4:981).

10. Aptly, the volume of the dictionary devoted to the letter *v,* largely comprised of *ver-* words, was plagued by unanticipated delays and took more than seventy years to complete (from around 1880 till 1956), as though the structural deferral in *ver-* had infected the attempt at a complete collection of its combinations.

11. Leopold, *Die Vorsilbe VER- und ihre Geschichte,* 264. Statistical

analyses of the prefix by more recent linguists have largely confirmed Leopold's findings; see the analysis of 1,133 *ver-* verbs in Mungan, *Die semantische Interaktion,* 133. The vast majority have "nasty" or excessive meanings; only in 3 percent of cases does *ver-* effect little or no change in the root verb (*meiden/vermeiden,* to avoid; *ändern/verändern,* to change).

12. I am grateful to Karl Guthke and Peter Höfle, who separately pointed out to me the double meaning of the word.

13. "Mit *zer/auf* lassen sich noch viele neue Worte <(Verba)> mach[en] (*be* auch gut zur Unbestimmtheit, auch *ge* vielleicht)," KA 16:455, No. 22. Angle brackets mark insertions by Schlegel into the manuscript.

14. I am grateful to David Elmer for calling my attention to this etymology.

15. Derrida, *La Dissémination,* 252/222.

16. Kleist, *Sämtliche Werke und Briefe,* 2:593.

17. Novalis, *Schriften,* 2:242, No. 445.

18. "die Ironie der Ironie," KA 2:369/TP 125.

19. "wenn man nicht wieder aus der Ironie herauskommen kann, wie es in diesem Versuch über die Unverständlichkeit zu sein scheint," KA 2:369/TP 125.

20. Freud, "Bemerkungen über einen Fall von Zwangsneurose," *Gesammelte Werke,* 7:381–463/"Notes upon a Case of Obsessional Neurosis," *Standard Edition,* 10:153–318; "Fetischismus," *Gesammelte Werke,* 14:311–17/"Fetishism," *Standard Edition,* 21:149–57.

21. Lacan, *Écrits,* 166.

22. Hegel, *Werke,* 13:94/*Aesthetics,* 1:65.

23. "erhabne Frechheit," KA 24:31.

24. "eine ganz neue Gattung," KA 24:51.

25. "von der umgebenden Welt ganz abgesondert und in sich selbst vollendet . . . wie ein Igel," KA 2:197, No. 206/PF 45.

26. "Ein Fragm.[ent] ist ein selbstbestimmter und selbstbestimmender Gedanke," KA 18:305, No. 1333.

27. "ein System von Fragmenten," KA 18:100, No. 857.

28. "Die Encycl[opädie] läßt sich schlechterdings und durchaus nur in *Fragmenten* darstellen," KA 18:485, No. 141.

29. Beda Allemann points out the connection between irony and chemistry in Schlegel in his *Ironie und Dichtung,* 61–69, as does Peter Szondi in "Antike und Moderne in der Ästhetik der Goethezeit" (Szondi, *Poetik und Geschichtsphilosophie,* 1:11–265, here 136–38), but both leave the insight largely undeveloped.

Two: The Fragment, Symptom of Aesthetics

1. "Sie will, und soll auch Poesie und Prosa, Genialität und Kritik, Kunstpoesie und Naturpoesie bald mischen, bald verschmelzen . . . und die Formen der Kunst mit gediegnem Bildungsstoff jeder Art . . . sättigen," KA 2:182, No. 116/PF 31. Imposing an *obligation* when a *will* to the same end has already been acknowledged ("it wants to and also should") is a strange gesture that requires further scrutiny.

2. "wo Vernunft und Unvernunft sich saturiren und durchdringen," KA 18:162, No. 471. For further examples of saturation, permeation, mixture, and fusion, see KA 18:342, No. 248; ibid., No. 243; KA 2:216, No. 304/PF 60.

3. "eine *Revoluzion* in dem aesthetischen Gebiet," KA 17:371, No. 258.

4. The audience consisted of three rich young merchants from Cologne in Paris to see the world (the brothers Sulpiz and Melchior Boisserée and their friend Johann Baptist Bertram, who would later become Schlegel's sponsors in his Cologne years) and Helmina von Hafster. See KA 11:xxix–xxx.

5. "die Neueren sind durch die Untersuchungen der Chemie zur höheren Naturansicht gekommen, die Alten aber direkt, und zwar durch Poesie und Religion," KA 11:105.

6. "eine Art von transcendentaler Chemie," KA 18:89, No. 716.

7. Lichtenberg, *Schriften und Briefe*, 2:393.

8. Ibid., 2:453–54. For a study of Lichtenberg's relation to the language of chemistry, see Winthrop-Young, *Lichtenberg und die französische Revolution*.

9. Kant, *Metaphysische Anfangsgründe der Naturwissenschaft*, AA 4:471.

10. Kant, *Prolegomena*, AA 4:366/*Prolegomena*, 115.

11. Paul de Man has suggested that "it would hardly be hyperbolic to say . . . that the whole discipline of *Germanistik* has developed for the single reason of dodging Friedrich Schlegel" (*Aesthetic Ideology*, 168). What he says a bit further about a passage in *Lucinde* can also be applied to this diagnosis: "It is a joke, but we know that jokes are not innocent" (169).

12. I capitalize the term to refer specifically to an intellectual formation in the eighteenth century, as distinct from the lower-case enlightenment of rationalism and scientific verifiability, which in the Occidental tradition is as old as philosophy itself.

13. Hegel, *Werke*, 13:92/*Aesthetics*, 1:63.

14. Bohrer, *Die Kritik der Romantik,* particularly 97–137 and 221–42.

15. See Mann, *Deutschland und die Deutschen,* especially 31–35 / 15–18. Lukács's critique of romanticism permeates his work. Just two examples: Lukács, *Skizze einer Geschichte der neueren deutschen Literatur,* 66–87, esp. 83; and Lukács, *Die Zerstörung der Vernunft* (first edition 1953), 84–172.

16. Habermas, *Der philosophische Diskurs der Moderne,* 110–15 / 88–92.

17. Frenzel and Frenzel, *Daten deutscher Dichtung,* 1:300.

18. Craig, *The Germans,* 190–91.

19. The reception of Schlegel's work by *Germanistik* under the Nazis by no means confirms the widespread diagnosis that he, always placed under the nebulous rubric of romanticism, helped prepare the way for Hitler. Quite the contrary: beginning as early as May 1933, barely four months after Hitler's election to the chancellorship, professors of German literature, eager to prove their ideological reliability, marginalize Schlegel and the Jena group in favor of Heidelberg romanticism with its supposed rootedness in the *Volk* and its deep attachment to nature. This move is legitimized by an insistence on the essential *continuity* of the work of Schlegel and his circle with the Enlightenment. Cf. Klausnitzer, "Blaue Blume unterm Hakenkreuz," 522–24. In 1926, Alfred Baeumler prepares the ground for the shift away from early romanticism by pointing out the indebtedness of Jena romanticism to the eighteenth century; he does so in order to distinguish Heidelberg romanticism from the shallow word games that in his view Schlegel and Novalis play. See his introduction to Bachofen, *Der Mythus von Orient und Occident,* clxix–clxx.

20. Eichner, "The Rise of Modern Science and the Genesis of Romanticism," 8.

21. Coleridge, *Collected Works,* vol. 4, pt.1, p. 471. For Coleridge's loathing of "French" chemistry, see Levere, "Coleridge, Chemistry, and the Philosophy of Nature."

22. Schelling's organic view of nature is articulated in *Ideen zu einer Philosophie der Natur* of 1797 (Schelling, *Historisch-Kritische Ausgabe,* pt. 1, vol. 5) and *Von der Weltseele, eine Hypothese der höheren Physik zur Erklärung des allgemeinen Organismus* of 1798 (Schelling, *Sämmtliche Werke,* vol. 1, pt. 2, pp. 345–583).

23. The main exponents of "romantic science" are Lorenz Oken, Friedrich Hufeland, Gottfried Reinhold Treviranus, Carl Gustav Carus, Henrik Steffens, and Johann Wilhelm Ritter. Some of their writings are anthologized in Bernoulli and Kern, *Romantische Naturphilosophie.* Gode-von Aesch, *Natural Science in German Romanticism,* contains a lot

of information about their projects. That not all of them were scientifically specious is argued by the essays in Cunningham and Jardine, eds.,
Romanticism and the Sciences. See Snelders, "Romanticism and Naturphilosophie," for an overview, and Wetzels, "Aspects of Natural Science
in German Romanticism," 52–59, for an account of the "romantic physi-
cist" Johann Wilhelm Richter.

24. Schanze, *Romantik und Aufklärung,* 11.

25. Dischner and Faber, eds., *Romantische Utopie-Utopische Romantik,* 12.

26. Blanchot, *L'Entretien infini,* 518/353.

27. Lacoue-Labarthe and Nancy, *L'absolu littéraire,* 17/8. For Hörisch
(*Die fröhliche Wissenschaft der Poesie,* 23) the early romantics not only
constituted an avant-garde in *their* time but continue to do so in ours.

28. See for instance the superb essays in Behler and Hörisch, eds., *Die
Aktualität der Frühromantik,* as well as the work of Ernst Behler, Manfred
Frank, and Winfried Menninghaus, cited below. Similarly, Rodolphe
Gasché: "If I contend that the fragments attempt to elaborate a *concept*
of the fragment . . . it is also to make the point that the Romantic frag-
ment is a *philosophical* conception" ("Identity in Fragmentation," PF x).

29. Cf. Hans Eichner, introduction, KA 16:xi.

30. On Schlegel's plans, see Ernst Behler, introduction, KA 18:xii–xvi,
xlix–lx.

31. Lacoue-Labarthe and Nancy, *L'Absolu littéraire,* 43/29.

32. Quoted in Jung, *Von der Mimesis zur Simulation,* 66.

33. Scarry, *On Beauty and Being Just.*

34. Baeumler, *Das Irrationalitätsproblem in der Ästhetik und Logik des
18. Jahrhunderts,* 2.

35. Burke, *Philosophical Enquiry into the Origin of our Ideas of the
Sublime and the Beautiful,* vol. 1 of *The Works of Edmund Burke,* 56.

36. Rousseau, *The Social Contract,* 44.

37. For a discussion of the political implications of this logic, see Eagleton, *The Ideology of the Aesthetic,* esp. 13–30.

38. "Das Prinzip, das das Verhältniß des Ganzen zu den Theilen und
der Theile zum Ganzen ausdrückt, hat man in der Kunst zu suchen," KA
12:18.

39. A small selection of Lichtenberg's aphorisms was published in
1800 and 1801 as *Georg Christoph Lichtenberg's vermischte Schriften,* though
the majority of what has come to be known as his *Sudelbücher* were published far too late for them to have influenced Schlegel's fragments.

40. "eine *kritische Chamfortade*," KA 24:21.

41. Mautner, "Der Aphorismus als literarische Gattung," 47, 49.

42. *Historisches Wörterbuch der Philosophie,* vol. 1, columns 437–38.

43. Gerhard Neumann, *Ideenparadiese,* 42. See also Neumann, *Der Aphorismus,* 5, where he characterizes the aphorism as a "*presentation of the conflict* between what is individual . . . and its sublation [*Aufhebung*] in the general."

44. Spicker, *Der Aphorismus,* 78–79.

45. Mautner acknowledges the discontinuity of the two genres suggested by the term *fragment.* "A tendency lurks in its etymological meaning," he writes, "that, as soon as one leaves the field of romantic theory, stands in direct opposition to the specific external *self-enclosed unity* [*Geschlossenheit*] of the literary aphorism" (Mautner, "Der Aphorismus als literarische Gattung," 34). It is taken for granted by him that *within* the field of romantic theory such unity is a feature of the fragment, thus making it continuous with the aphorism (cf. 54).

46. Lichtenberg, *Schriften und Briefe,* 2:166.

47. Nietzsche, *Kritische Gesamtausgabe,* pt. 6, vol. 3, p. 147.

48. *The Wit and Humor of Oscar Wilde,* 58.

49. "Der Historiker ist ein rückwärts gekehrter Prophet," KA 2:176, No. 80/PF 27.

50. "Das Druckenlassen verhält sich zum Denken, wie eine Wochenstube zum ersten Kuß," KA 2:174, No. 62/PF 26.

51. "Eine gute Vorrede muß zugleich die Wurzel und das Quadrat ihres Buchs sein," KA 2:148, No. 8/PF 1.

52. "Alles beurteilen zu wollen, ist eine große Verirrung oder eine kleine Sünde," KA 2:159, No. 102/PF 12.

53. One comparatively modest example: Fr = x√Δρ, which the editor of the critical edition decodes as "Fragment = reduced drama" (KA 16:165, No. 952).

54. "Viele Werke der Alten sind Fragmente geworden. Viele Werke der Neuern sind es gleich bei der Entstehung," KA 2:169, No. 24/PF 21.

55. "*Studium* ist absichtl.[iches] Fragment," KA 16:129, No. 536.

56. I owe this insight to Szondi, *Antike und Moderne in der Ästhetik der Goethezeit,* in *Poetik und Geschichtsphilosophie,* 1:103–5. Szondi points out that a form of historical understanding, usually clothed in organic metaphors of generation, maturation, and death, is already present in Winckelmann, 40–42, something which Schlegel had sensed: "Winkelmann [*sic*] was the first to feel the antinomy of antiquity and modernity"

(Die Antinomie der Antik[e] und d[er] Moderne hat Winkelmann zuerst gefühlt [KA 16:104, No. 236]).

57. Panofsky, *Idea,* 29, 37.

58. Tatarkiewicz, *History of Aesthetics,* 3:452.

59. Luhmann makes this point in his *Ausdifferenzierung des Kunstsystems,* 24–25.

60. In the sense of Eco's *The Open Work.*

61. With a certain justification, for a fragment does not in fact fit the rubric of what was being collected, namely "work." Cf. a note from 1797: "Writings that are *not* works . . . *Fragment* . . ." (Schriften die *nicht* Werke sind . . . *Fragment* . . . [KA 16:163, No. 918]).

62. The reason that "criticism" is a more adequate translation of Benjamin's title word *Kunstkritik* than the more literal "art criticism," understood mainly as the criticism of *visual* art, has everything to do with the early romantic notion of the work of art. For reasons I will discuss below, Schlegel (as well as Novalis) regards the quintessential artwork as *verbal,* a view recognized and criticized by Benjamin. Samuel Weber makes a similar point in Weber, "Criticism Underway," 308 n17.

63. Barthes, *S/Z,* 10/4.

64. "Der synthetische Schriftsteller konstruiert und schafft sich einen Leser, wie er sein soll," KA 2:161, No. 112/PF 14.

65. "ruhend und tot, sondern lebendig und entgegenwirkend," ibid.

66. "tritt mit ihm in das heilige Verhältnis der innigsten Symphilosophie oder Sympoesie," ibid.

67. The sociological implication is clear: the demand for innovation elicits from writers ever greater activity and variety, which, to be recognized and appreciated, demands a new, active reader. Both developments further the differentiation of the sphere of literature. Cf. Luhmann, *Die Kunst der Gesellschaft,* 85.

68. Blanchot, *L'écriture du désastre,* 72/42.

69. This totality is not, as we shall see, confined to the fragments Schlegel wrote, but stretches into infinity.

70. "das ist ihr eigentliches Wesen, daß sie ewig nur werden, nie vollendet sein kann," KA 2:183, No. 116/PF 32.

71. "Ein einziges analytisches Wort, auch zum Lobe, kann den vortrefflichsten witzigen Einfall, dessen Flamme nun erst wärmen sollte, nachdem sie geglänzt hat, unmittelbar löschen," KA 2:149, No. 22/PF 3.

72. "Wenn manche mystische Kunstliebhaber, welche jede Kritik für

Zergliederung, und jede Zergliederung für Zerstörung des Genusses halten, konsequent dächten: so wäre Potztausend das beste Kunsturteil über das würdigste Werk," KA 2:154, No. 57/PF 7.

73. "Streng genommen ist der Begriff eines wissenschaftlichen Gedichts wohl so widersinnig, wie der einer dichterischen Wissenschaft," KA 2:154, No. 61/PF 8.

74. "Die ganze Geschichte der modernen Poesie ist ein fortlaufender Kommentar zu dem kurzen Text der Philosophie: Alle Kunst soll Wissenschaft, und alle Wissenschaft soll Kunst werden; Poesie und Philosophie sollen vereinigt sein," KA 2:161, No. 115/PF 14.

75. "Es gibt so viel Poesie, und doch ist nichts seltner als ein Poem! Das macht die Menge von poetischen Skizzen, Studien, Fragmenten, Tendenzen, Ruinen, und Materialien," KA 2:147, No. 4/PF 1.

76. "Auch in der Poesie mag wohl alles Ganze halb, und alles Halbe doch eingentlich ganz sein," KA 2:148, No. 14/PF 2.

77. "Es ist gleich tödlich für den Geist, ein System zu haben, und keins zu haben. Er wird sich also wohl entschließen müssen, beides zu verbinden," KA 2:173, No. 53/PF 24.

78. "Jeder Satz jedes Buch, so sich nicht selbst widerspricht, ist unvollständig," KA 18:83, No. 647.

79. Of the 451 *Athenäum* fragments, scholars have identified 219 as Friedrich's work, 127 as the work of the three other collaborators (August Wilhelm 85, Schleiermacher 29, and Novalis 13), and 4 as collective products, while the authorship of the remaining 101 is open (though it is likely that Friedrich wrote most of those). I owe these figures to Hans Eichner's account in the introduction to volume 2 of the critical edition (KA 2:cxi–cxiv).

80. "es soll die Gestalt eines kleinen Dialogs gewinnen, eine Form die den Fragmenten gewiß nicht fremd ist," KA 24:8. The multiplicity of voices that laces the fragments also extends to the lively correspondence between the members of the Jena group. The passage I just cited, for example, is from a letter Friedrich Schlegel and Schleiermacher write to A. W. Schlegel on January 15, 1798, in which Schleiermacher claims, not without irony, to "speak merely as [Friedrich's] voice, without wanting to take responsibility for anything" (rede bloß als sein Organ ohne irgend etwas verantworten zu wollen [ibid.]).

81. "ein bunter Haufen von Einfällen," KA 2:159, No. 103/PF 12.

82. "wie das überraschende Wiedersehen zwei befreundeter Gedanken nach einer langen Trennung," KA 2:171, No. 37.

83. "Ein Dialog ist eine Kette, oder ein Kranz von Fragmenten," KA 2:176, No. 77/PF 27.

84. "[daß] die Worte sich selbst oft besser verstehen, als diejenigen von denen sie gebraucht werden," KA 2:364/TP 119.

85. "geheime Ordensverbindungen," ibid.

86. Bohrer, *Kritik der Romantik,* 39–94.

87. In a rich article, Christopher Kubiak has reflected productively both on the "genre" (or nongenre) of the fragment and its implication in the notion of system; see Kubiak, "Sowing Chaos."

88. "ein System von Fragmenten," KA 18:100, No. 857. See also KA 18:98, No. 829; ibid., No. 832; KA 18:108, No. 950; KA 18:232, No. 462; KA 18:359, No. 473.

89. Lacoue-Labarthe and Nancy, "Noli me frangere," 87.

90. *"Ich strebe nach Allheit d[es] Wissens,"* KA 18:5, No. 18.

91. "Da ich überall in π [Poesie] und φ [Philosophie] zuerst und aus Instinkt auf das συστ [System] gegangen bin, so bin ich wohl ein Universalsystematiker," KA 18:38, No. 214.

92. Cf. Ostermann, *Das Fragment,* 13.

93. Gasché, "Ideality in Fragmentation," PF vii.

94. Frank, *"Unendliche Annäherung,"* 936.

95. Neumann, *Ideenparadiese,* 569.

96. The homology of fragment, individual, and universe is sponsored by the tight connection that the philosophical tradition maintains between the notions of *organic* and of *system.* For Kant, a proper organization of knowledge is only imaginable if it takes the form of a system. For a system provides "the unity of the manifold cognitions under an idea" in order to form a totality (cf. *Kritik der reinen Vernunft,* AA vols. 3 and 4/*Critique of Pure Reason,* A 832/B 860 [A refers to the first, B to the second edition of the *Critique*]). But to be a system, the totality must have a particular shape: "The whole is articulated [*gegliedert*] (*articulatio*) and not accumulated [*gehäuft*] (*coacervatio*). It can indeed grow internally . . . but not externally . . .; i.e., it can grow only like an animal body" (A 833 /B 861; cf. B xxiii). The mechanical connotations of the Greek root of *system* (*synistanai:* to combine, to put together) have been superseded by an organic model; for all the architectural metaphors that pervade Kant's critical philosophy, it is ultimately the articulated body that serves as the model for the system. Thus Krug's philosophical dictionary of 1829 has no trouble putting the scientific system into a metonymic chain with "skeletal system, solar system, state system, etc." (*Allgemeines Wörterbuch*

der philosophischen Wissenschaft, 4:103), for all these systems are thought to draw their metaphorical force from the body. The connection of the two is so powerfully evident to Enlightenment and post-Enlightenment thinking that the very first meaning of *System* given by Grimm's *Deutsches Wörterbuch* is "a sensible *articulated* [*gegliedertes*] whole" (DW 20:1433, my emphasis).

97. Lacoue-Labarthe and Nancy, *L'Absolu littéraire,* 64/44.

98. "Just as the fragment of Antiquity manifests the essential originality of the ancient work, the modern fragment 'characterizes' this originality, and thereby sketches out the 'project' of the future work whose individuality will dialectically reunite and sublate (art aside, we are very close to Hegel) the thinking, living, and working dialogue of ancient and modern fragments" (Lacoue-Labarthe and Nancy, *L'Absolu littéraire,* 68/47).

99. As so often in the critical literature, here too the authors take the romantic notion of "symphilosophy" perhaps more seriously than is warranted; put differently, they adduce evidence from some authors to make judgments about every author belonging to the Jena "group," thus blurring important distinctions. Here, in a section that in the French edition of the book is devoted to introducing Schlegel's *Lyceum* and *Athenäum* fragments, the cited evidence for the "genre of generation" comes from Novalis's "Blüthenstaub" collection ("Fragments of this kind are literary seeds") and from *Athenäum* fragment 338 ("In the Self everything is formed organically"), written by Schleiermacher. For a more extensive critique of the *Literary Absolute,* see Newmark, "*L'absolut littéraire.*"

100. Gasché, "Identity in Fragmentation," PF xi.

101. Peter Szondi relies on a similar organic homology in developing a utopian (i.e., future-oriented) narrative: "The fragment is understood as a project, as the 'subjective seed of a becoming object,' as preparation for the longed-for synthesis. What is seen in the fragment is no longer what is unachieved or what has remained fragmentary, but rather the anticipation, the promise" (Szondi, *Satz und Gegensatz,* 13/*On Textual Understanding,* 64–65).

102. Behler, "Das Fragment der Frühromantik," in *Studien zur Romantik und zur idealistischen Philosophie,* 2:36.

103. "als Idee . . . völlig überzeugt," KA 7:8.

104. Behler, "Die Kunst der Reflexion," in *Studien zur Romantik und zur idealistischen Philosophie,* 1:120.

105. "Das Leben des universellen Geistes ist eine ununterbrochne Kette innerer Revolutionen," KA 2:255, No. 451/PF 93.

106. Behler points out for example that Schlegel rejects Fichte's attempt at limiting the infinite progress of reflection as unjustified because "such an obstacle cannot . . . be put in the way of the consciousness in pure thought" (*Studien zur Romantik und zur idealistischen Philosophie,* 1:126).

107. Schelling, *Sämmtliche Werke,* 1:3, 625, 626 / *System of Transcendental Idealism (1800),* 230.

108. Frank, *Einführung in die frühromantische Ästhetik,* 244.

109. I rely here on Frank's exposition in *Einführung in die frühromantische Ästhetik,* 287–306, largely reproduced in Frank, "*Unendliche Annäherung,*" 929–44.

110. By relying on a similar understanding of the concept of allegory, Gary Handwerk's impressive reading of Schlegel's concept and deployment of irony ends up redeeming it for a "higher" purpose by claiming it for a hermeneutically productive notion of conversation; see Handwerk, *Irony and Ethics in Narrative,* 18–30.

111. For another, far less elaborate attempt at using the idea of infinite approximation to redeem the fragments, see Ueding, "Das Fragment als literarische Form der Utopie," esp. 353–55.

112. Frank, *Einführung in die frühromantische Ästhetik,* 293–94.

113. De Man, *Blindness and Insight,* 191.

114. Frank, *Einführung in die frühromantische Ästhetik,* 312.

115. Frank, *Das Problem "Zeit" in der deutschen Romantik,* 501.

116. Frank brings the concept of infinite approximation to bear on Schlegel differently, though no less redemptively, in his "'Wechselgrundsatz'"; there, the "deferral of the limit of knowledge" is interpreted as providing "a prospect on the growth of knowledge," 32 (see also 43–44), when in fact the *loss* of knowledge and meaning is an equally possible outcome.

117. "Je organischer, je systematischer," KA 16:164, No. 940.

118. "*Systeme* müssen wachsen; der Keim in jedem System muß *organisch* sein," KA 16:165, No. 953.

119. "Wo die Philosophie aufhört, muß die Poesie anfangen," KA 2:61, No. 48 / PF 98.

120. "Die Philosophie lehrte uns, daß alles Göttliche sich nur andeuten, nur mit Wahrscheinlichkeit voraussetzen lasse, und daß wir daher die Offenbarung für die höchste Wahrheit annehmen müssen. Die Offenbarung aber ist eigentlich eine für den sinnlichen Menschen zu erhabene Erkenntnis, und so tritt die Kunst sehr gut ins Mittel, um durch

sinnliche Darstellung und Deutlichkeit dem Menschen die Gegenstände der Offenbarung vor Augen zu stellen," KA 13:174.

121. Many critics, Frank among them, draw heavily on just these lectures for quotations evincing a telic coherence in Schlegel's work.

122. "Wer Sinn fürs Unendliche hat, . . . sieht in ihm das Produkt sich ewig scheidender und mischender Kräfte, denkt sich seine Ideale wenigstens chemisch [. . .] nur der vollendete Geist könnte Ideale organisch denken," KA 2:243, No. 412/PF 83.

123. "Die οργ [organische] Poesie die göttliche," KA 18:235, No. 501.

124. Blanchot, *L'écriture du désastre*, 98/59.

125. "Man soll der Philosophie . . . nicht bloß die Unphilosophie, sondern die Poesie entgegensetzen," KA 2:261, No. 48/PF 98.

126. Behler, *Studien zur Romantik und zur idealistischen Philosophie*, 1:119.

127. "wechseld zwischen χα [Chaos] und συστ [System], χα [Chaos] zu συστ [System] bereitend und dann neues χα [Chaos]," KA 18:283, No. 1048.

128. "das Produzierende mit dem Produkt darstellte," KA 2:204, No. 238/PF 50.

129. Matthew Tanner recognizes the disruptive potential of chemistry in Schlegel's fragments, yet proceeds to contain this possibility in a manner similar to Frank's: here the organic provides "the promise of teleology [that] acts, for Schlegel, as a *regulative idea* legitimizing chemical fragmentarity" (Tanner, "Chemistry in Schlegel's *Athenäum* Fragments," 149 [my emphasis]). But the chemical is not a stage toward the organic, but always within it.

130. "Die φ [Philosophie] ein επος, fängt in d.[er] Mitte an," KA 18:82, No. 626.

131. Menninghaus, *Unendliche Verdopplung*, esp. chap. 3.

132. Benjamin, *Gesammelte Schriften*, vol. 1, pt. 1, p. 87/*Selected Writings*, 1:165.

133. De Man, *Blindness and Insight*, 220.

134. De Man's strange reintroduction of a direction ("the *narrowing* spiral," "*more and more* remote") may be connected to the fact that he frequently imagines language as a mathematical construct. Here he is led by the metaphor of the spiral; elsewhere he thinks of hyperbole, ellipsis, and parabola, indeed of tropes in general, as mathematical entities: "Tropes are quantified systems of motion. The indeterminations of imitation and of hermeneutics have at last been formalized into a mathe-

matics that no longer depends on role models or on semantic intentions" ("Aesthetic Formalization: Kleist's *Über das Marionettentheater*," in *The Rhetoric of Romanticism*, 286. For a sustained argument about the mathematics of tropes, see Paul de Man, "Pascal's Allegory of Persuasion," in *Aesthetic Ideology*, 51–69.) De Man echoes some lines that Novalis jotted down while reading the *Neues Organon* (1764) by the eighteenth-century scientist and logician Johann Heinrich Lambert: "Tropical expressions point to [*deuten auf*] the art of determining, and thus rendering *figural*, our cognition. Mental mathesis would be founded by means of a completed tropics" (*Schriften*, 3:130). I prefer the model of chemistry to that of mathematics, because chemistry (in its late-eighteenth-century version) leaves a *remainder*, both material and intellectual. Things dissolve and bind as imperfectly as their elemental structures and the logic of their reactions are understood at the time. This seems to me to provide a better model of poetic writing as it is described and practiced by the young Schlegel.

135. Occasionally de Man makes this move as well: "The ironist invents a form of himself that is 'mad' but that does not know its own madness; he then proceeds to reflect on his madness thus objectified" (*Blindness and Insight*, 216). This model of irony as a double consciousness, which may be correct as a *psychological* account, does not help us with textual analysis.

136. As we shall see in chapter 3, beginning in the early nineteenth century, chemistry increasingly and successfully abstracts from the material particularity that makes substances puzzlingly unique a more formal understanding of combinations and divisions. Such formalization is needed in order to develop the mathematical accounts that earlier chemists had sought and failed to attain.

137. De Man, *Aesthetic Ideology*, 90.

138. See his "Monologue," quoted in the Introduction above, *Schriften*, 2:672/TP 145–46. See also *Schriften*, 3:50, and ibid., 360, No. 547.

139. Read, *Through Alchemy to Chemistry*, 14.

Three: Chemistry in the Eighteenth Century

1. "Wenn der kritische Anatom die schöne Organisation eines Kunstwerks erst zerstört, in elementarische Masse analysiert, und mit dieser dann mancherlei physische Versuche anstellt, aus denen er stolze Resultate zieht: so täuscht er sich selbst auf eine sehr handgreifliche Weise:

denn das Kunstwerk existiert gar nicht mehr," KA 1:326. A closer examination of the essay would reveal, I think, a more equivocal distinction between the organic and the chemical than I claim above, drawing some of its passages closer to the group of texts that privilege the chemical. Schlegel revised the text before including it in volume 5 of his *Sämtliche Werke*, published in 1823; that version sharpens the line between destructive analysis and constructive synthesis: the critical anatomist, now called a "judging art-anatomist" (beurteilender Kunst-Anatom) destroys "like an experimenting natural scientist" (wie ein experimentierender Naturforscher) not the organization of the artwork but its "harmony and organic structure" (Harmonie und den organischen Zusammenhang) (ibid. n3, n4, n7). Indeed, Schlegel's revisions can be read as a systematic effort at reducing the ambiguity in the early version of the essay: thus the potentially neutral phrase "chemical process" (chymischen Prozeß [327]) becomes, twenty-five years later, "process of destructive analysis" (Verfahren zerstörender Analyse [ibid. n18]).

2. Frank, "'Wechselgrundsatz': Friedrich Schlegels philosophischer Ausgangspunkt," 29–30.

3. "Sie will, und soll auch Poesie und Prosa, Genialität und Kritik, Kunstpoesie und Naturpoesie bald mischen, bald verschmelzen," KA 2:182, No. 116/PF 31.

4. "innigst verschmolzen," KA 18:342, No. 248.

5. "π [Poesie] und ϕ [Philosophie] werden sich immer inniger durchdringen," KA 18:342, No. 243.

6. "wo Vernunft und Unvernunft sich saturiren und durchdringen," KA 18:162, No. 471.

7. "Wo [Poesie und Praxis] sich ganz durchdringen und in eins schmelzen, da entsteht Philosophie," KA 2:216, No. 304/PF 60.

8. "Wer Sinn fürs Unendliche hat, . . . sieht in ihm das Produkt sich ewig scheidender und mischender Kräfte, denkt sich seine Ideale wenigstens chemisch, und sagt, wenn er sich entschieden ausdrückt, lauter Widersprüche," KA 2:243, No. 412/PF 83.

9. "eine Art von transcendentaler Chemie," KA 18:89, No. 716.

10. "die Wissenschaft aller sich ewig mischenden und wieder trennenden Wissenschaften, eine logische Chemie," KA 2:200, No. 220/PF 47.

11. "Eine vollendete χ [kritische] ϕ [Philosophie] wäre doch immer nur chemisch vollendet, nicht organisch," KA 18:131, No. 114.

12. "$\chi\rho$ [Kritik] die $\phi\sigma$ [philosophische] Kunst d[er] $\frac{\chi\epsilon\mu}{o}$ [reinen Chemie]," KA 18:232, No. 466.

13. "Die chemische Klassifikation der Auflösung in die auf dem trocknen und in die auf dem nassen Wege, ist auch in der Literatur auf die Auflösung der Autoren anwendbar, die nach Erreichung ihrer äußersten Höhe sinken müssen. Einige verdampfen, andre werden zu Wasser," KA 2:150, No. 32/PF 4.

14. "Ironie ist χεμ [chemische] Genialität," KA 18:232, No. 465.

15. "Ironie ist Universelles Experiment," KA 18:217, No. 279.

16. "Ironie ist innerlich; der Witz nur die Erscheinung derselben," KA 18, 203, No. 76.

17. "Witz ist Universalchemie," KA 18:230, No. 440. Schlegel is not alone in this characterization; Jean Paul, in his *Vorschule der Ästhetik,* writes of wit (*Witz*): "It is for the spirit what chemistry [*Scheidekunst*] is for fire and water" (Jean Paul, *Werke,* 5:200).

18. "Witz ist eine Explosion von gebundnem Geist," KA 2:158, No. 90/PF 11.

19. "Was man gewöhnlich Vernunft nennt, ist nur eine Gattung derselben; nämlich die dünne und wäßrige. Es gibt auch eine dicke feurige Vernunft, welche den Witz eigentlich zum Witz macht," KA 2:159, No. 104/PF 12–13.

20. "Ein witziger Einfall ist eine Zersetzung geistiger Stoffe, die also vor der plötzlichen Scheidung innigst vermischt sein mußten. Die Einbildungskraft muß erst mit Leben jeder Art bis zur Sättigung angefüllt sein, ehe es Zeit sein kann, sie durch die Friktion freier Geselligkeit so zu elektrisieren, daß der Reiz der leisesten freundlichen oder feindlichen Berührung ihr blitzende Funken und leuchtende Strahlen, oder schmetternde Schläge entlocken kann," KA 2:150, No. 34/PF 4.

21. "Es ist natürlich, daß die Franzosen etwas dominieren im Zeitalter. Sie sind eine chemische Nation, der chemische Sinn ist bei ihnen am allgemeinsten erregt, und sie machen ihre Versuche auch in der moralischen Chemie immer im Großen. Das Zeitalter ist gleichfalls ein chemisches Zeitalter. Revolutionen sind universelle nicht organische, sondern chemische Bewegungen. Der große Handel ist die Chemie der großen Ökonomie . . . Die chemische Natur des Romans, der Kritik, des Witzes, der Geselligkeit, der neuesten Rhetorik und der bisherigen Historie leuchtet von selbst ein," KA 2:248, No. 426/PF 87.

22. For a detailed biographical account, see Schwedt, *Goethe als Chemiker,* 3–224.

23. For example, in his most extensive contributions to natural philosophy, *Ideen zu einer Philosophie der Natur* of 1797, Schelling, *His-*

torisch-Kritische Ausgabe, pt. 1, vol. 5, pp. 59–306, and *Von der Weltseele* of 1798, Schelling, *Sämmtliche Werke,* pt. 1, vol. 2, pp. 345–583.

24. This is confirmed by Peter Kapitza in his study of the idea of "mixture" in early romanticism, the first to demonstrate the link between chemical and poetic theory in detail: "At the time of early romanticism the word mixture [*Mischung*] can be found in a firmly established context. It is the quintessence of chemical science and can therefore be transferred to the spiritual realm" (Kapitza, *Die frühromantische Theorie der Mischung,* 14).

25. De Man, *Blindness and Insight,* 207.

26. "Der romant.[ische] Imperativ fodert [sic] d.[ie] Mischung aller Dichtarten," KA 16:134, No. 586.

27. For a brief history of chemical mixtures, see Bensaude-Vincent and Stengers, *A History of Chemistry,* 29–31.

28. Gren, *Systematisches Handbuch der gesamten Chemie,* 1:32–33, cited in Kapitza, *Die frühromantische Theorie der Mischung,* 72. This is not far from Aristotle's definition of mixture (cf. *Of Generation and Corruption,* 328a), with one important terminological difference: Aristotle calls the transformative mixture *misis* or *krasis,* while the aggregate in which the original elements remain *un*changed is called *synthesis;* in Gren's formulation, by contrast, *synthesis* (rendered through a literal translation as *Zusammen-setzung,* putting or positing together) signifies precisely the *change* to which the original elements yield. What assures the term *synthesis* a dazzling career in philosophy is one small but crucial step from here: it is to regard change as *progress,* and thus the synthesis as higher (in many senses) than the elements that gave rise to it.

29. Klaproth, *Chemie,* 6.

30. Ibid., 1. For other instances, see Kapitza, *Die frühromantische Theorie der Mischung,* 12–13.

31. Gren, *Systematisches Handbuch der gesamten Chemie,* 1:1, cited in Kapitza, *Die frühromantische Theorie der Mischung,* 13.

32. Gmelin, *Grundriß der allgemeinen Chemie zum Gebrauch bei Vorlesungen,* 1:75, cited in Kapitza, *Die frühromantische Theorie der Mischung,* 12.

33. Knight, "German Science in the Romantic Period," 161.

34. Messiness is, in a way, endemic to chemistry: "Of all the sciences, chemistry exhibits, it seems to us, a peculiarity in the definition of its territory. Here is a body of knowledge with multiple facets and innumerable ramifications: it applies in the depths of the Earth as well as in space,

and it is as important to agriculture as it is to heavy and fine industry and to pharmacy. Here is a science that spans the borders between the inert and the living, between the microscopic and the macroscopic. How can we assign an identity to a discipline that seems to be everywhere and nowhere at once? . . . Chemistry has always been heir to a heterogeneous territory, one that defied all a priori definition" (Bensaude-Vincent and Stengers, *A History of Chemistry,* 4–5).

35. Kuhn, *The Structure of Scientific Revolutions,* 56; for his discussion of the chemical revolution, see 53–56 and 69–72.

36. Cohen, *Revolution in Science,* 239–46.

37. Quoted in Crosland, "Chemistry and the Chemical Revolution," 402.

38. "*Revoluzion* in dem aesthetischen Gebiet," KA 17:371, No. 258.

39. "eine ganz neue Gattung," KA 24:51.

40. For documentation, see Cohen, *Revolution in Science,* 240.

41. The revolution that demonstrably did profit from the new research in chemistry was not the French but the American: "Lavoisier . . . had worked on the improvement of gunpowder. . . . French gunpowder was superior to British in 1776 and thus helped the American colonists to win the War of Independence" (Knight, *Ideas in Chemistry,* 44).

42. "*neue Schule,*" KA 17:371, No. 258.

43. The standard work is Partington, *A History of Chemistry,* vol. 3.

44. Bensaude-Vincent and Stengers, *A History of Chemistry,* 86.

45. Lavoisier, *Traité élémentaire de chimie,* 1:192/175.

46. Girtanner, *Neue chemische Nomenklatur für die deutsche Sprache,* 11–12.

47. Klaproth, *Chemie,* 5.

48. Lavoisier, *Traité élémentaire de chimie,* 1:xvi–xvii/xxiv. Translations significantly modified.

49. Klaproth and Wolff, *Chemisches Wörterbuch,* 1:322.

50. Elements 114, 116, and 118 have been produced by some scientists but as yet not duplicated by others. See Service, "Berkeley Crew Bags Element 118."

51. Brock, *The Norton History of Chemistry,* 119.

52. Bensaude-Vincent and Stengers, *A History of Chemistry,* 39.

53. Dietrich von Engelhardt, in his *Hegel und die Chemie,* points out that the contrast between phlogistic and antiphlogistic chemistry is "far smaller than is not infrequently assumed by scientific accounts" (33).

54. Bensaude-Vincent and Stengers, *A History of Chemistry,* 3.

55. Bettina Haupt has shown the persistent flux between the self-description of chemistry as art and as science in a study of chemical textbooks written in German that appeared between 1775 and 1850 (Haupt, *Deutschsprachige Chemielehrbücher,* 56–76).

56. Klaproth, *Chemie,* 1.

57. Adelung, *Grammatisch-kritisches Wörterbuch,* 1:1335.

58. Fourcroy, *Système des connaissances chimiques,* 1:4/1:3–4.

59. Lavoisier, *Traité élémentaire de chimie,* 1:xiii/xxi.

60. See Kuhn, *The Structure of Scientific Revolutions,* 130–34.

61. Lavoisier, *Traité élémentaire de chimie,* 1:xii–xiii/xx.

62. Klaproth, *Chemie,* 1.

63. Knight, *Ideas in Chemistry,* 65.

64. Read, *Through Alchemy to Chemistry,* 145.

65. Roger, "The Living World," 270 n36.

66. See Dijksterhuis, *The Mechanization of the World-Picture,* and Butterfield, *The Origins of Modern Science.*

67. Knight, *Ideas in Chemistry,* 28.

68. Quoted in Brock, *The Norton History of Chemistry,* 66.

69. Stewart, *Selected Philosophical Papers of Robert Boyle,* 141, cited in Knight, *Ideas in Chemistry,* 37.

70. Boyle, *Sceptical chymist,* 562.

71. Durner, "Theorien der Chemie," 11.

72. Brock, *The Norton History of Chemistry,* 68.

73. Ibid., 63.

74. Bensaude-Vincent and Stengers, *A History of Chemistry,* 33–36.

75. See Kuhn, "Robert Boyle and the Structural Chemistry of the Seventeenth Century."

76. Klaproth, *Chemie,* 6.

77. Knight, *Ideas in Chemistry,* 49.

78. Modern physics, in pursuing the goal of homogeneous matter, has only managed to create an ever-expanding menu of distinct particles (quarks, for example, turn out to come in six "flavors").

79. Bensaude-Vincent and Stengers, *A History of Chemistry,* 31.

80. Quoted in Brock, *The Norton History of Chemistry,* 58.

81. Newton, *Opticks,* 376.

82. Knight, "Romanticism and the Sciences," 18.

83. Cunningham and Jardine, *Romanticism and the Sciences,* xix.

84. Eichner, "The Rise of Modern Science and the Genesis of Romanticism," 8.

85. Bensaude-Vincent and Stengers, *A History of Chemistry*, 31.

Four: "Theory of the Combinatorial Method" of Poetry

1. "Ich muß durchaus eine ganz neue Methode constituiren. . . . Theorie der combinator[ischen] Methode," KA 18:448, No. 190.

2. "Die Sphäre des combinatorischen Geistes ist durchaus unbestimmt. Aber es muß eine Methode geben, nach welcher dabey verfahren wird. Diese Methode wird Experimentiren seyn. Wer nach dieser Methode verfährt, der darf sich die kühnsten Versuche erlauben. Er wird gewiß auf Realität stoßen," KA 12:102.

3. "nichts als ein Experiment sei, ist sehr wahr," KA 18:135, No. 160.

4. "Der Ess.[ay] nicht *Ein* Exp.[eriment] sondern ein beständiges Experimentiren," KA 18:215, No. 248.

5. "die ganze Kette meiner Versuche," KA 2:364/TP 119.

6. "die Mitteilung der Ideen . . . überhaupt möglich sei; und wo hätte man nähere Gelegenheit über die Möglichkeit oder Unmöglichkeit dieser Sache mancherlei Versuche anzustellen, als wenn man ein Journal wie das *Athenäum* entweder selbst schreibt, oder doch als Leser an demselben teilnimmt?" KA 2:363/TP 119.

7. "Der romant.[ische] Imperativ fodert [*sic*] d.[ie] Mischung aller Dichtarten," KA 16:134, No. 586.

8. "In der ächt romantisch[en] Prosa müsssen [*sic*] alle Bestandtheile bis zur Wechselsättig[un]g verschmolzen sein," KA 16:134, No. 589.

9. His innovations are of course not sui generis but occur in a literary-historical context rich with experiments. Mixing and matching genres is a practice well-known among other romantics. See Ryan, "Hybrid Forms in German Romanticism."

10. "kann mir einen Roman kaum anders denken, als gemischt aus Erzählung, Gesang und andern Formen," KA 2:336/DP 102. For further cross-genre characterization of novels ("the Socratic dialogues of our time," "a compendium, an encyclopedia") see KA 2:149, No. 26/PF 3; KA 2:156, No. 78/PF 10.

11. Schlegel's descriptions in his letters of how he gathers fragments for his collections offer evidence for both "methods": there are fragments that he chisels and fragments he finds (by reading, for example, his own correspondence).

12. "Die neue Poesie oder sogenannte *neue Schule* entspricht sehr bestimmt der Naturφ [Philosophie]," KA 17:371, No. 258.

13. "χεμ [chemische] Fr.[agmente]," KA 18:199, No. 30.

14. "Zerstückelung *eines Ganzen,*" KA 24:102.

15. "Die επιδειξις der Universalität, und der Synfonismus der Fr.[agmente] würde durch die reale Abstrakzion . . . des Ganzen in beyden Stücken eine formale Destrukzion erleiden," KA 24:105.

16. August Wilhelm's letter has not been preserved, but his position can be inferred from Friedrich's response (KA 24:102).

17. "Wie schön sind die einzelnen, und wie erst in Masse," KA 24:91. See also KA 24:88.

18. "Mitglied einer Masse, die sich nicht trennen läßt. Ueberhaupt hängen die verdammten Dinger so zusammen," KA 24:97.

19. "Ironie ist die Form des Paradoxen. Paradox ist alles, was zugleich gut und groß ist," KA 2:153, No. 48/PF 6.

20. Neumann, *Ideenparadiese,* 418.

21. "logische Schönheit," KA 2:152, No. 42.

22. "eine der ursprünglichen Handlungsweisen des menschlichen Geistes," KA 2:209, No. 256.

23. "innre Geselligkeit," KA 2:225, No. 339.

24. "unbedingt geselliger Geist," KA 2:148, No. 9.

25. "Explosion von gebundenem Geist," KA 2:158, No. 90/PF 11.

26. "überraschende Zufälligkeit," KA 2:200, No. 220/PF 47.

27. Jakobson, "Closing Statement: Linguistics and Poetics," 358.

28. Ibid.

29. "daß die Worte sich selbst oft besser verstehen, als diejenigen von denen sie gebraucht werden," KA 2:364/TP 119.

30. "Ironie ist χεμ [chemische] Genialität," KA 18:232, No. 465.

31. "Ironie ist Univ[erselles] Experiment," KA 18:217, No. 279.

32. "eine Definition die nicht witzig ist, taugt nichts, und von jedem Individuum gibt es doch unendlich viele reale Definitionen," KA 2:177, No. 82/PF 28.

33. "Die besten sind *echappées de vue* ins Unendliche," KA 2:200, No. 220/PF 47.

34. De Man, *Allegories of Reading,* 301. This is a conception of allegory he develops by way of reading Schlegel.

35. Cf. Schreiber, "Stop Making Sense," 174.

36. "Ironie der Ironie," KA 2:369/TP 125.

37. Benjamin, *Gesammelte Schriften,* vol. 1, pt. 1, p. 84 / *Selected Writings,* 1:163.

38. "eine *Revoluzion* in dem aesthetischen Gebiet," KA 17:371, No. 258.

39. "den Schein des Verkehrten und Verrückten, oder des Einfältigen und Dummen," KA 2:319 / DP 86.

40. Blanchot, *L'Entretien infini,* 518 / 353.

41. Blanchot, *L'écriture du désastre,* 98 / 59.

42. "Durch die chemische Ansicht wird die Natur zum Schein; auf d[en] ersten Blick macht dieß d.[em] Enthusiasmus der π [Poesie] durchaus ein Ende. Näher betrachtet giebts ein großes Fundament," KA 18:162, No. 464.

43. "kann man den Witz als das Vermögen, die Ähnlichkeiten zwischen Gegenständen aufzufinden, die sonst sehr unabhängig, verschieden und getrennt sind, und so das Mannigfaltigste, Verschiedenartigste zu Einheit zu verbinden, den *kombinatorischen Geist* nennen," KA 12:403.

44. "blitzende Funken und leuchtende Strahlen, oder schmetternde Schläge entlocken kann," KA 2:150, No. 34 / PF 4.

45. "Wit, ars combinatoria, criticism, the art of invention is all the same" ("Witz, ars combinat.[oria], Kritik, Erfindungskunst, ist alles einerlei," KA 18:124, No. 20).

46. "Witz ist Universalchemie," KA 18:230, No. 440.

47. "Die wahre Methode der φσ [Philosophie] wäre eine combinator.[ische] Analysis," KA 18:354, No. 404. For more evidence along the same lines, see KA 18:448, No. 190; KA 18:471, No. 8; KA 18:344, No. 267.

48. "Dieses Kombinatorische ist es, was ich . . . als wissenschaftlichen Witz bezeichnete. Es kann nicht entstehen ohne Universalität, denn nur wo eine Fülle verschiedenartiger Stoffe vereinigt ist, können neue chemische Verbindungen und Durchdringungen derselben vor sich gehen," KA 3:84.

49. It is an unaccountability that chemistry has managed to lessen but not eliminate entirely: to this day, the particular features of a chemical compound (including whether it will even take place) cannot be predicted accurately. Thus a branch of the science, aptly called combinatorial chemistry, specializes in rapidly testing thousands of different compounds for their usefulness in pharmaceutical and medical research. For an overview, see Thompson and Ellman, "Synthesis and Applications of Small Molecule Libraries."

50. "Die neue Poesie oder sogenannte *neue Schule* entspricht sehr bestimmt der Naturφ [Philosophie]. Es war eine *Revoluzion* in dem aes-

thetischen Gebiet. Die romantische π [Poesie] als eine combinatorische und universelle gehört hieher," KA 17:371, No. 258.

51. "erhabne Frechheit," KA 24:31;"ganz neue Gattung," KA 24:51; "kritische Dictatoren Deutschl.[ands]," KA 24:32. The German poet and the dictator are, at least etymologically, closely linked: *dictator* derives from the same word, *dictare* ("to dictate," "to compose"), that gives us the German word *Dichter* (poet).

52. We can find a point of transition between this radical, scientifically imagined combinatorics and Schlegel's later organicist mysticism in one of the "Ideas," fragments published in the penultimate issue of the *Athenäum* in 1800. These announce, in their word choice and the piousness of their tone, some of the religious motifs that come to dominate Schlegel's future career. Idea 123 (KA 2:268/PF 105) declares that a "true universality" (wahre Universalität) that would render "art more artificial, . . . poetry more poetic, criticism more critical, history more historical" (die Kunst . . . künstlicher . . . die Poesie poetischer, die Kritik kritischer, die Historie historischer) arises "when the simple light ray of religion and morality touches and inseminates a chaos of combinatorial wit. There the highest poetry and philosophy blossom by themselves" (wenn der einfache Strahl der Religion und Moral ein Chaos des kombinatorischen Witzes berührt und befruchtet. Da blüht von selbst die höchste Poesie und Philosophie.).

One can almost feel the dread to which the idea of the "combinatorial chaos," of wit—*Witz*—imagined as "an explosion of bound spirit," has given rise in its author. While merely two years earlier *Witz,* egged on by its fortuitous rhyme with *Blitz* (lightning), could "electrify" the imagination and "elicit brilliant sparks and luminescent lightning, or smashing thunderbolts," here *Witz* is controlled by a simple *Strahl.* The shades of meaning in *Strahl* (lightning, but also a ray of light) help Schlegel bridge the divide between the tempestuousness of chemistry (behind us, yet semantically preserved) and the nurturing warmth of sunlight before us. The pillars supporting the bridge are religion and morality; they are meant to rearrange the chemical chaos into the harmony of organic nature ("inseminate," "blossom").

53. "das Kombinatorische," KA 2:200, No. 220.

54. "Die Encycl.[opädie] muß experimentieren," KA 18: 348, No. 323.

55. "Der wahre Standpunkt ist d[er] centrale oder der Encykl[opädische]. Die Methode viell[eicht] transc.[endental] oder combinat[orisch]. Zur Methode und zum Standpunkt bedarf man noch einer bestimmten

Tendenz, um von der Stelle zu kommen Diese Tendenz ist die combi-nat[orische]," KA 18:362, No. 498.

56. "Magic is not polemical but combinatorial" (Die Mag[ie] nicht polemisch sondern combinatorisch [KA 18:388, No. 805]).

57. "*Unbeschränkter Umfang* ist der eine große Vorzug der Poesie," KA 1:294.

58. "π [Poesie] und φ [Philosophie] sollen sich immer innigst durch-dringen; das wird ganz neue Erscheinungen geben," KA 18:342, No. 243. See also KA 12:101.

59. By contrast, Peter Kapitza lets the *difference* wrought by chemical mixture transmute into an *improvement:* that the new chemical poetry "must stand qualitatively higher than philosophy or poetry by themselves becomes evident through the determination of the chemical mixture, which points to a new substance with changed qualities" (Kapitza, *Die frühromantische Theorie der Mischung,* 109).

60. "die alte Natur und Kraft . . ., wo der naive Tiefsinn den Schein des Verkehrten und Verrückten, oder des Einfältigen und Dummen durchschimmern läßt," KA 2:319/DP 86. Twenty-three years later, in 1823, Schlegel changes this passage for his collected works to "the glim-mer of the peculiar and even of the paradoxical or of a childish but still ingenious simplicity" (den Schein des Sonderbaren und selbst des Widersinnigen oder auch einer kindlichen aber doch geistreichen Einfalt [ibid., note 4]). Though this is entirely in keeping with Schlegel's usual pattern of toning down (or eliminating) the most daring parts of his early writings in later editions, Paul de Man oddly gets the chronology backwards, without, however, damaging his main argument. Cf. de Man, *Aesthetic Ideology,* 180–81.

61. Barthes, *Le Bruissement de la langue, 66/54.* We can also think of this responsiveness to internal mandates in terms of the differentiation of the literary system (in which the rules of writing are but one element) articulated by sociological systems theory. Indeed, the particular concep-tion of writing at work here, allegorically modeled on chemistry, can it-self in turn serve as an allegory for the larger process of the differen-tiation of literature as a social system. See Luhmann, *Die Kunst der Gesellschaft,* and Schmidt, *Die Selbstorganisation des Literatursystems.*

62. I am indebted to Eco, *The Search for the Perfect Language,* 53–72, for information about Llull, and 269–92 about Leibniz.

63. Leibniz, *Die philosophischen Schriften,* 7:192.

64. Neubauer, *Symbolismus und symbolische Logik,* 11.

65. Valéry, *Oeuvres,* 1:635.

66. It is true that twentieth-century mathematics has had to confront the specter of regions of undecidability and incoherence within its borders, but this has not changed the validity of the two features I mentioned earlier: algorithms continue to work mechanically (if not always universally), and the formalistic distinction between rule and input continues to obtain. I am grateful to Barry Mazur for clarifying this issue for me.

67. "Die wichtigsten wissenschaftlichen Entdeckungen sind *bonmots* der Gattung. Das sind sie durch die überraschende Zufälligkeit ihrer Entstehung, durch das Kombinatorische des Gedankens," KA 2:200, No. 220/PF 47.

68. "Die Encycl[opädie] läßt sich schlechterdings und durchaus nur in *Fragmenten* darstellen—Diese *combinat[orischen] Ideen* . . . ," KA 18:485, No. 141.

69. "Wo man die Bestandtheile nicht bloß *gleichartig* sondern auch verschiedenartig zu bilden strebt, da strebt man nach *Ganzheit* nicht bloß nach *Einheit,*" KA 16:89, No. 46.

70. "Die class.[ischen] Gedichtarten haben nur *Einheit;* die progressiven allein *Ganzheit,*" KA 16:122, No. 446.

71. "Many people consider something to be a system only when it has a big lump in the middle" (Viele Leute halten nur das für ein System, was einen großen Klumpen in d[er] Mitte hat [KA 18:63, No. 432]).

72. "Er wird sich also wohl entschließen müssen, beides zu verbinden," KA 2:173, No. 53/PF 24.

73. Mallarmé, *Oeuvres complètes,* 867.

74. Foucault, *Les mots et les choses,* 103/89.

75. "in Berührung gesetzt," KA 2:182, No. 116/PF 31.

76. Wordsworth, "Preface to *Lyrical Ballads* and Appendix," in *Selected Prose,* 283. Even in the *Lyrical Ballads* this "spontaneous overflow" is far from spontaneous but carefully modulated by meter.

77. "daß alles poetisiert werden soll," KA 2:205, No. 239/PF 51.

78. "Diesen chemischen Prozeß des Philosophierens. . . . [D]ie Philosophie, welche sich immer von neuem organisieren und desorganisieren muß," KA 2:216, No. 304/PF 60.

79. "deren Werkzeug, die willkürliche Zeichensprache, Menschenwerk und also unendlich perfektibel und korruptibel ist," KA 1:294. See also KA 18:94, No. 784.

80. "progressive Universalpoesie . . . die Aussicht auf eine grenzenlos wachsende Klassizität," KA 2:182–83, No 116/PF 32.

81. ". . . wie sie [die romantische Dichtart] allein frei ist . . . ," ibid.; "der höchsten und allseitigsten Bildung," ibid.; "zu d.[em] *combinatorischen Chaos* in d[en] Fragmenten," KA 18:476, No. 57.

82. For a very different view, see Ernst Behler: "According to the early Romantic model, the poetic work is the result of conscious artistry, and the poet is in absolute control of his creation" (Behler, *German Romantic Literary Theory,* 302).

83. "ich wollte zeigen, daß die Worte sich oft besser verstehen, als diejenigen von denen sie gebraucht werden, wollte aufmerksam darauf machen, daß es unter den philosophischen Worten, die oft in ihren Schriften wie eine Schar zu früh entsprungener Geister alles verwirren und die unsichtbare Gewalt des Weltgeistes auch an dem ausüben, der sie nicht anerkennen will, geheime Ordensverbindungen geben muß," KA 2:364/TP 119.

84. "Princ[ipien] der φσ [Philosophie] und π [Poesie] giebts eben nicht außer ihnen selbst," KA 18:344, No. 267.

85. "eine reelle Sprache, daß wir aufhören möchten mit Worten zu kramen, und schauen alles Wirkens Kraft und Samen," KA 2:364/TP 119. What are we to make of the rhyme *kramen/Samen?* Does it, in a sentence expressing the hope that the use of words may cease, attempt to play out music against language? But does the "semantic propinquity" of the rhyming words not rely on the chemistry that insures that, as Roman Jakobson puts it, "words similar in sound are drawn together in meaning"? Does the expressed wish for a "real language" not rely on the very chemistry it would wish to dislodge?

86. "den heiligen, zarten, flüchtigen, luftigen, duftigen gleichsam imponderablen Gedanken," ibid.

87. "Nur ganz kürzlich wurde dieser Gedanke einer reellen Sprache mir von neuem erregt. . . . Im neunzehnten Jahrhundert, versichert uns Girtanner, im neunzehnten Jahrhundert wird man Gold machen können . . .: 'Jeder Chemiker, jeder Künstler wird Gold machen; das Küchengeschirr wird von Silber, von Gold sein.' . . . Schon oft hatte ich die Objektivität des Goldes im stillen bewundert, ja ich darf wohl sagen angebetet. Bei den Chinesen, dachte ich, bei den Engländern, bei den Russen, auf der Insel Japan, bei den Einwohnern von Fetz und Marokko, ja sogar bei den Kosaken, Tscheremissen, Baschkiren und Mulatten, kurz überall wo es nur einige Bildung und Aufklärung gibt, ist das Silber, das Gold verständlich und durch das Gold alles übrige. Wenn nun erst jeder Künstler diese Materien in hinreichender Qualität besitzt, so darf er ja

nur seine Werke in Basrelief schreiben, mit goldnen Lettern auf silbernen Tafeln. Wer würde eine so schön gedruckte Schrift, mit der groben Äußerung, sie sei unverständlich, zurückweisen wollen?" KA 2:365/TP 120–21.

88. Christoph Girtanner, "Untersuchung, ob der Salpeterstoff ein einfacher, oder ein zusammengesetzter Körper sei," *Allgemeines Journal der Chemie* 2.9 (1800): 248, quoted in Schumacher, *Ironie der Unverständlichkeit*, 192. Girtanner's claim provides further evidence of how thoroughly convoluted the state of late-eighteenth-century chemistry is. His crackpot idea may lead one to believe that he belonged to the last of the alchemists. Far from it: as we saw in chapter 3, Girtanner is among the early converts to Lavoisier's theory in Germany. His *Neue chemische Nomenklatur*, which attempts to bring German terminology up to date, appears just two years after Lavoisier's *Elements* of 1789; a year later he follows up with a broad critique of phlogistic chemistry.

89. "nur Hirngespinste oder Ideale," KA 2:365/TP 121. Through a reading of contemporary economic theorists, most notably Adam Smith, Eckhard Schumacher points out that by the late eighteenth century not even gold could count as the absolute standard of value; rather, gold, much like paper money, was thought of as a medium of exchange. See his *Ironie der Unverständlichkeit*, 193–95 and 207–12. Thanks to one of those contingent yet chemically fortuitous substitutions dear to Schlegel that transforms one set of letter combinations into another one, the "objectivity" of *Gold* turns into the uncertainty of reference that mere *Geld* (money) offers.

Five: αβ *& LMN*

1. Amalia: "Ist denn alles Poesie?" . . . Ludoviko: "[J]ede [Kunst und jede Wissenschaft], die auch nicht in den Worten der Sprache ihr Wesen treibt, hat einen unsichtbaren Geist, und der ist Poesie," KA 2:304/DP 75–76.

2. For a shrewd reading of this issue, to which the following paragraph is indebted, see Derrida, "Economimesis," 70–93/11–25.

3. This claim is made in Kittler, "Musik als Medium," 83, and, seven decades earlier, in Mauthner, *Wörterbuch der Philosophie*, 2:563.

4. I attempt a more detailed analysis of this matter in an essay, still in progress, on the place of voice in Kant's third *Critique*.

5. The "consumption" of poetry is to be taken quite literally here, as

this *Lyceum* fragment suggests: "A critic is a reader who ruminates. Therefore he ought to have more than one stomach" (Ein Kritiker ist ein Leser, der wiederkäut. Er sollte also mehr als einen Magen haben [KA 2:149, No. 27/PF 3]).

6. Whether visual or musical combinatorics contains the impurities, contingencies, and failures that we have noted in Schlegel's conception of poetic language and for which the state of chemistry in the late eighteenth century served him as an apt allegory, or whether it aspires to the universality and uniformity of a mathematical operation, or to another model altogether, can only be determined through detailed analysis of specific works.

7. Kittler, *Aufschreibesysteme,* 232/184.

8. Foucault, *Les mots et les choses,* 92–95/78–81.

9. The published translation omits the all-important adjective "mathematical."

10. "die reinste und gediegenste Unverständlichkeit gerade aus der Wissenschaft und aus der Kunst erhält, die ganz eigentlich aufs Verständigen und Verständlichmachen ausgehn," KA 2:364/TP 119.

11. "Das ganz vollendete und vollkommne Verstehen selbst aber . . . ," KA 10:534.

12. It is all there: the last words are written (rather than exhaled together with his soul); a fragment (rather than a pithy aperçu); they end in the contrary *aber* (rather than in a satisfying closure); and they perform not one but *two* paradoxes, one in the form, the other in the content of the utterance: they describe completion and perfection in an incomplete and imperfect sentence, and while discussing perfect comprehension, leave us finally with enough incomprehension that a reader, including this reader, is called upon to compensate for it with interpretation.

13. "Ich bin eine grammatische Natur und verstehe Dich besser geschrieben als sprechend," KA 24:155.

14. "Dann werde ich auch mit Euch leben, und nicht mehr schreiben, was sich nicht sagt, sondern wieder reden lernen. Es wird eine glückliche, seelige, herrliche Zeit seyn," KA 23:305.

15. "Ich komme nun mein Versprechen zu halten . . . wäre es auch nur um eine so entschiedene Verächterin alles Schreibens und Buchstabenwesens mit meiner Liebhaberei für diese Dinge zu necken. Dir wäre ein Gespräch vielleicht lieber. Aber ich bin nun einmal ganz und gar ein Autor. Die Schrift hat für mich ich weiß nicht welchen geheimen Zauber vielleicht durch die Dämmerung von Ewigkeit, welche sie umschwebt.

Ja ich gestehe Dir, ich wundre mich, welche geheime Kraft in diesen toten Zügen verborgen liegt. . . . Fast möchte ich in der etwas mystischen Sprache unsers H. sagen: Leben sei Schreiben; die einzige Bestimmung des Menschen sei, die Gedanken der Gottheit mit dem Griffel des bildenden Geistes in die Tafeln der Natur zu graben," KA 8:42/TP 420.

16. Kittler, *Aufschreibesysteme,* 82–88/63–69.

17. Kittler, *Grammophon Film Typewriter,* 275–76.

18. Ibid., 18.

19. "Es ist wohl schön, daß wir endlich einmal wieder miteinander gesprochen haben; ich bin es auch zufrieden, daß Du durchaus nicht schreiben wolltest, und auf die armen unschuldigen Buchstaben schiltst, weil Du wirklich zum Sprechen mehr Genie hast. Aber ich habe doch noch eins und das andre auf dem Herzen, was ich nicht sagen konnte und was ich versuchen will, Dir brieflich anzudeuten.

Warum aber auf diesem Wege?—O mein Freund, wenn ich nur noch ein feineres gebildeteres Element der Mitteiling wüßte . . . ," KA 5:76/LF 124.

20. "*Apologie d[es] Buchstabens,* d.[er] als einziges ächtes *Vehikel d[er] Mittheilung sehr ehrwürdig ist,*" KA 18:5, No. 15.

21. "Der Buchstabe als Princip der K[unst] und Wss [Wissenschaft]," KA 18:260, No. 797.

22. "Der Buchstabe muß grade thätig, lebendig seyn, agil oder progreßiv," KA 18:364, No. 510.

23. "In den Alten sieht man den vollendeten Buchstaben der ganzen Poesie: in den Neuern ahnet man den werdenden Geist," KA 2:158, No. 93/PF 11.

24. "In d[er] Würde d.[es] Buchstabens könnte der Keim der neuen φσ [Philosophie] dicht an die Gränze der alten gelegt werden," KA 18:260, No. 797.

25. "*Geist und Buchstabe* ist ein religiöser Unterschied," KA 18:39, No. 221.

26. One symptom of the reach of the hermeneutic theory implied by the verse in second Corinthians lies in the interesting quandary into which it puts translators, especially Christian ones. For would it not follow that if they believed in its spiritual message—"Don't read (me) literally!"—they would have to ignore its letter? Would they not be prohibited from translating Paul's original *gramma* (as well as of course *pneuma*) literally? Twentieth-century translations, such as the New English and Good News Bibles, do just that: they take *gramma* metonymically and

render it as "written law." (To accomplish this, they need to stretch the letter of *gramma,* since according to Liddell and Scott's *Greek-English Lexicon* only the plural *grammata* means law or rule, while Bauer's more germane *Greek-English Lexicon of the New Testament and Other Early Christian Literature* does not list this definition for *gramma* at all, singular or plural.) By contrast, the King James version, which I use above, courts the charge of performative contradiction by remaining faithful to the dead letter, *against* the "Pauline spirit." So does Luther: "Denn der Buchstabe tötet, aber der Geist macht lebendig." The issue of a literal vs. figurative translation raises the larger question of how any *writer,* including Paul himself, can be adequate to his injunction to abandon the letter and embrace the spirit (Romans 7:6 and 2:28–29). Would one not have to stop writing?

27. For an account of the letter-spirit distinction around 1800 in philosophical terms, see Weissberg, *Geistersprache,* chap. 6, esp. 161–67.

28. For an analysis of Luther's—implicit and explicit—media theory, see Schneider, "Luther mit McLuhan."

29. Lessing, "Eine Parabel," *Werke,* 8:125–26.

30. For a detailed reading of how the issue of letter and spirit is mapped on the "cultural dialogue" of Jews and Christians in Enlightenment and post-Enlightenment German literature, see Jeffrey Librett's thoughtful study *The Rhetoric of Cultural Dialogue.* Librett provides shrewd readings of Schlegel's reformulation of the spirit / letter distinction (esp. in chapters 3 and 4), which resonate with some of the arguments I attempt to advance here.

31. Herder, *Briefe zur Beförderung der Humanität,* 2:207–8; Heine, *Zur Geschichte der Religion und Philosophie in Deutschland,* in *Historisch-kritische Gesamtausgabe der Werke,* vol. 8, pt. 1, pp. 76–77. In his 1797 essay "Über Lessing," Schlegel quotes the sentence immediately following the passage from Lessing that I quote, and provides this summary: "In general, *boundless contempt for the letter* was one of the main traits in Lessing's character" (Überhaupt war *unbegrenzte Verachtung des Buchstabens* ein Hauptzug in Lessings Charakter [KA 2:109]). The context leaves it open how Schlegel evaluates this character trait.

32. Goethe, *Die Leiden des jungen Werther, Werke,* 6:58 / *Collected Works,* 11:40.

33. Does Goethe register this fact after all? Is he winking at us when he lets Werther sigh, not by means of the rasping *ach* of the German soul, but via the round and empty letter *O,* whose entanglement with *E*

will come to play such a prominent part in his *Elective Affinities*? I suspect not, though there is surely no harm in our imagining such a wink.

34. Goethe, *Italienische Reise, Werke,* 11:399 / *Collected Works,* 12:319.

35. Schiller, *Kabale und Liebe, Sämtliche Werke,* 1:836 / *Plays,* 79. Many equally blatant passages from Schiller could be cited: "As surely as a visible presentation has more powerful effects than dead letter or cold narration, the theater has more profound and lasting effects than morals and laws" (Was kann eine gute stehende Schaubühne eigentlich wirken? [*Sämtliche Werke,* 5:824]).

36. Schiller, "Über Matthissons Gedichte," *Sämtliche Werke,* 5:1000.

37. I am thinking here of Erich Auerbach's marvelous reading of "Odysseus' Scar" in *Mimesis,* 3–23.

38. McLuhan, *The Gutenberg Galaxy,* 26.

39. Kittler, *Aufschreibesysteme,* 152 / 119.

40. Schlegel offers a peculiar version of inner vision in which the other senses are not denied but rather absorbed by "a pure mass of gentle light," a development not entirely surprising in a novel with the title *Lucinde:* "A new sense seemed to have opened up in me: I discovered in myself a pure mass of gentle light. . . . This new sense perceived so clearly and precisely, like a spiritual eye directed inwards; yet at the same time its perceptions were as deep and silent as those of the sense of hearing, and as immediate as the sense of touch" (Ein neuer Sinn schien mir aufgegangen; ich entdeckte in mir eine reine Masse von mildem Licht. . . . Er sah so klar und bestimmt, wie ein geistiges nach Innen gerichtetes Auge: dabei waren aber seine Wahrnehmungen innig und leise wie die des Gehörs, und so unmittelbar wie die des Gefühls [KA 5:19 / LF 57]).

In what can be taken as a commentary on this passage, Kittler has remarked that "such sensuousness (and sensuality) stored in Poetry is characteristic of an age in which the medium of the book is for the first time universal . . . and for the last time without competition from other sound and image media" (*Aufschreibesysteme,* 149 / 117). But something more and odder than a "wallowing in audiovisual sensuality" (*Aufschreibesysteme,* 150 / 117) is happening in the passage from *Lucinde,* for it projects on the mind's screen not only a movie but also a feelie ("its perceptions were . . . as immediate as the sense of touch"). And the condition for the success of such projection is not sensuality but its analogue, for hearing and touch are only likenesses ("wie die des Gehörs, . . . wie die des Gefühls") and the only reality inner vision.

41. Hölderlin, *Werke und Briefe,* 2:648 / TP 72. Though this text was

not published until 1917 and thus most likely remained unknown to Schlegel, it condenses many published and unpublished ideas with which he was intimately familiar.

42. Novalis, "Glauben und Liebe," *Schriften* 2:491/TP 135.

43. Similarly at Novalis, *Schriften,* 3:283–84, No. 245. For a very different view, see Novalis's fragment in his collection *Blüthenstaub:* "The designation through tones and lines is a wonderful abstraction. Three letters designate the word 'God,' a few lines designate a million things. How easy handling the universe becomes, how vivid the concentricity of the world of spirits. One word of command moves armies, the word 'freedom' nations" (Novalis, *Schriften,* 2:413, No. 2). To be sure, this stands in sharp contrast to the remarks in "Faith and Love," quoted above, but it seems to me that the slippage between "tones and lines" still permits a view of language in which written marks are nothing but the mnemonic devices for sounded words, bereft of any productive abilities of their own.

44. Eichendorff, *Werke,* 3:605.

45. McLuhan, *The Gutenberg Galaxy,* 13.

46. See Freud's essay on fetishism in Freud, *Gesammelte Werke,* 14:311–17/*Standard Edition* 21:147–58.

47. "bloß auf die Form wie die Buchstabengelehrten . . . auf den Geist, auf das innere Leben," KA 8:263/AM 499. See also KA 2:348/DP 114.

48. "Man redet schon lange von einer Allmacht des Buchstabens, ohne recht zu wissen was man sagt. Es ist Zeit daß es Ernst damit werde, daß der Geist erwache und den verlornen Zauberstab wieder ergreife," KA 2:262, No. 61/PF 100.

49. Kittler, *Aufschreibesysteme,* 19/12.

50. "Die γρ [Grammatik] folgendermaßen in der φσ [Philosophie] zu behandeln 1) das Gegebne; die Buchstaben," KA 19:154, No. 10.

51. "Es gibt keinen Philologen ohne Philologie in der ursprünglichsten Bedeutung des Worts, ohne grammatisches Interesse," KA 2:241, No. 404/PF 81.

52. Though Schlegel knew both well: an example of the former can be found in his Cologne lectures of 1805–6 (KA 13:186–87), an example of the latter in *Über die Sprache und Weisheit der Indier* (KA 8:113–90/AM 428–65).

53. To insist on the *gramma* in *grammar* entails the insight that the codification of the combinatorial rules of spoken language epistemologically relies on the availability of writing. The linguistic or cognitive

theories (for instance Chomsky's) that find grammar in the mind or even in the brain overlook the fact that the condition of possibility of recognizing concepts such as "word" or "sentence" lies in a writing system that *creates* these units. Cf. Stetter, *Schrift und Sprache,* esp. 75–115.

54. Compare this with how the magic of the sign is treated at about the same time by another reader: Faust's calling forth of the Earth Spirit by means of the sign of the microcosm. That written mark, far from being read as puzzling or ambiguous, flatters Faust into self-aggrandizement ("I look and feel my powers growing, / As if I'd drunk new wine I'm glowing") because it cancels itself as written sign and turns into a living speaker ("You have implored me to appear, / Make known my voice, reveal my face"). See J. W. Goethe, *Faust, Werke,* 3:23, lines 462–63; 486–87 / *Faust,* 101–3.

55. Lacan, *Écrits,* 153.

56. "Es gibt keinen Philologen ohne Philologie in der ursprünglichsten Bedeutung des Worts, ohne grammatisches Interesse. Philologie ist ein logischer Affekt, das Seitenstück der Philosophie, Enthusiasmus für chemische Erkenntnis: denn die Grammatik ist doch nur der philosophische Teil der universellen Scheidungs-und Verbindungskunst," KA 2:241, No. 404 / PF 81.

57. "Alles Wz [Witzige] ist doch zuerst γρ [grammatisch] und in sofern φσ [philosophisch]," KA 18:232, No. 462.

58. "Der Buchstabe als . . . Organ des Witzes," KA 18:260, No. 797.

59. "Der Buchstabe jedes Werks ist *Poesie,* der Geist φσ [Philosophie]," KA 16:167, No. 984.

60. Bolz, "Der Geist und die Buchstaben," 79.

61. "die Mitteilung der Ideen . . . überhaupt möglich sei," KA 2:363 / TP 119.

62. "*Bin* mit *in* verwandt. asse und esse wirklich vielleicht ein Wort?" KA 17:18, No. 113.

63. "Bezieht sich *Danken* auf *Dank* oder auf Ding?" KA 17:24, No. 125.

64. "Die *Consonanten* einzutheilen nach EISEN, *Wasser, Luft,*" KA 18:178, No. 627.

65. "die einen alkalinisch die andren Säuren?" KA 16:328, No. 890.

66. "die Consonant[en] [entsprechen] d[en] chem.[ischen] Stoff[en], die Vokale dem Licht," KA 16:375, No. 96.

67. "Die *Vokale* vielleicht nicht bloß Licht sondern auch das bindende und verschmelzende *Wasser* in d[er] Sprache.—Die *Consonanten* drücken allerdings *Stein* und *Luft* aus.—<oder Conson[anten] =

Wasser + Stein[,] Vok[ale] = Licht + Luft,>" KA 16:329, No. 897. Angle brackets mark Schlegel's later insertions.

68. "Die Consonanten können auch die chemischen Grundstoffe bedeuten," KA 17:27, 138.

69. "*Verwandtschaftstafeln der Buchstaben,*" KA 16:378, No. 129.

70. Foucault, *Les Mots et les choses,* 89/75.

71. For example: "*g* has more affinity for *h* than the other letters" (g hat immer noch mehr Affinität zu h als d[ie] andern Buchstaben [KA 16:380, No. 132]); "*S* and *i* match well—*F* and *o*—*K* and *a*—but also *T* <*D*> and *u*?" (S und i paßt gut zusammen—F und o—K und a—nun aber auch T <D> und u? [KA 16:445, No. 252]).

72. Foucault maintains that in the epistemic assumption of the "Classical age" (roughly from the middle of the seventeenth to the end of the eighteenth centuries) "the world, as the totality of what is representable, must be able to become, in its totality, an Encyclopaedia" (*Les Mots et les choses,* 100/85). On the "Classical period" : "To know is to speak correctly, and as the steady progress of the mind dictates. . . . The sciences are well-made languages, just as languages are sciences lying fallow" (101/87).

73. Kittler, *Aufschreibesysteme,* 56/42.

74. For an overview, as well as for an interesting account of language genesis, see the popular accounts of Dunbar, *Grooming, Gossip, and the Evolution of Language,* and Deacon, *The Symbolic Species.*

75. Foucault, *Les mots et les choses,* 119/103. The published English translation might lead us to believe that Foucault's model carries a stronger sense of chemical logic than we find in the original French. The translation divides "each word, down to the least of its *molecules,*" while Foucault uses the flatly mechanical *parcelle* ("particle," "part," "piece of land").

76. Kittler, *Aufschreibesysteme,* 56/42.

77. Lacan, *Écrits,* 158.

78. Herder, *Ueber die Wirkung der Dichtkunst auf die Sitten der Völker in alten und neuen Zeiten, Sämtliche Werke,* 8:340.

79. Klaproth, *Vorlesungen über die Experimentalchemie,* 1.

80. "den Schein des Verkehrten und Verrückten, oder des Einfältigen und Dummen durchschimmern läßt," KA 2:319/DP 86.

81. Jürgen Trabant makes the interesting observation that the late eighteenth century does not (re-)discover the *voice* but the *ear,* that it is thus not primarily an instance of phonocentrism but of otocentrism (Trabant, "Vom Ohr zur Stimme," 64). In that case, the "inner eye"

could just as well have been called the "inner ear," had that term not already been in use for a physical organ.

82. Stephani, *Fibel für Kinder von edler Erziehung, nebst einer genauen Beschreibung meiner Methode für Mütter, welche sich die Freude verschaffen wollen, ihre Kinder selbst in kurzer Zeit lesen zu lehren,* quoted in Kittler, *Aufschreibesysteme,* 64/50.

83. Kittler, *Aufschreibesysteme,* 64/50.

84. Lafont et al., *Anthropologie de l'écriture,* 56–90.

85. Coulmas, *The Writing Systems of the World,* 159. This is a paraphrase of what the grammatologist Ignace Gelb has called the "principle of reduction" (Gelb, *A Study of Writing,* 182) according to which writing systems evolve unidirectionally from the least abstract (pictogram) to the most abstract (alphabet) (200–201).

86. Whether in pre-Greek scripts the relationship between the letter and its name is arbitrary or not is a matter of some debate among scholars: some believe that the names derive from the shapes of the letters (the letter *beth* originally is supposed to have looked like a house, for instance), others maintain that the objects are merely chosen because of their mnemonic function (as in our "*A* is for apple . . ."); see Diringer, *The Alphabet,* 1:167–69, for an overview. The question of what sort of writing system merits the name alphabet is debated with great passion among scholars, hence also the question of its historical and geographic origin(s). For an overview see Drucker, *The Alphabetic Labyrinth,* 22–48. As Derrida, among others, has shown, claims about the superiority of a writing system often stand in for fervently held ethno-mythic claims (Derrida, *De la grammatologie,* 11/3). For a complete list of letter names and their meanings, see Coulmas, *The Writing Systems of the World,* 163.

87. McLuhan, *The Gutenberg Galaxy,* 61.

88. Foucault, *Les mots et les choses,* 128/112. As so often, here too it remains unclear whether Foucault's paraphrase (in this case, of Condillac) also reflects his own thinking about the issue.

89. "*Unbeschränkter Umfang* ist der eine große Vorzug der Poesie," KA 1:294.

90. Kittler, *Aufschreibesysteme,* 266/212.

91. "12 Consonanten und 5 Vokale / dazwisch[en] alle mögl[ichen] Versetzungen—wie viele können das sein?— 1 V[okal] 1 C[onsonant] = 60 und 60. 1 V[okal] 2 C[onsonaten] = 720," KA 16:392, No. 238.

92. "Unter diesen Worten sind gewiß eine Menge bedeutungslos," KA 16:393, No. 238.

93. "d[ie] ursprüngl[ichen] Begriffe," ibid.

94. "Die 720 . . . sollten *tellur[ische]* Elemente bedeuten," ibid. (The editors of KA give 920 [corrected from 980], while in my view the manuscript clearly indicates 720 [corrected from 780], a number that is also far more plausible in this context.) It is unlikely that Schlegel is referring here to the element tellurium, discovered but a dozen years before this note was written and isolated for the first time by Martin Heinrich Klaproth; the plural "telluric elements" would make little sense in that case.

95. Havelock, "Chinese Characters and the Greek Alphabet," 1. In his view, the meaninglessness of alphabetic letters recommends them as conveyors of information, for the reader is not detained by complications in decipherment. Thus, he argues, alphabetic writing (by which he means the Greek script and those deriving from it) frees the reader's mind, permitting the writer to experiment with a larger range of meanings than would be possible in nonalphabetic scripts, where the need for redundancy to assist the reader is more acutely felt by the writer. The alphabet thus becomes the engine of the rapid philosophical and scientific innovation in European cultures. Cf. Havelock, *The Literate Revolution in Greece,* esp. chapters 1, 3, and 13. Derrick de Kerckhove and others have attempted to support Havelock's argument with a neurophysiological and biological basis in Kerckhove and Lumsden, eds., *The Alphabet and the Brain,* but most linguists remain skeptical, suspecting a Western cultural bias. See for example Coulmans, *The Writing Systems of the World,* 160–61.

96. Drucker, *The Alphabetic Labyrinth,* 59.

97. Bayley, *The Lost Language of Symbolism,* 294.

98. Drucker, *The Alphabetic Labyrinth,* 12.

99. Schlegel decorated the title pages of all of his philosophical notebooks with elaborate calligraphic writing (KA 18:xlii); for an example see the plate after KA 18:xxxii.

100. For a detailed catalog of the nonphonetic functions of the letters in English spelling, see Coulmans, *The Writing Systems of the World,* 167–77.

101. This reading shares with Winfried Menninghaus's study of nonsense the aim of locating a theory and practice of nonsense in romanticism. Yet while that study locates such a theory and practice in the narrative (il)logic of the fairy tale and explicitly *not* in the combinatorial game peculiar to nonsense poetry, I propose to find it in the model of the chemical contamination of sense and nonsense in the agency of the letter. See Menninghaus, *Lob des Unsinns,* 15–16/7.

102. "L, R, M, N / L und N bloß kindisch—R und M zu d[em]

Großen sehr schicklich. [. . .] *K* Tiefe, *T* Kraft, Muth, *W* Begeisterung, Schnelle, Sturmwind, *Sch* Wollust, Höchstes," KA 16:445, No. 252.

103. Around 1800, there are theories that assign a semantic value to the letters of the alphabet in *non*arbitrary ways; thus it is taken as appropriate that members of the family—papa, mama—are designated with gentle labials, while the *O* outlines the wide-open eyes of astonishment. See Foucault, *Les mots et les choses*, 118 / 102.

104. Kittler, *Aufschreibesysteme*, 266 / 212.

105. Morgenstern, *Alle Galgenlieder*, 23.

106. "Viell.[eicht] ist der der Luc.[inde] *Natur* und *Liebe*, nur daß d[ie] Natur hier ganz untergeordnet ist," KA 16:236, No. 56.

107. Kittler, *Aufschreibesysteme*, 267 / 212.

108. Foucault, *Les mots et les choses*, 95 / 81.

109. Lacan, *Écrits*, 160.

110. "die reinste und gediegenste Unverständlichkeit," KA 2:364 / TP 119.

111. Foucault, *Les mots et les choses*, 103 / 89.

112. Brock, *The Norton History of Chemistry*, 156–57.

113. Thus Guyton de Morveau et al., *Méthode de nomenclature chimique*, 12. To be sure, like the conceptual revolution in chemistry, the linguistic revolution makes heavy use of precisely those traditional ideas and words that it sets out to overcome; see Engelhardt, *Hegel und die Chemie*, 36–37. In this sense too, chemistry is a volatile mixture of incompatible elements.

114. Lavoisier, *Traité élémentaire de chimie*, 1:vi / xiv.

115. The volume edited by Bensaude-Vincent and Abbri, *Lavoisier in European Context*, provides a detailed country-by-country account of the adoption of the new nomenclature in which Germany, however, is missing. For the importance of Lavoisier's language reform, see also Beretta, *The Enlightenment of Matter*, esp. chapters 4 and 5.

116. Bensaude-Vincent and Stengers, *A History of Chemistry*, 89.

117. Brock, *The Norton History of Chemistry*, 116.

118. Bergman, *Dissertation on Elective Attractions*, 3.

119. Goethe, *Werke*, 6:276; *Works*, 11:116. In his commentary, Benno von Wiese reasonably assumes that Goethe borrows the notion of "elective affinity" from Bergman (see Goethe, *Werke*, 6:656). Jeremy Adler concurs, pointing out, however, that there is only circumstantial evidence for this judgment. See his *"Eine fast magische Anziehungskraft*," 75–77.

120. See the beautiful iconography in the tables of affinities and re-actions in Bergman's *Dissertation* (figs. 1a–b, and 3) as well as the simpler but no less striking table inside the back cover of Pierre Joseph Macquer's *Élémens de chymie.*

121. As David Wellbery notes in his foreword to the English transla-tion (*Discourse Networks,* xii), "notation systems" or "systems of writing down" renders Kittler's term more literally and, I believe, more accu-rately than "discourse networks."

122. In order to be dependable, data processing must be independent of the medium in which it is conducted. Whether I perform a calcula-tion with pencil and paper, an abacus, a computer, or buttons, the result should be the same. This neutrality vis-à-vis the material in which it is performed has allowed the notion of computing to be extended to en-tirely new domains. Researchers have recently harnessed the properties of DNA to perform mathematical calculations usually solved in other me-dia (paper, computer). The seminal paper here is Adleman, "Molecular Computation of Solutions to Combinatorial Problems."

123. Coogan, "Alphabets and Elements." I owe this reference to Gre-gory Nagy, *Poetry as Performance,* 216. For a theory that explains the di-vision of the alphabet into two parts by relying on the physiology of sound production, see Sittig, "Abecedarium und Elementum," 133. These theories are speculative, since, as Walter Burkert points out, "the linguis-tic derivation of *elementum* poses insurmountable difficulties" (Burkert, "Στοιχειον," 167).

124. For Nagy, this feature makes *elementum* into a "fitting symbol for the elements of authorship in oral tradition" (ibid.).

125. "fängt in d.[er] Mitte an," KA 18:82, No. 626.

Six: The Politics of Permanent Parabasis

1. Barthes, *S/Z,* 11/5.

2. Ibid., back cover of the French edition.

3. Menninghaus has offered the most rigorous version of such a read-ing in his *Unendliche Verdopplung.* See the Afterword for an account and a critique of his approach. For another reading of the fragments in the context of poststructuralism, see Ostermann, *Das Fragment.*

4. Hörisch, *Die fröhliche Wissenschaft der Poesie,* 140.

5. Kaltenbrunner, "'Revolution und Faulheit' I/II," 141.

6. For documentation see Weiland, *Der junge Friedrich Schlegel,* esp.

17–25; the book registers only the thematic manifestations of Schlegel's interest in radical politics and is unconcerned with the political implications of his formal innovations. A detailed account of Schlegel's political thought, which, however, pays hardly any attention to poetic practice or theory, can be found in Hendrix, *Das politische Weltbild Friedrich Schlegels.*

7. "Diese Begeisterung für eine große öffentliche Sache macht trunken," KA 23:144.

8. "Ich will Dirs nicht läugnen, daß mir der Republikanismus noch ein wenig näher am Herzen liegt, als die göttliche Kritik, und die allergöttliche Poesie," KA 23:305.

9. For examples see Behler's introduction, KA 7:xxii–xxv.

10. Kant, "Zum ewigen Frieden," AA 8:352 / *Philosophy of Kant,* 439.

11. "nur in der Welt der reinen Gedanken existiert . . . Das Einzelne und das Allgemeine ist überhaupt durch eine unendliche Kluft voneinander geschieden, über welche man nur durch einen Salto mortale hinüber gelangen kann. Es bleibt hier nichts übrig, als durch eine *Fiktion* einen empirischen Willen als *Surrogat* des a priori gedachten absolut allgemeinen Willens gelten zu lassen," KA 7:16.

12. "Der *Wille der Mehrheit* soll als Surrogat des allgemeinen Willens gelten. *Der Republikanismus ist also notwendig demokratisch,* und das unerwiesene Paradoxon (S. 26), daß der Demokratismus notwendig despotisch sei, kann nicht richtig sein," KA 7:17.

13. "daß dem Menschen, außer den Vermögen, die das rein isolierte Individuum als solches besitzt, auch noch im Verhältnis zu andern Individuen seiner Gattung, das *Vermögen der Mitteilung* (der Tätigkeiten aller übrigen Vermögen) zukomme," KA 7:14.

14. "das Fundament und Objekt der *Politik,*" KA 7:15.

15. Eichner, *Friedrich Schlegel,* 15–16, 112.

16. Haym, *Die romantische Schule,* 253–55.

17. "Republikanismus der Tragödie," KA 11:209.

18. "Repräsentation des Volks," KA 11:208.

19. "Die Grenzen der dramatischen Sphäre bestimmt der stärkste Wille der Maße des Publikums, welcher nothwendig die dramatische Darstellung beherrscht und lenkt. Wenn etwa höhere Stände oder der Wille Weniger herrscht, so werden diese ihre *konventionellen* und zufälligen Begriffe zum Gesetz erheben; ihre Engherzigkeit wird die Grenze der Kunst. Dergl. Schranken sind dann Decenz pp. Diese Schranken stören die Freiheit der Kunst. Ist aber der Wille wirklich öffentlich und giebt es nur das Gesetz, daß die Darstellungen *bürgerlich* seyn sollen, re-

publikanisch, öffentlich: das setzt dem Dichter eigentlich gar keine Schranken," KA 11:207.

20. "Manche witzige Einfälle sind wie das überraschende Wiedersehen zwei befreundeter Gedanken nach einer langen Trennung," KA 2:171, No. 37/PF 23.

21. "ein bunter Haufen von Einfällen . . . Diese verbindet doch jenes freie und gleiche Beisammensein, worin sich auch die Bürger des vollkommnen Staats . . . dereinst befinden werden," KA 2:159, No. 103/PF 12.

22. "*Experimentiren* ist sehr im Geist d[er] revoluz.[ionären] Praxis," KA 18:342, No. 246.

23. "Poesie ist eine republikanische Rede; eine Rede, die ihr eignes Gesetz und ihr eigner Zweck ist, wo alle Teile freie Bürger sind, und mitstimmen dürfen," KA 2:155, No. 65/PF 8.

24. "Das Zeitalter ist gleichfalls ein chemisches Zeitalter. Revolutionen sind universelle nicht organische, sondern chemische Bewegungen," KA 2:248, No. 426/PF 87.

25. Hörisch, *Die fröhliche Wissenschaft der Poesie,* 142.

26. Tanner, "Chemistry in Schlegel's *Athenäum* Fragments," 147.

27. "des Verkehrten und Verrückten, oder des Einfältigen und Dummen," KA 2:319/DP 86.

28. Foucault, *Les mots et les choses,* 95/81.

29. Klaus Scherpe, "Zur Faszination des Organischen," in *Faszination des Organischen,* ed. Hartmut Eggert et al. (Munich: Iudicum, 1995), 7–11, here 10.

30. "Meine Praxis (Oxygene, Azote = Theorie) endigt mit Schwindsucht wie d.[as] Athmen im Oxygene," KA 18:135, No. 162.

31. "eine gewisse chemische Besessenheit," KA 18:135, No. 162.

32. "Schellings φσ [Philosophie] ist suroxydirt," KA 18:136, No. 169.

33. "Die Chemie muß drei Princ.[ipien] haben. φ [Philosophie] und π [Poesie] = Azote? Oxygen η [ethische] Atmosphäre. Die jetzige φ [Philosophie] wohl reine Lebensluft," KA 18:231, No. 458.

34. "Die Menschheit selbst als Proceß ist d[ie] höchste Potenz der Oxydation für diese Epoche d[er] Erde," KA 18:165, No. 500.

35. "Jedes Verbrennen nur ein Wiederholen d[er] ältesten Liebesgeschichte. Das Oxyg.[en] stürzt mit Ungestüm auf das Hydrog[en] und dieses entflieht. Kein andrer Liebender ist so wüthend, kein Weib so leicht und spröde," KA 18:184, No. 700.

36. "Der χεμ [chemische] Proceß als böses Princip und als *Krankheit* zu betrachten," KA 18:88, No. 740. Similarly KA 18:179, No. 634.

37. "Ist χεμ [Chemie] überhaupt d[as] böse Princip in d[er] Natur, so ist das *Wasser* d[er] erste grosse Sündenfall d[er] Erdoberfläche," KA 18:182, No. 679.

38. "Viell.[eicht] sind die Elemente Krankheiten," KA 18:151, No. 337.

39. "Viell.[eicht] ist jede *Kunstfertigkeit* eine *Krankheit d[es] Geistes,* die man sich künstlich inokuliren muß," KA 18:158, No. 415.

40. "Daher das Epidemische d[er] Kunst," ibid.

41. "Nach der Analogie jenes Gedankens würde auf das chemische ein organisches Zeitalter folgen," KA 2:248–49, No. 426/PF 87.

42. For an overview, see Roger, "The Living World," 270–78. We may speculate that the seductive charge of the organic lies in offering a coherent and homogeneous picture of the world at precisely the time— the late eighteenth century—when human life itself becomes imaginable as mechanical. Since the mechanization of life has not let up, the hold that the notion of the organic enjoys on our consciousnesses has not weakened. On the contrary: the more our control of nature spreads, the more desperately we cling to the holistic "ecosystem." The "sacredness" of life stands in direct proportion to the successes of biological engineering. If this wishful notion of nature is, as we like to say, "romantic," then romanticism—in the form of Schlegel's writing—also provides a glimpse into a nature running amok, not a sublime nature mocking our efforts at taming it (which would still adhere to the notion of the organic organization of nature), but a nature that is rotten to its very core.

43. Lenoir, "Morphotypes and the Historical-Genetic Method in Romantic Biology," 120.

44. Did Schlegel perhaps know the no doubt fanciful etymology that Adelung's dictionary provides for *Keim,* the seed—and metonymic embodiment of organicism—with which so much romantic writing is compared, indeed with which it compares itself (e.g., Novalis about his *Blüthenstaub* fragments, *Schriften,* 2:413)? *Keim,* according to Adelung, goes back to the Greek *chyma,* which, it so happens, is exactly the same root he suggests, less fancifully, for *Chemie* (*Grammatisch-kritisches Wörterbuch,* 1:1335; 2:1538).

45. "Es müßte möglich sein vor Gesundheit zu sterben," KA 18:192, No. 785.

46. "Die Keime der künftigen Organisation sind zuvor Gift und auch die Schlacken der Verwesung sind es," KA 18:169, No. 536.

47. "Es gibt nur eine organische Materie—GIFT," KA 18:172, No. 562.

48. "Lessing endlich war einer von den *revolutionären* Geistern, die

überall . . ., gleich einem scharfen Scheidungsmittel, die heftigsten Gärungen und gewaltigsten Erschütterungen allgemein verbreiten," KA 2:101.

49. "kann nicht schließen, nur abschneiden, oder aufhören; sie endigt also immer nothwendig annihilirend oder ironirend," KA 16:162, No. 902.

50. De Man, *Aesthetic Ideology,* 178–79. See also de Man, *Allegories of Reading,* 300–301.

51. "permanente Parekbase," KA 18:85, No. 668.

52. "Der einzige Unterschied besteht in der Parekbasis, einer Rede, die in der Mitte des Stücks vom Chor im Namen des Dichters an das Volk gehalten wurde. Ja, es war eine gänzliche Unterbrechung und Aufhebung des Stückes, in welcher, wie in diesem, die größte Zügellosigkeit herrschte und dem Volk von dem bis an die äußerste Grenze des Proszeniums heraustretenden Chor die größten Grobheiten gesagt wurden. Von diesem Heraustreten (εχβασιζ) kommt auch der Name," KA 11:88.

53. "*reine Komödie* [. . .] allen Zweck und alle Absicht sich in sich selbst auflöst [. . .] die Unform selbst ist . . . die höchste Kunst," KA 11:89.

54. "Es gehört ihm [dem Witz] ein Publikum, worin jeder mündig ist und die Freiheit nicht mißbraucht," KA 11:94.

55. "soll es ein Gedicht des Witzes geben, . . . so muß der Witz unumschränkt frei sein. Diese Freiheit ist nun wohl zu gestatten, wenn es für ein kleines Publikum bestimmt ist, welches das Recht hat, an einer solchen Freiheit Anteil zu nehmen. Keineswegs ist dies aber für die gemischte Menge, die des Genusses dieser Freiheit gar nicht würdig ist, und wobei die allerunangenehmsten, schädlichsten Folgen zu befürchten wären," ibid.

56. "Der Magistrat sah sich hier wirklich genötigt, sowohl die persönliche Satire als auch den Chor mit der Parekbase zu verbieten. Dies fällt aber zugleich mit dem Verfall des Republikanismus und der Demokratie zusammen," ibid.

57. "In jedem συστ [systematischen] Werk muß ein *Prolog* sein, ein *Epilog* und ein *Centrolog* (oder eine *Parekbase*)," KA 16:164, No. 942.

58. "Nur durch eine fortdauernde immer wiederhohlte Störung ist Leben möglich," KA 18:419, No. 1181.

59. "Bei einem Menschen, der eine gewisse Höhe und Universalität d[er] Bildung erreicht hat, ist sein Inneres eine fortgehende Kette der ungeheuersten Revoluzionen," KA 18:82–83, No. 637.

60. "*wir sind nur ein Stück von uns selbst* . . . Diejenige Tätigkeit aber,

wodurch das Bewußtsein sich am meisten als Bruchstück kundgibt, ist der *Witz,* sein Wesen besteht eben in der Abgerissenheit und entspringt wieder aus der Abgerissenheit und Abgeleitetheit des Bewußtseins selber," KA 12:392.

61. "ein Blitz aus der unbewußten Welt, die für uns immer neben der bewußten besteht, und stellt auf diese Weise den fragmentarischen Zustand unseres Bewußtseins sehr treffend dar. Es ist eine Verbindung und Mischung des Bewußten und Unbewußten," KA 12:393.

62. "Ohne alle Absicht und bewußtlos wird plötzlich etwas gefunden, was mit dem Vorhergehenden gar keinen Zusammenhang hat, vielmehr im Gegenteil immer gleichsam in einem grellen Widerspruche steht," ibid.

63. The editor informs us of this possibility, KA 18:xlvii–xlix.

64. "Das Leben des universellen Geistes ist eine ununterbrochne Kette innerer Revolutionen; alle Individuen, die ursprünglichen, ewigen nämlich leben in ihm. Er ist echter Polytheist und trägt den ganzen Olymp in sich," KA 2:255, No. 451/PF 93.

65. "Selbst ein freundschaftliches Gespräch, was nicht in jedem Augenblick frei abbrechen kann, aus unbedingter Willkür, hat etwas Illiberales," KA 2:151, No. 37/PF 5.

66. "Alle Gemüter, die sie lieben, befreundet und bindet Poesie mit unauflöslichen Banden," KA 2:284/DP 53. The critical edition reads "unauflöslischen," an error, as a glance at the first printing of the essay shows; see *Athenaeum* 3.1: 58.

67. By contrast, Gary Handwerk's reading, neglecting the debilitating effects of interruption, finds in irony a normative standard for mutual understanding: "Objectivity is thus interpreted by irony as an intersubjectivity that can serve as a guarantor of general validity" (*Irony and Ethics in Narrative,* 33).

68. "deren Zweck die Organisation des Republikanismus ist [. . .] eine unechte und *permanente Insurrektion:* denn die echte und politisch mögliche ist notwendig transitorisch," KA 7:25.

69. "nicht nur gerechtfertigt, sondern auch praktisch notwendig," KA 7:16.

70. Žižek, *The Sublime Object of Ideology,* 28–33.

71. "Überdem gelten diese Regeln des Schicklichen und Anständigen . . . nur für das Leben, nie für die Kunst," KA 11:90.

Afterword: The Chemical Critique of Idealism

1. "eine Art von transcendentaler Chemie," KA 18:89, No. 716.

2. "die Wissenschaft aller sich ewig mischenden und wieder trennen-den Wissenschaften, eine logische Chemie," KA 2:200, No. 220/PF 47.

3. "π [Poesie] und φ [Philosophie] werden sich immer inniger durch-dringen," KA 18:342, No. 243; "bald mischen, bald verschmelzen," KA 2:182, No. 116/PF 31.

4. Luhmann, *Die Wissenschaft der Gesellschaft*, 8.

5. Fichte, *Wissenschaftslehre*, 1:124. Since both German and English editions provide the pagination of the widely cited J. G. Fichte, *Sämmtliche Werke*, ed. I. H. Fichte (Berlin: Veit und Co., 1845–46), only that page number is given.

6. The latter, Fichte concedes, can be effected through a "completed approximation to infinity, which as such is impossible" (1:115).

7. "une sçiençe absolument experimentale"; "Sa marche rigoureuse peut ressembler à present . . . à celle de l'immortel Lavoisier," KA 18:543. Original in French. "Die Methode des Idealismus ist ein *combinatorisches Experimentiren*," KA 12:21. Schlegel's usage of "experiment" is not always consistent; here it is, by way of Lavoisier, clearly associated with chem-istry and thus the sort of endless deferral embedded in that model. Else-where, e.g. in his notes for a lecture course on transcendental philosophy at the University of Jena in 1800/1801, he limits his emphatic assertion that "*philosophy is an experiment*" (*Die Philosophie ist ein Experiment* [KA 12:3]) by adding that it involves an "*experimentation* like in physics" (ein *Experimentiren*, wie in der Physik [ibid.]). For Schlegel, that seems to hold the promise of a method with the aid of which "every step we take *would be necessary* [and] contain nothing hypothetical" (daß jeder Schritt, den wir thun, *nothwendig sey*, nichts Hypothetisches enthalte [ibid.]). While he may be appealing to the different statuses that physics and chemistry hold at the end of the eighteenth century, and while we need to mark this difference, it is not an absolute one: the disciplines (in-sofar as this term even applies to them) and their concepts of the ex-periment share a great deal of overlap. Well into the last third of the eighteenth century, chemistry is often regarded as a branch of physics. Cf. Durner, "Theorien der Chemie," 8.

8. "fängt in d.[er] Mitte an," KA 18:82, No. 626.

9. "wahre φ [Philosophie]," KA 18:7, No. 34.

10. "Wenn die Möglichkeit einer Grundwissenschaft zugegeben

wird, so läßt sich a priori beweisen, daß *sie aus lauter Thesen und Antithesen bestehen muß,*" KA 18:8, No. 45.

11. "Die φ [Philosophie] muß mit unendl[ich] vielen Sätzen anfangen, d[er] Entstehung nach (nicht mit Einem)," KA 18:26, No. 93.

12. Bensaude-Vincent and Stengers, *A History of Chemistry,* 63. A leading historian of science takes this to be the case still today: "The chemist cannot get very far from experiment; and indeed probably has to think with his hands in a way not necessary in theoretical physics" (Knight, *Ideas in Chemistry,* 3). Lower prestige is one consequence of chemistry's laborious implication in matter: "By and large, a pejorative view of the methodological sophistication of chemical science has prevailed, notably in comparison to physics. The structure of scientific explanation in chemistry has often been deemed child's play, or kitchen work. Chemistry is frequently characterized as a handmaiden" (Nye, *From Chemical Philosophy to Theoretical Chemistry,* 57).

13. After this study was completed, Frederick Beiser was kind enough to show me drafts of some of his essays on this subject that deepen our understanding of the romantic critique of idealism significantly. I am grateful for his generosity and regret not being able to discuss them here in the detailed manner they deserve.

14. Lacoue-Labarthes and Nancy, *L'absolut littéraire,* 69/48.

15. Menninghaus, *Unendliche Verdopplung,* 26.

16. It remains unclear in this otherwise lucid study what philosophical or historical insight is to be gained from imagining the romantics as standing in competition with a late-twentieth-century philosopher.

17. For an overview of the project see Henrich, *Konstellationen.* The group of skeptical thinkers includes Friedrich Immanuel Niethammer, Johann Benjamin Erhard, Carl Christian Erhard Schmid, Carl Immanuel Diez, and Friedrich Carl Forberg. For a panoramic overview, see Frank, *"Unendliche Annäherung"*; for Schlegel's place in the network see 858–944.

18. Frank, *"Unendliche Annäherung,"* 858–59.

19. Frank, *Das Problem "Zeit" in der deutschen Romantik,* 501.

20. Kant, *Metaphysische Anfangsgründe der Naturwissenschaft,* AA 4:471.

21. Schelling, *Historisch-Kritische Ausgabe,* pt. 1, vol. 5, p. 243.

22. Ibid., 238. In order to rescue his view of the basic homogeneity of matter, Schelling assumes that nature, by means of an "artful device [*Kunstgriff*]," has divided "substances that were homogeneous according

to their nature, and has kept them apart for as long as possible, because, once joined [*verbunden*], they are not capable of further separation and are nothing but dead, inert matter" (ibid., 176). It is not hard to see that the real "artful device" is employed not by nature but by Schelling's philosophy; its generosity (or is it megalomania?) lies in lending this quality to its object of analysis.

23. "Daß man eine Philosophie annihiliert, wobei sich der Unvorsichtige leicht gelegentlich selbst mit annihilieren kann, oder daß man ihr zeigt, sie annilihiere sich selbst, kann ihr wenig schaden. Ist sie wirklich Philosophie, so wird sie doch wie ein Phönix aus ihrer eignen Asche immer wieder aufleben," KA 2:180, No. 103/PF 30.

Sources Cited

Adelung, Johann Christoph. *Grammatisch-kritisches Wörterbuch der hochdeutschen Mundart, mit beständiger Vergleichung der übrigen Mundarten, besonders aber der Oberdeutschen.* 2d ed. Leipzig: Breitkopf, 1793–1801.

Adleman, L. M. "Molecular Computation of Solutions to Combinatorial Problems." *Science* 266 (1994): 1021–24.

Adler, Jeremy. *"Eine fast magische Anziehungskraft": Goethes "Wahlverwandtschaften" und die Chemie seiner Zeit.* Munich: C. H. Beck, 1987.

Adorno, Theodor W. *Ästhetische Theorie* Frankfurt: Suhrkamp, 1973.

Allemann, Beda. *Ironie und Dichtung.* Pfullingen: Neske, 1956.

Aristotle. *The Complete Works of Aristotle.* Edited by Jonathan Barnes. Princeton: Princeton University Press, 1984.

Athenaeum. Eine Zeitschrift von August Wilhelm Schlegel und Friedrich Schlegel. 1798–1800. Reprint. Stuttgart: Cotta, 1960.

Auerbach, Erich. *Mimesis: The Representation of Reality in Western Literature.* Translated by Willard Trask. Princeton: Princeton University Press, 1953.

Bachofen, Johann Jakob. *Der Mythus von Orient und Occident. Eine Metaphysik der alten Welt.* Edited by Manfred Schröter. Munich: C. H. Beck, 1926.

Baeumler, Alfred. *Das Irrationalitätsproblem in der Ästhetik und Logik des 18. Jahrhunderts bis zur Kritik der Urteilskraft.* Reprint. Darmstadt: Wissenschaftliche Buchgesellschaft, 1967.

Barthes, Roland. *Le Bruissement de la langue.* Paris: Éditions du Seuil, 1984/ *The Rustle of Language.* Translated by Richard Howard. New York: Hill & Wang, 1986.

——. *S/Z.* Paris: Éditions du Seuil, 1970/ *S/Z.* Translated by Richard Howard. New York: Hill & Wang, 1974.

Bauer, Walter. *Greek-English Lexicon of the New Testament and Other Early Christian Literature.* 4th ed. Translated by William Arndt and F. Wilbur Gingrich. Chicago: University of Chicago Press, 1960.

Bayley, Harold. *The Lost Language of Symbolism*. Reprint. New York: Carol, 1993.

Behler, Ernst. *German Romantic Literary Theory.* Cambridge: Cambridge University Press, 1993.

———. *Studien zur Romantik und zur idealistischen Philosophie*. Paderborn: Schöningh, 1988–93.

Behler, Ernst, and Jochen Hörisch, eds. *Die Aktualität der Frühromantik*. Paderborn: Schöningh, 1987.

Benjamin, Walter. *Gesammelte Schriften*. Edited by Rolf Tiedemann and Hermann Schweppenhäuser. Frankfurt: Suhrkamp, 1980.

———. *Selected Writings*. Vol. 1. Edited by Marcus Bullock and Michael Jennings. Cambridge: Harvard University Press, 1996.

Bensaude-Vincent, Bernadette, and Ferdinando Abbri, eds. *Lavoisier in European Context: Negotiating a New Language for Chemistry.* Canton, Mass.: Science History Publications, 1995.

Bensaude-Vincent, Bernadette, and Isabelle Stengers. *A History of Chemistry.* Translated by Deborah van Dam. Cambridge: Harvard University Press, 1996.

Beretta, Marco. *The Enlightenment of Matter: The Definition of Chemistry from Agricola to Lavoisier.* Canton, Mass.: Science History Publications, 1993.

Bergman, Torbern. *A Dissertation on Elective Attractions.* Translated by J. A. Schufle. New York: Johnson Reprint Corp., 1968.

Bernoulli, Christoph, and Hans Kern. *Romantische Naturphilosophie.* Jena: Diederichs, 1926.

Blanchot, Maurice. *L'Entretien infini.* Paris: Gallimard, 1969 / *The Infinite Conversation.* Translated by Susan Hanson. Minneapolis: University of Minnesota Press, 1993.

———. *L'écriture du désastre.* Paris: Gallimard, 1980 / *The Writing of the Disaster.* Translated by Ann Smock. Lincoln: University of Nebraska Press, 1995.

Bohrer, Karl Heinz. *Die Kritik der Romantik. Der Verdacht der Philosophie gegen die literarische Moderne.* Frankfurt: Suhrkamp, 1989.

Bolz, Norbert. "Der Geist und die Buchstaben: Friedrich Schlegels hermeneutische Postulate." In *Texthermeneutik: Aktualität, Geschichte, Kritik,* ed. Ulrich Nassen, 79–112. Paderborn: Schöningh, 1979.

Boyle, Robert. *The sceptical chymist: Or Chymico-Physical Doubts and Paradoxes, touching the experiments, Whereby vulgar Spagyrists are wont to evince their Salt, Sulphur and Mercury, to be the true Principle of*

Things. In *The Works of the Honourable Robert Boyle,* ed. Thomas Birch, 1:474–586. London: J. and F. Rivington et al., 1772.

Brock, William. *The Norton History of Chemistry.* New York: Norton, 1993.

Burke, Edmund. *The Works of Edmund Burke.* London: George Bell & Sons, 1909.

Burkert, Walter. "Στοιχειου." *Philologus* 103 (1959): 167–97.

Butterfield, Herbert. *The Origins of Modern Science, 1300–1800.* Rev. ed. New York: Free Press, 1965.

Cohen, I. B. *Revolution in Science.* Cambridge: Harvard University Press, 1985.

Coleridge, Samuel Taylor. *The Collected Works of Samuel Taylor Coleridge.* Edited by Kathleen Coburn. Princeton: Princeton University Press, 1969– .

Coogan, Michael D. "Alphabets and Elements." *Bulletin of the American Schools for Oriental Research* 216 (1974): 61–63.

Coulmas, Florian. *The Writing Systems of the World.* Oxford: Basil Blackwell, 1989.

Craig, Gordon. *The Germans.* New York: Meridian, 1991.

Crosland, Maurice. "Chemistry and the Chemical Revolution." In Rousseau and Porter, eds., *The Ferment of Knowledge,* 389–416.

Cunningham, Andrew, and Nicholas Jardine, eds. *Romanticism and the Sciences.* Cambridge: Cambridge University Press, 1990.

Deacon, Terrence. *The Symbolic Species: The Co-Evolution of Language and the Brain.* New York: Norton, 1997.

De Man, Paul. *Aesthetic Ideology.* Edited by Andrzej Warminski. Minneapolis: University of Minnesota Press, 1996.

———. *Allegories of Reading: Figural Language in Rousseau, Nietzsche, Rilke, and Proust.* New Haven: Yale University Press, 1979.

———. *Blindness and Insight: Essays in the Rhetoric of Contemporary Criticism.* 2d ed. Minneapolis: University of Minnesota Press, 1983.

———. *The Rhetoric of Romanticism.* New York: Columbia University Press, 1984.

Derrida, Jacques. *La Dissémination.* Paris: Éditions du Seuil, 1972/*Dissemination.* Translated by Barbara Johnson. Chicago: University of Chicago Press, 1981.

———. "Economimesis." In Sylviane Agacinski et al., *Mimesis des articulations,* 55–93. Paris: Aubier-Flammarion, 1975/trans. Richard Klein, *Diacritics* 11 (1981): 3–25.

————. *De la grammatologie.* Paris: Éditions de Minuit, 1967/ *Of Grammatology,* translated by Gayatri Chakravorti Spivak, corrected edition. Baltimore: Johns Hopkins University Press, 1998.

Dijksterhuis, Eduard Jan. *The Mechanization of the World-Picture.* Translated by C. Dikshoorn. Oxford: Clarendon, 1961.

Diringer, David. *The Alphabet: A Key to the History of Mankind.* 3d ed. New York: Funk & Wagnalls, 1968.

Dischner, Gisela, and Richard Faber, eds. *Romantische Utopie-Utopische Romantik.* Hildesheim: Gerstenberg, 1979.

Drucker, Johanna. *The Alphabetic Labyrinth: The Letters in History and Imagination.* London: Thames & Hudson, 1995.

Dunbar, Robin. *Grooming, Gossip, and the Evolution of Language.* Cambridge: Harvard University Press, 1996.

Durner, Manfred. "Theorien der Chemie." In Schelling, *Historisch-Kritische Ausgabe,* Supplement to vols. 5–9, pp. 1–161.

Eagleton, Terry. *The Ideology of the Aesthetic.* Oxford: Basil Blackwell, 1990.

Eco, Umberto. *The Open Work.* Translated by Anna Cancogni. Cambridge: Harvard University Press, 1989.

————. *The Search for the Perfect Language.* Translated by James Fentress. Oxford: Blackwell, 1995.

Eichendorff, Joseph von. *Werke.* Edited by Ansgar Hillach. Munich: Winkler, 1970–88.

Eichner, Hans. *Friedrich Schlegel.* New York: Twayne, 1970.

————. "The Rise of Modern Science and the Genesis of Romanticism." *PMLA* 97 (1982): 8–30.

Engelhardt, Dietrich von. *Hegel und die Chemie. Studie zur Philosophie und Wissenschaft der Natur um 1800.* Wiesbaden: Pressler, 1976.

Fichte, Johann Gottlieb. *Grundlage der gesamten Wissenschaftslehre (1794).* Hamburg: Felix Meiner, 1988/ *Science of Knowledge.* Edited and translated by Peter Heath. Cambridge: Cambridge University Press, 1982.

Foucault, Michel. *Language, Counter-Memory, Practice.* Edited by Donald Bouchard. Ithaca: Cornell University Press, 1977.

————. *Les Mots et les choses: Une archéologie des sciences humaines.* Paris: Gallimard, 1966/ *The Order of Things: An Archeology of the Human Sciences.* New York: Random House, 1971.

Fourcroy, Antoine François de. *Système des connaissances chimiques, et leurs applications aux phénomènes de la nature et de l'art.* Paris: Baudouin, 1800–1801/ *A General System of Chemical Knowledge and its Ap-*

plication to the Phenomena of Nature and Art. Translated by William Nicholson. London: Cadell & Davies, 1804.

Frank, Manfred. *Einführung in die frühromantische Ästhetik.* Frankfurt: Suhrkamp, 1989.

———. *Das Problem "Zeit" in der deutschen Romantik: Zeitbewußtsein und Bewußtsein von Zeitlichkeit in der frühromantischen Philosophie und in Tiecks Dichtung* 2d ed. Paderborn: Schöningh, 1990.

———. *"Unendliche Annäherung": Die Anfänge der philosophischen Frühromantik.* Frankfurt: Suhrkamp, 1997.

———. "'Wechselgrundsatz': Friedrich Schlegels philosophischer Ausgangspunkt." *Zeitschrift für philosophische Forschung* 50 (1996): 26–50.

Frenzel, H. A., and E. Frenzel. *Daten deutscher Dichtung: Chronologischer Abriss der deutschen Literaturgeschichte.* 23d ed. Munich: Deutscher Taschenbuch Verlag, 1987.

Freud, Sigmund. *Gesammelte Werke.* Frankfurt: S. Fischer, 1940–68 / *Standard Edition of the Complete Psychological Works of Sigmund Freud.* Edited by James Strachey et al. London: Hogarth, 1953–74.

Gelb, I. J. *A Study of Writing.* Rev. ed. Chicago: University of Chicago Press, 1963.

Girtanner, Christoph. *Neue chemische Nomenklatur für die deutsche Sprache.* Berlin: Johann Friedrich Unger, 1791.

Gode-von Aesch, Alexander. *Natural Science in German Romanticism.* New York: Columbia University Press, 1941.

Goethe, Johann Wolfgang von. *Collected Works.* Edited by Victor Lange et al. New York: Suhrkamp, 1983–89.

———. *Faust.* Translated by Walter Kaufmann. New York: Doubleday, 1961.

———. *Gedenkausgabe der Werke, Briefe und Gespräche.* Edited by Ernst Beutler. Zürich: Artemis, 1948–64.

———. *Werke* (Hamburger Ausgabe). Edited by Erich Trunz. 12th ed. Munich: Beck, 1981.

Grimm, Jacob, and Wilhelm Grimm. *Deutsches Wörterbuch.* 1854–1960. Reprint, Munich: Deutscher Taschenbuch Verlag, 1984.

Gumbrecht, Hans Ulrich, and K. Ludwig Pfeiffer, eds. *Materialität der Kommunikation.* Frankfurt: Suhrkamp, 1988 / *Materialities of Communication.* Translated by William Whobrey. Stanford: Stanford University Press, 1994.

Guyton de Morveau, Louis Bernard, et al. *Méthode de nomenclature chimique.* Paris: Cuchet, 1787.

Habermas, Jürgen. *Der philosophische Diskurs der Moderne.* Frankfurt: Suhrkamp, 1985 / *The Philosophical Discourse of Modernity.* Translated by Fredrick G. Lawrence. Cambridge: MIT Press, 1987.

Handwerk, Gary. *Irony and Ethics in Narrative: From Schlegel to Lacan.* New Haven: Yale University Press, 1985.

Haupt, Bettina. *Deutschsprachige Chemielehrbücher (1775–1850).* Stuttgart: Deutscher Apothekerverlag, 1987.

Havelock, Eric. "Chinese Characters and the Greek Alphabet." *Sino-Platonic Papers* 5 (December 1987): 1–4.

———. *The Literate Revolution in Greece and Its Cultural Consequences.* Princeton: Princeton University Press, 1982.

Haym, Rudolf. *Die romantische Schule. Ein Beitrag zur Geschichte des deutschen Geistes* 5th ed. Edited by Oskar Walzel. Berlin: Weidmann, 1928.

Hegel, Georg Wilhelm Friedrich. *Aesthetics.* Translated by T. M. Knox. Oxford: Clarendon Press, 1975.

———. *Werke.* Edited by Eva Moldenhauer and Karl Markus Michel. Frankfurt: Suhrkamp, 1970.

Heine, Heinrich. *Historisch-kritische Gesamtausgabe der Werke.* Edited by Manfred Windfuhr. Hamburg: Hoffmann & Campe, 1973–1997.

Hendrix, Gerd Peter. *Das politische Weltbild Friedrich Schlegels.* Bonn: Bouvier, 1962.

Henrich, Dieter. *Konstellationen. Probleme und Debatten am Ursprung der idealistischen Philosophie (1789–1795).* Stuttgart: Klett-Cotta, 1991.

Herder, Johann Gottfried. *Briefe zu Beförderung der Humanität.* Edited by Heinz Stolpe. Berlin: Aufbau, 1971.

———. *Sämtliche Werke.* Edited by Bernhard Suphan. Berlin: Weidmann, 1877–1913.

Hölderlin, Friedrich. *Werke und Briefe.* Edited by Friedrich Beißner and Jochen Schmidt. Frankfurt: Insel, 1969.

Hörisch, Jochen. *Die fröhliche Wissenschaft der Poesie. Der Universalitätsanspruch der Dichtung in der frühromantischen Poetologie.* Frankfurt: Suhrkamp, 1976.

Jakobson, Roman. "Closing Statement: Linguistics and Poetics." In *Style in Language,* ed. Thomas A. Sebeok, 350–77. Cambridge: MIT Press, 1960.

Jean Paul. *Werke.* Edited by Norbert Miller and Gustav Lohmann. Munich: Hanser, 1959–63.

Jung, Werner. *Von der Mimesis zur Simulation. Eine Einführung in die Geschichte der Ästhetik.* Hamburg: Junius, 1995.

Kaltenbrunner, Gerd-Klaus. "'Revolution und Faulheit' I/II." In Dischner and Faber, *Romantische Utopie-Utopische Romantik,* 135–48.

Kant, Immanuel. *Critique of Pure Reason.* Translated by Werner Pluhar. Indianapolis: Hackett, 1996.

———. *Kants gesammelte Schriften.* Edited by Königlich Preußische Akademie der Wissenschaften. Berlin: Walter de Gruyter, 1902– .

———. *Kritik der Urteilskraft,* AA 5:165–486 / *Critique of Judgment.* Translated by Werner S. Pluhar. Indianapolis: Hackett, 1987.

———. *The Philosophy of Kant: Immanuel Kant's Moral and Political Writings.* Edited by Carl Friedrich. New York: Modern Library, 1949.

———. *Prolegomena to Any Future Metaphysics.* Translated by P. Carus. Indianapolis: Bobbs-Merrill, 1950.

Kapitza, Peter. *Die frühromantische Theorie der Mischung. Über den Zusammenhang von romantischer Dichtungstheorie und zeitgenössischer Chemie.* Munich: Max Hueber Verlag, 1968.

Kerckhove, Derrick de, and Charles J. Lumsden, eds. *The Alphabet and the Brain: The Lateralization of Writing.* Berlin: Springer-Verlag, 1988.

Kittler, Friedrich. *Aufschreibesysteme 1800/1900.* 3d ed. Munich: Fink, 1995 / *Discourse Networks 1800/1900.* Translated by Michael Metteer, with Chris Cullens. Stanford: Stanford University Press, 1990.

———. *Grammophon Film Typewriter.* Berlin: Brinkmann & Bose, 1986/ *Gramophone, Film, Typewriter.* Translated by Geoffrey Winthrop-Young and Michael Wutz. Stanford: Stanford University Press, 1999.

———. "Musik als Medium." In *Wahrnehmung und Geschichte: Markierungen zur Aisthesis materialis,* ed. Bernhard Dotzler and Ernst Müller, 83–99. Berlin: Akademie Verlag, 1995.

Kittler, Friedrich, et al., eds. *Diskursanalysen 1: Medien.* Opladen: Westdeutscher Verlag, 1987.

Klaproth, Martin Heinrich. *Chemie. Nach der Abschrift von Stephan Friedrich Barez, Winter 1807/08.* Edited by Brita Engel. Berlin: Verlag für Wissenschafts- und Regionalgeschichte, 1994.

———. *Vorlesungen über die Experimentalchemie. Nach einer Abschrift aus dem Jahre 1789.* Edited by Rüdiger Stolz et al. Berlin: Verlag für Wissenschafts- und Regionalgeschichte, 1993.

Klaproth, Martin Heinrich, and Friedrich Wolff. *Chemisches Wörterbuch.* Berlin: Vossische Buchhandlung, 1807–10.

Klausnitzer, Ralf. "Blaue Blume unterm Hakenkreuz. Zur literaturwissenschaftlichen Romantikrezeption im Dritten Reich." *Zeitschrift für Germanistik* 7 (1997): 521–42.

Kleist, Heinrich von. *Sämtliche Werke und Briefe.* Edited by Helmut Sembdner. 7th ed. Munich: Hanser, 1984.

Knight, David. "German Science in the Romantic Period." In *The Emergence of Science in Western Europe,* ed. Maurice Crosland, 161–78. London: Macmillan, 1975.

———. *Ideas in Chemistry: A History of the Science.* London: Athlone Press, 1992.

———. "Romanticism and the Sciences." In Cunningham and Jardine, *Romanticism and the Sciences,* 13–24.

Krug, Wilhelm Traugott. *Allgemeines Handwörterbuch der philosophischen Wissenschaft nebst ihrer Literatur und Geschichte.* Leipzig: Brockhaus, 1827–29.

Kubiak, Christopher. "Sowing Chaos: Discontinuity and the Form of Autonomy in the Fragment Collections of the Early German Romantics." *Studies in Romanticism* 33 (1994): 411–49.

Kuhn, Thomas. "Robert Boyle and the Structural Chemistry of the Seventeenth Century." *Isis* 43 (1952): 12–16.

———. *The Structure of Scientific Revolutions.* 2d ed. Chicago: University of Chicago Press, 1970.

Lacan, Jacques. *Écrits: A Selection.* Translated by Alan Sheridan. New York: Norton, 1977.

Lacoue-Labarthe, Philippe, and Jean-Luc Nancy. *L'absolu littéraire: Théorie de la littérature du romantisme allemand.* Paris: Éditions du Seuil, 1978 / *The Literary Absolute: The Theory of Literature in German Romanticism.* Translated by Philip Barnard and Cheryl Lester. Albany: State University of New York Press, 1988.

———. "Noli me frangere." *Revue des Sciences Humaines* 185 (1982): 83–92.

Lafont, Robert, et al. *Anthropologie de l'écriture.* Paris: Centre Georges Pompidou, 1984.

La Mettrie, Julien. *L'Homme machine: A Study in the Origins of an Idea.* Edited by Aram Vartanian. Princeton: Princeton University Press, 1960.

Lavoisier, Antoine-Laurent. *Traité élémentaire de chimie, présenté dans un ordre nouveau, et d'après les découvertes modernes.* 3d ed. Paris: Deterville, 1801 / *Elements of Chemistry in a New Systematic Order Contain-*

ing All the Modern Discoveries. Translated by Robert Kerr. Edinburgh: W. Creech, 1790.

Leibniz, Gottfried Wilhelm. *Die philosophischen Schriften.* Edited by Carl Gerhardt. Berlin: Weidmann, 1875–90.

Lenoir, Timothy. "Morphotypes and the Historical-Genetic Method in Romantic Biology." In Cunningham and Jardine, eds., *Romanticism and the Sciences,* 119–29.

Leopold, Max. *Die Vorsilbe VER- und ihre Geschichte.* Breslau: M. & H. Marcus, 1907.

Lessing, Gotthold Ephraim. *Werke.* Edited by Herbert Göpfert et al. Munich: Hanser, 1970–79.

Levere, Trevor. "Coleridge, Chemistry, and the Philosophy of Nature." *Studies in Romanticism* 16 (1977): 349–79.

Librett, Jeffrey. *The Rhetoric of Cultural Dialogue: Jews and Germans from Moses Mendelssohn to Richard Wagner and Beyond.* Stanford: Stanford University Press, 2000.

Lichtenberg, Georg Christoph. *Georg Christoph Lichtenberg's vermischte Schriften.* Edited by Ludwig Christian Lichtenberg and Friedrich Kries. Göttingen: Johann Christian Dietrich, 1800–1804.

———. *Schriften und Briefe.* Edited by Wolfgang Promies. Munich: Hanser, 1967.

Liddell, George, and Robert Scott. *Greek-English Lexicon.* Oxford: Clarendon Press, 1983.

Lord, Albert. *The Singer of Tales.* Cambridge: Harvard University Press, 1960.

Luhmann, Niklas. *Die Ausdifferenzierung des Kunstsystems.* Bern: Benteli, 1994.

———. *Die Gesellschaft der Gesellschaft.* Frankfurt: Suhrkamp, 1997.

———. *Die Kunst der Gesellschaft.* Frankfurt: Suhrkamp, 1995.

———. "A Redescription of 'Romantic Art.'" *MLN* 111 (1996): 506–22.

———. *Die Wissenschaft der Gesellschaft.* Frankfurt: Suhrkamp, 1994.

Lukács, Georg. *Skizze einer Geschichte der neueren deutschen Literatur.* Darmstadt: Luchterhand, 1974.

———. *Die Zerstörung der Vernunft.* Vol. 1: *Irrationalismus zwischen den Revolutionen.* Darmstadt: Luchterhand, 1981.

Macquer, Pierre Joseph. *Élémens de chymie.* Paris: Herissant, 1753.

Mallarmé, Stéphane. *Oeuvres complètes.* Edited by Henri Mondor and G. Jean-Aubry. Paris: Bibliothèque de la Pléiade, 1945.

Mann, Thomas. *Deutschland und die Deutschen, 1945.* Hamburg: Europäische Verlagsanstalt, 1992 / *Germany and the Germans*. Washington: Library of Congress, 1945.

Mauthner, Fritz. *Wörterbuch der Philosophie. Beiträge zu einer Kritik der Sprache* (1923–24). Reprint, Wien: Böhlau, 1997.

Mautner, Franz. "Der Aphorismus als literarische Gattung." In Neumann, ed. *Der Aphorismus*, 19–74.

McLuhan, Marshall. *The Gutenberg Galaxy.* Toronto: University of Toronto Press, 1962.

Menninghaus, Winfried. *Lob des Unsinns. Über Kant, Tieck und Blaubart.* Frankfurt: Suhrkamp, 1999 / *In Praise of Nonsense: Kant and Bluebeard.* Translated by Henry Pickford. Stanford: Stanford University Press, 1999.

———. *Unendliche Verdopplung: Die frühromantische Grundlegung der Kunsttheorie im Begriff absoluter Selbstreflexion.* Frankfurt: Suhrkamp, 1987.

Morgenstern, Christian. *Alle Galgenlieder. Galgenlieder, Palmström, Palma Kunkel, Gingganz.* Frankfurt: Insel, 1949.

Mungan, Güler. *Die semantische Interaktion zwischen dem präfigierenden Verbzusatz und dem Simplex bei deutschen Partikel-und Präfixverben.* Frankfurt: Lang, 1986.

Nagy, Gregory. *Poetry as Performance: Homer and Beyond.* Cambridge: Cambridge University Press, 1996.

Neubauer, John. *Symbolismus und symbolische Logik. Die Idee der ars combinatoria in der Entwicklung der modernen Dichtung.* Munich: Wilhelm Fink, 1978.

Neumann, Gerhard, ed. *Der Aphorismus. Zur Geschichte, zu den Formen und Möglichkeiten einer literarischen Gattung.* Darmstadt: Wissenschaftliche Buchgesellschaft, 1976.

———. *Ideenparadiese. Untersuchungen zur Aphoristik von Lichtenberg, Novalis, Friedrich Schlegel und Goethe.* Munich: Wilhelm Fink, 1976.

Newmark, Kevin. "*L'absolut littéraire:* Friedrich Schlegel and the Myth of Irony." *MLN* 107 (1992): 905–30.

Newton, Isaac. *Opticks, or, A Treatise of the Reflections, Refractions, Inflections and Colours of Light.* 4th ed. New York: Dover, 1952.

Nietzsche, Friedrich. *Kritische Gesamtausgabe.* Edited by Giorgio Colli and Mazzino Mantinari. Berlin: de Gruyter, 1967–97.

Novalis (Friedrich von Hardenberg). *Schriften.* Edited by Paul Kluckhohn and Richard Samuel. 3d ed. Stuttgart: Kohlhammer, 1977– .

Nye, Mary Jo. *From Chemical Philosophy to Theoretical Chemistry: Dy-*

namics of Matter and Dynamics of Disciplines, *1800–1950.* Berkeley: University of California Press, 1993.

Ostermann, Eberhard. *Das Fragment. Geschichte einer ästhetischen Idee.* Munich: Wilhelm Fink, 1991.

Panofsky, Erwin. *Idea. Ein Beitrag zur Begriffsbestimmung der älteren Kunsttheorie.* 5th ed. Berlin: V. Spiess, 1985.

Partington, J. R. *A History of Chemistry.* London: Macmillan, 1961–70.

Rasch, William. "Injecting Noise into the System: Hermeneutics and the Necessity of Misunderstanding." *SubStance* 67 (1992): 61–76.

Read, John. *Through Alchemy to Chemistry: A Procession of Ideas and Personalities.* London: G. Bell & Sons, 1957.

Ritter, Joachim, et al., eds. *Historisches Wörterbuch der Philosophie.* Basel: Schwabe, 1971– .

Roger, Jacques. "The Living World." In Rousseau and Porter, eds., *The Ferment of Knowledge,* 255–83.

Rousseau, G. S., and Roy Porter, eds. *The Ferment of Knowledge: Studies in the Historiography of Eighteenth-Century Science.* Cambridge: Cambridge University Press, 1980.

Rousseau, Jean-Jacques. *The Social Contract.* Translated by G. D. H. Cole. London: J. M. Dent & Sons, 1913.

Ryan, Judith. "Hybrid Forms in German Romanticism." In *Prosimetrum: Crosscultural Perspectives on Narrative in Prose and Verse,* ed. Joseph Harris and Karl Reichl, 165–81. Cambridge: D. S. Brewer, 1997.

Santner, Eric. *Friedrich Hölderlin: Narrative Vigilance and the Poetic Imagination.* New Brunswick: Rutgers University Press, 1986.

Scarry, Elaine. *On Beauty and Being Just.* Princeton: Princeton University Press, 1999.

Schanze, Helmut. *Romantik und Aufklärung: Untersuchungen zu Friedrich Schlegel und Novalis.* Erlanger Beiträge zur Sprach-und Kunstwissenschaft 27. 2d ed. Nürnberg: Verlag Hans Carl, 1976.

Schelling, Friedrich Wilhelm Joseph. *Historisch-Kritische Ausgabe.* Edited by Hans Michael Baumgartner et al. Stuttgart: Frommann-Holzboog, 1976– .

———. *Sämmtliche Werke.* Edited by K. F. A. Schelling. Stuttgart: J. G. Cotta'scher Verlag, 1856–1964.

———. *System of Transcendental Idealism (1800).* Translated by Peter Heath. Charlottesville: University Press of Virginia, 1978.

Schiller, Friedrich. *Plays: "Intrigue and Love" and "Don Carlos."* Edited by Walter Hinderer. New York: Continuum, 1983.

————. *Sämtliche Werke*. Edited by Gerhard Fricke and Herbert Göpfert. Munich: Hanser, 1958–59.

Schlegel, Friedrich. *Aesthetic and Miscellaneous Works of Friedrich von Schlegel*. Translated by E. J. Millington. London: G. Bell & Sons, 1915.

————. *Dialogue on Poetry and Literary Aphorisms*. Translated by Ernst Behler and Roman Struc. University Park: Pennsylvania State University Press, 1968.

————. *Kritische Friedrich-Schlegel-Ausgabe*. Edited by Ernst Behler et al. Paderborn: Schöningh, 1958– .

————. *Lucinde and the Fragments*. Translated by Peter Firchow. Minneapolis: University of Minnesota Press, 1971.

————. *Philosophical Fragments*. Translated by Peter Firchow. Minneapolis: University of Minnesota Press, 1991.

————. *Sämmtliche Werke*. Vienna: Jacob Mayer, 1822–25.

Schmidt, Siegfried J. *Die Selbstorganisation des Literatursystems im 18. Jahrhundert*. Frankfurt: Suhrkamp, 1989.

Schneider, Manfred. "Luther mit McLuhan: Zur Medientheorie und Semiotik heiliger Zeichen." In Kittler et al., eds., *Diskursanalysen*, 1:13–25.

Schreiber, Jens. "Stop Making Sense." In Kittler et al., eds., *Diskursanalyse*, 1:172–88.

Schulte-Sasse, Jochen, et al., eds. and trans. *Theory as Practice: A Critical Anthology of Early German Romantic Writings*. Minneapolis: University of Minnesota Press, 1997.

Schumacher, Eckhard. *Die Ironie der Unverständlichkeit: Johann Georg Hamann, Friedrich Schlegel, Jacques Derrida, Paul de Man*. Frankfurt: Suhrkamp, 2000.

Schwedt, Georg. *Goethe als Chemiker*. Berlin: Springer, 1998.

Service, Robert. "Berkeley Crew Bags Element 118." *Science* 284 (1999): 1751.

Sittig, Ernst. "Abecedarium und Elementum." In *Satura. Früchte aus der antiken Welt. Otto Weinreich zum 13. März dargebracht*, 131–38. Baden-Baden: Verlag für Kunst und Wissenschaft, 1952.

Snelders, H. A. M. "Romanticism and Naturphilosophie and the Inorganic Natural Sciences 1797–1840: An Introductory Survey." *Studies in Romanticism* 9 (1970): 193–215.

Spicker, Friedemann. *Der Aphorismus. Begriff und Gattung von der Mitte des 18. Jahrhunderts bis 1912*. Berlin: de Gruyter, 1997.

Stetter, Christian. *Schrift und Sprache*. Frankfurt: Suhrkamp, 1997.

Szondi, Peter. *Poetik und Geschichtsphilosophie*. Edited by Senta Metz and Hans-Hagen Hildebrandt. Frankfurt: Suhrkamp, 1974.

———. *On Textual Understanding, and Other Essays*. Translated by Harvey Mendelsohn. Minneapolis: University of Minnesota Press, 1986.

———. *Satz und Gegensatz*. Frankfurt: Insel, 1964.

Tanner, Matthew. "Chemistry in Schlegel's *Athenäum* Fragments." *Modern Language Studies* 31 (1995): 140–53.

Tatarkiewicz, Wladyslaw. *History of Aesthetics*. The Hague: Mouton, 1970–74.

Thompson, Lorin A., and Jonathan A. Ellman. "Synthesis and Applications of Small Molecule Libraries." *Chemical Review* 96 (1996): 555–600.

Trabant, Jürgen. "Vom Ohr zur Stimme. Bemerkungen zum Phonozentrismus zwischen 1770 und 1830." In Gumbrecht and Pfeiffer, eds., *Materialität der Kommunikation*, 63–79.

Ueding, Gert. "Das Fragment als literarische Form der Utopie." *Etudes Germaniques* 41 (1986): 351–62.

Valéry, Paul. *Oeuvres*. Edited by Jean Hytier. Paris: Gallimard, 1957.

Weber, Samuel. "Criticism Underway: Walter Benjamin's *Romantic Concept of Criticism*." In *Romantic Revolutions: Criticism and Theory*, ed. Kenneth R. Johnston et al., 302–19. Bloomington: Indiana University Press, 1990.

Weiland, Werner. *Der junge Friedrich Schlegel, oder Die Revolution in der Frühromantik*. Stuttgart: Kohlhammer, 1968.

Weissberg, Liliane. *Geistersprache. Philosophischer und literarischer Diskurs im späten achtzehnten Jahrhundert*. Würzburg: Königshausen & Neumann, 1990.

Wellek, René. *Concepts of Criticism*. New Haven: Yale University Press, 1963.

Wetzels, Walter. "Aspects of Natural Science in German Romanticism." *Studies in Romanticism* 10 (1971): 44–59.

Wilde, Oscar. *The Wit and Humor of Oscar Wilde*. Edited by Alvin Redman. New York: Dover, 1959.

Winthrop-Young, Geoffrey. "Lichtenberg und die französische Revolution: Zum Verhältnis von Sprache, Naturwissenschaft und Aufklärung." Ph.D. diss., University of British Columbia, 1991.

Wordsworth, William. *Selected Prose*. Edited by John Hayden. Harmondsworth: Penguin, 1988.

Žižek, Slavoj. *The Sublime Object of Ideology*. London: Verso, 1989.

Index

Index